OCR AS

Physical Education

Carl Atherton   Symond Burrows   Sue Young

Philip Allan Updates, an imprint of Hodder Education, part of Hachette Livre UK, Market Place, Deddington, Oxfordshire OX15 0SE

Orders

Bookpoint Ltd, 130 Milton Park, Abingdon, Oxfordshire OX14 4SB
tel: 01235 827720
fax: 01235 400454
e-mail: uk.orders@bookpoint.co.uk

Lines are open 9.00 a.m.–5.00 p.m., Monday to Saturday, with a 24-hour message answering service. You can also order through the Philip Allan Updates website: www.philipallan.co.uk

© Philip Allan Updates 2008

ISBN 978-1-84489-641-7

Impression number   5 4 3 2 1
Year   2012 2011 2010 2009 2008

Printed in Italy.

Hachette Livre UK's policy is to use papers that are natural, renewable and recyclable products and made from wood grown in sustainable forests. The logging and manufacturing processes are expected to conform to the environmental regulations of the country of origin.

P01151

Contents

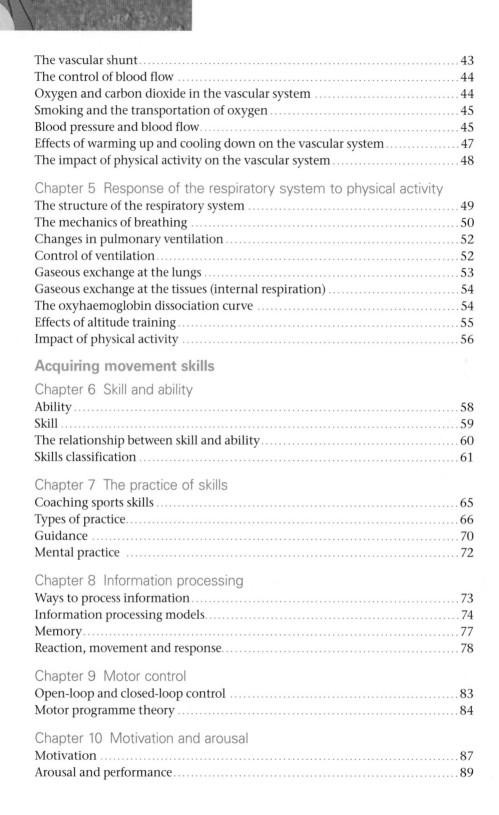

Unit G452 Acquiring, developing and evaluating practical skills in physical education

Answers

Index

Introduction

About this book

This textbook has been written specifically to meet the needs of students taking the OCR specification for Physical Education from September 2008. The book is divided according to the OCR specification. The first Unit (G451) comprises three sections. The first looks at anatomy and physiology, the second section concentrates on acquiring movement skills and the third section looks at the sociocultural studies relating to participation in physical activity. The final part of this book gives advice on the practical and coursework sections of the OCR course known as Unit G452: Acquiring, developing and evaluating practical skills in physical education.

It is common for the AS Physical Education course to be taught in accordance with the way this book is structured. Students tend to follow lessons on anatomy and physiology, acquiring skills and then sociocultural issues as separate entities and indeed the exam at the end of the course asks questions that are related to these three sections. The way to use the book, therefore, is to link the appropriate section of the book to the lessons you are currently undertaking. Each section is set out to form a logical progression so that knowledge gained in earlier chapters can be used as a basis for some of the concepts detailed in later chapters.

Special Features

This book contains several special features designed to aid your understanding of the requirement of the OCR AS Physical Education course.

Key Terms

These are concise definitions of the main terms needed throughout the course. You are often required to define such key terms in the early part of exam questions. The answers to most exam questions will be based on a clear recollection of such definitions and the examiner will very often have these key terms listed in the examiners' marks scheme. If you can remember them and explain them, you are almost guaranteed to score a mark.

Top Tips

This feature offers advice on what you should do and, equally importantly, what you should not do, in order to ensure exam success. The authors use their examination experience to give students valuable advice on how to answer exam questions, using typical examples and relevant knowledge.

Tasks to Tackle

The authors have included some activities throughout each chapter that are designed to improve and reinforce your understanding of the main concepts covered in each chapter. As you do the activities, you should look back over the chapter to help you complete each task. Some tasks can be carried out individually or in groups, so you may be able to do them as part of your lesson or with your fellow students as part of the revision process. Where appropriate, answers to tasks are given at the back of the book.

Practice makes perfect

At the end of each chapter there is a set of questions appropriate to that particular section of work. The questions are based on examiner knowledge of the main topics and are often divided so that early questions may ask for definitions and lists, while later questions may require more of an explanation. The answers to these questions are offered at the end of the book and it is strongly recommended that you use this feature to help gauge your understanding of the relevant topics. Having read the chapter and perhaps covered that same topic as part of your course, you should attempt the questions without looking at the answers. Once you have completed the questions and checked them, it may then be possible to look back over the chapter to see if you can uncover any answers that you may have missed. Repeat this process so that you know the answers to some of the questions you might face during the exam. This is a great way to do your revision and ensure exam success.

Scheme of Assessment

Unit G451 is assessed by a 2-hour written paper. This question paper has three sections, with one question in each section. The three sections relate directly to the structure of this book, in other words, Section A asks a question on anatomy and physiology, Section B asks a question on acquiring movement skills and Section C asks a question on sociocultural studies relating to participation in physical activity. Candidates must answer all parts of the question in each of sections A, B and C and will be asked to demonstrate knowledge, analysis and evaluation.

Each question is divided into five parts labelled (a) to (e) and is stepped to increasingly test your knowledge. In other words, part (a) is easier than part (b) and so on. The written exam is worth 60% of the total AS marks, and is marked out of a total of 90 marks. Part of the marks awarded are for the quality of written communication. Candidates should therefore ensure that spelling, punctuation and grammar are accurate and that the meaning of what they have written is clear. They should also organise information in a coherent manner and use relevant specialist vocabulary when appropriate.

In the AS examination the quality of written communication mark is specifically awarded in the last part of each question, part (e). Parts (a)–(d) still require clear expression, punctuation and grammar but will be stepped so that more detailed knowledge and explanations are required as the question develops. Parts (a) and (b), for example, may require a definition or a simple list, whereas parts (c), (d) and (e) will require more discussion, evaluation and application. As a student, you may now begin to appreciate the value of the Top Tips, Key Terms and Practice Makes Perfect sections that are special features of this book.

Unit G452, which is the practical, coursework-based unit is externally set, internally assessed and externally moderated. Candidates are assessed in two chosen activities from two different activity profiles and in a response to a live performance. This unit is awarded 80 marks and accounts for 40% of the total AS marks.

There are many different 'activity profiles' that you can do in your practical coursework, but for your final assessment they need to be from two different categories chosen from:

- athletic activities
- combat activities
- dance activities
- invasion game activities
- net/wall game activities
- striking/fielding games
- target game activities
- gymnastic activities
- outdoor and adventurous activities
- swimming activities
- safe and effective exercise activities

You are expected to develop an understanding and appreciation of the various pathways to success. The concept of **success** underpins this unit. OCR identifies a variety of pathways to success, including:

- outwitting opponents
- accurately replicating skills/movements
- exploring and communicating ideas, concepts and emotions
- performing to your 'maximum' level
- identifying and solving problems
- exercising safely and effectively

Any activity may include a variety of pathways to success.

OCR recommends that you should have the opportunity to experience a variety of roles:

- performing, for example different playing positions in invasion games, or singles and doubles in racket games
- coaching/teaching, for example teaching skills/application of tactics to a fellow student
- officiating, for example judging/refereeing to appropriate rules, regulations and codes of conduct

You need to be aware of the short- and long-term health and fitness benefits of the activity and of the opportunities for participation and progression, both locally and nationally. You also need to be able to explain the factors that contribute to an effective performance through development of your knowledge and understanding of the relationship between skill, strategy and fitness.

Assessment information

Coursework assessment is divided into two main areas:

- performance
- evaluation and planning for performance improvement

Studying for the exam

Read each chapter thoroughly

On completion of each topic, make sure that you have read each page of the relevant chapter and use the Tasks to Tackle to test yourself. If you adopt this approach for every chapter of the book, then your revision will be just that, i.e. revising what you have already learned rather than learning material for the first time.

Complete the Practice Makes Perfect exercises

If you tackle these specific exam-style questions at the end of each chapter, you will have checked that you have understood the key concepts. You will also gain useful examination practice and perhaps build some confidence based on a realisation of what you can achieve in the exam. You will also develop good exam technique, especially if, as you answer the questions, you adopt the strategies listed below.

Develop your practical skills

40% of the marks for this course are gained from practical performance and the evaluation of the performance in terms of coaching, performing and/or officiating. These are skills you can practise in your own time away from the classroom and you should follow the advice given in the last chapter in this book to help you perfect them.

Read the Chief Examiner's Report

This report will alert you to the strengths and weaknesses shown by previous students and will help you to refine your approach. Along with previous examination papers and mark schemes, these reports are available in pdf format from the OCR website (www.ocr.org.uk).

Make your own notes

As you progress through this book, build up your own index of terms or small explanations of key topics and write them down in a format that you find easy to relate to. When it comes to revision, you can then use these notes to help you and much of your revision will seem to have been done for you.

Keep up to date

This book contains many topical examples and these are a vital part of any examination answer. However the world of sport is constantly changing and if you read newspapers and magazines or simply refer to sport programmes on television, you might be able to find even more up-to-date examples to use in the exam. You will also find that by researching these examples yourself you are more likely to remember them.

Advice on exam technique

Success in the exam is not just based on subject knowledge. A successful student needs to marry subject knowledge to the question set. In order to succeed on the exam there are four main pieces of advice that the successful student may need.

Key words

Most exam questions require the definition, explanation, evaluation or application of key phrases and terms, which are featured throughout this book. Students should identify such key definitions, which are often asked directly for in the question, and then be able to write about them thoroughly. The examiner will have a list of these key terms in their mark scheme and if you mention them you are almost certain to be awarded marks.

Read the question

It is no use knowing all your key terms if you write about the wrong one, or one that is not asked for in the question, so make sure you take some time before you start to write any answers to read the whole question carefully. This will prevent silly errors such as mistaking the cognitive theory of learning with the cognitive phase of learning, two similarly worded concepts that appear in the acquiring movement skills section of the specification. When you have read the question, it might be a good idea to use a highlighter pen to identify the key phrases mentioned above and you may even jot down some key answers to these phrases before you begin to answer a question properly. Take a few minutes to plan each answer before you begin.

More answers than marks

Each question identifies the maximum number of marks that are available for each part. If the question part is worth 3 marks, then it would be unwise to give only two answers! Successful students will often write more answers than there are marks available to act as an insurance policy for success. Examiners award credit for correct answers, and do not deduct marks for any incorrect answers, so the more you write, the more chance you have of success. It is also worth using examples to back up each point you make, mainly because many questions ask you to do exactly this and they will often start with the phrase 'using examples from sport...' In any case, the example you give may indicate a thorough understanding of what the question is asking and the examiner may give you credit for showing your knowledge in this way.

Unit G451

An introduction to physical education

- Anatomy and physiology

- Acquiring movement skills

- Sociocultural studies relating to participation in physical activity

Chapter *1*

The skeletal and muscular systems

What you need to know

By the end of this chapter you should be able to:

- classify the following synovial joints — wrist, radio-ulnar, elbow, shoulder, spine, hip, knee and ankle
- identify the bones that articulate at these joints
- use correct anatomical terminology to describe the movements that these joints can perform
- explain the muscular functions of agonists, antagonists and fixators
- identify the agonist and antagonist muscle(s) for each of the movements at the synovial joints
- explain concentric, eccentric and isometric muscle contraction
- identify the three muscle fibre types (slow oxidative, fast oxidative glycolytic and fast glycolytic) and explain which are recruited depending on the type of physical activity
- describe the structure and function of these muscle fibre types
- analyse the effects of a warm-up and cool-down on the muscular system
- evaluate the impact of different types of physical activity — such as contact sports, high-impact sports and those involving repetitive actions — on both the skeletal and muscular systems

The skeleton

The skeleton (Figure 1.1) is made up of 206 bones. It comprises the axial skeleton, which is made up of the skull, the vertebral column, the sternum and the ribs, and the appendicular skeleton, which comprises the shoulder girdle, the hip girdle, and the bones of the arms, hands, legs and feet.

The skeleton has a number of functions:

- Support — the skeleton provides a rigid framework to the body.
- Levers — the bones act as a lever system, allowing movement.
- Attachment — the skeleton provides suitable sites for the attachment of muscles.
- Protection — the skeleton protects the internal organs. For example, the cranium protects the brain and the ribcage protects the heart and lungs.
- Blood cell production — both red and white blood cells are produced in the bone marrow. Red blood cells are produced at the ends of long bones, such as the femur in the leg and the humerus in the arm.
- Shape — the skeleton gives the body shape.

Joints

The skeleton is a framework connected by joints. Joints are necessary for muscles to lever bones, thus creating movement. A joint is formed where two or more bones meet. Joints are classified by how much movement they allow. There are three types:

- fibrous
- cartilaginous
- synovial

Fibrous joints allow no movement at all — they are completely fixed. There is no joint cavity and the bones are held together by fibrous, connective tissue. Examples of this type of joint can be found in the cranium, the facial bones and the pelvic girdle.

Cartilaginous joints occur where the bones are separated by cartilage. They allow only a slight amount of movement. Examples of this type of joint are the ribs joining the sternum and the vertebrae joining to form the spine.

Synovial joints (Figure 1.4) allow movement in one or more directions and are the most common of the three joints. These joints have a fluid-filled cavity surrounded by an articular capsule. Hyaline or articular cartilage is found at the ends of the bones where they come into contact with each other. This prevents friction between the articulating bones. There are six types of synovial joint:

- ball and socket
- condyloid
- hinge
- gliding
- pivot
- saddle

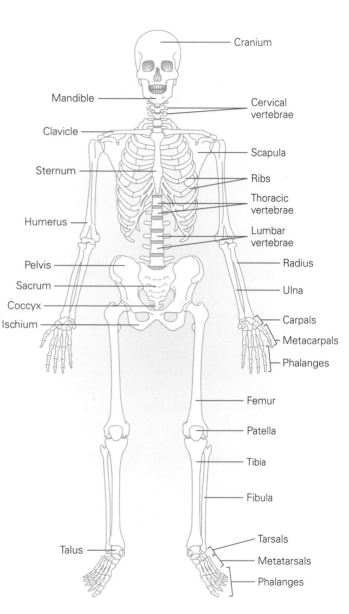

Figure 1.1 The human skeleton

You will not be asked to label a skeleton in the exam but you do need to know the names of the bones that articulate at the joints.

Top tip

Ball-and-socket joints allow the most movement. They are formed by the round head of one bone fitting into the cup-shaped capsule of the connecting bone. The hip and the shoulder are ball-and-socket joints.

Hinge joints allow movement in one plane only, owing to the shape of the bones that make up the joint. Examples of this type of joint are the ankle, the knee and the elbow.

Pivot joints allow rotational movement only, where the head of one bone fits into a notch on another. The atlas and axis vertebrae in the neck (cervical 1 and 2) and the joint between the radius and the ulna are pivot joints.

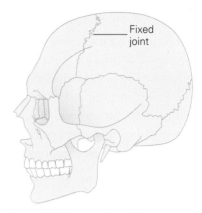

Figure 1.2 Fibrous joints of the cranium

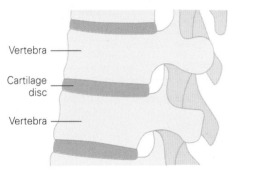

Figure 1.3 Cartilaginous joint in the spine

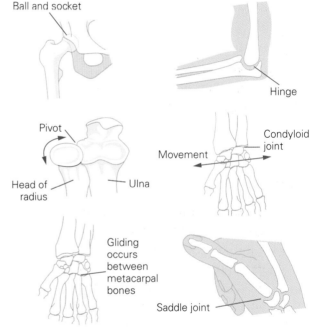

Figure 1.4 Synovial joints

Top tip

The fibula ends before it reaches the knee so is not an articulating bone at this joint. The inclusion of this bone in exam answers about the knee is a common error.

Condyloid joints are similar to hinge joints but instead of allowing movement in just one plane they allows sideways motion too. The dome-shaped surface of one bone fits into the hollow-shaped depression of the other. Examples of this type of joint are found in the wrist.

Gliding joints allow slight movement in all directions between two flat surfaces. Examples are found between the small bones of the wrist (metacarpals) and feet (metatarsals) as well as the articular processes of the vertebrae.

The bones that make up a saddle joint are either concave or convex. The surfaces are placed together, allowing movement at right angles. The thumb joint is an example.

Tasks to tackle 1.1

Use the labelled skeleton on page 3 to work out the articulating bones for the joints listed in the table below. Copy the table and complete it.

Joint	Joint type	Articulating bones
Ankle	Hinge	
Knee	Hinge	
Hip	Ball and socket	
Spine	Gliding	
Shoulder	Ball and socket	
Elbow	Hinge	
Wrist	Condyloid	

Structure of a synovial joint

A basic knowledge of the structure of synovial joints will help your understanding of the impact that different types of physical activity can have on the skeletal system. All synovial joints have four common features:

- cartilage
- a joint capsule
- synovial fluid
- ligaments

Articular or hyaline cartilage covers the ends of the bones at a joint. It forms a smooth surface, which reduces friction between the bones and thus protects the bone tissue and helps the smooth movement of the joint.

The joint capsule is a tough, fibrous, double layer of tissue encasing the joint. It adds stability and encloses the joint completely, making it airtight. Being airtight, the joint has to manufacture its own lubricants and nutrients. The synovial membrane is the inner layer or lining to the joint capsule. It covers the internal joint surfaces, except for the articular cartilage, and secretes synovial fluid.

Synovial fluid is the yellowish oily fluid that fills the joint capsule. Its functions are:

- to lubricate the cartilage surfaces by reducing friction between them, which permits even smoother movement
- to form a cushion of fluid between the bone surfaces, stopping the bones from grinding against each other and thus reducing wear and tear on the joint
- to nourish the cartilage

The ligaments are strong bands of tough, fibrous connective tissue, which provide stability by joining bone to bone (Figure 1.5).

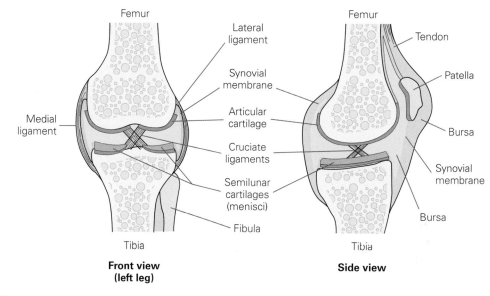

Figure 1.5 The structure of the knee (a synovial joint)

Some synovial joints have other structural features:

- Pads of fat in the gaps in and around the joint act as shock absorbers, for example in the elbow between the fibrous capsule and the adjoining muscles.
- Bursae are fluid-filled sacs located between the tendon and a bone. They reduce friction and hence wear and tear. They can be found in the shoulder joint between the head of the humerus and the ligament.
- The menisci are two pads of cartilaginous tissue found in the knee joint. They reduce friction between the tibia and the femur. The menisci improve the fit between the tibia and the femur by filling the gap with a rounded surface next to the femur and a flat surface next to the tibia.

Movement terminology

Flexion involves a *decrease* in the angle that occurs around a joint. For example, bending the arm at the elbow causes the angle between the radius and the humerus to decrease (Figure 1.6).

Extension involves an *increase* in the angle that occurs around a joint. For example, straightening the knee causes an increase in the angle between the femur and the tibia (Figure 1.7).

Plantarflexion is a term used solely for the ankle joint. It involves bending the foot downwards, away from the tibia (standing on your tiptoes).

Dorsiflexion is bending the foot upwards towards the tibia, or bending the hand backwards (Figure 1.8).

Abduction is movement away from the midline of the body — for example, raising the arms out to the side, away from the body.

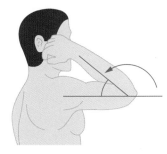

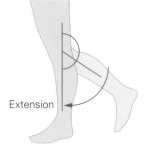

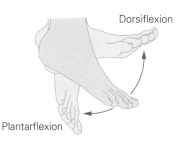

Figure 1.6 Elbow flexion   **Figure 1.7** Extension of the knee   **Figure 1.8** Plantarflexion and dorsiflexion

Adduction is movement towards the midline of the body — for example, lowering the arms back to the sides of the body (Figure 1.9).

Horizontal flexion (also called **horizontal adduction**) is movement of the arm forward across the body at 90° to shoulder abduction. For example, raise your arm out to the side until it is parallel to the floor (abduction of the shoulder) and then move it back across the body, keeping it parallel to the floor (Figure 1.10).

Horizontal extension (also called **horizontal abduction**) is movement of the arm backwards across the body to shoulder abduction. For example, raise your arm forward and hold it at 90° (flexion of the shoulder), then move it away from the body, keeping it parallel to the floor (Figure 1.11).

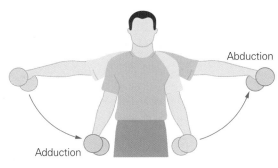

Figure 1.9 Adduction and abduction

Figure 1.10 Horizontal adduction

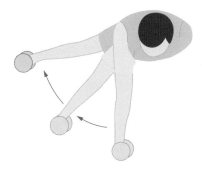

Figure 1.11 Horizontal abduction

Remember adduction and abduction as follows. If something is *abducted*, it is *taken away*. Look at the word *add*uction — think of *adding* the arm or leg back to the body.

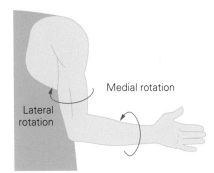

Figure 1.12 Lateral and medial rotation

Rotation is movement of a bone about its axis. This can be inward (medial) or outward (lateral) — see Figure 1.12.

Circumduction involves the lower end of the bone moving around in a circle. It is a combination of flexion, extension, abduction and adduction. Circumduction occurs at the shoulder and hip joints (Figure 1.13).

Pronation and **supination** are terms unique to the radio-ulnar joint, used to describe rotational movement. Pronation is when the palm faces down and supination is when the palm faces up (Figure 1.14).

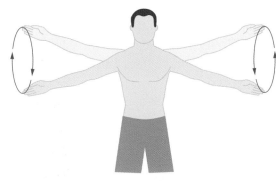

Figure 1.13 Circumduction at the shoulders

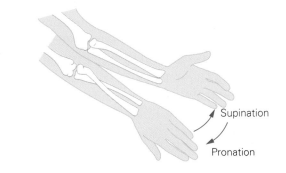

Figure 1.14 Pronation and supination of the forearm

Tasks to tackle 1.2

Work out the types of movement that can take place at each joint and then copy and complete the table.

	Wrist	Elbow	Radio-ulnar	Shoulder	Spine	Hip	Knee	Ankle
Flexion								
Extension								
Abduction								
Adduction								
Rotation								
Horizontal flexion								
Horizontal extension								
Plantarflexion								
Circumduction								
Dorsiflexion								
Palmarflexion								
Supination								
Pronation								
Lateral flexion								

Muscles

There are over 600 muscles in the human body, comprising approximately 45% of the total body weight. There are three main types of muscle tissue:

- skeletal
- cardiac
- smooth

Skeletal muscle is often referred to as voluntary, striped or striated muscle (Figure 1.15). It is attached to bone and produces movement. Skeletal muscle can occur in layers, where 'deep' muscles lie below 'superficial' muscles (Figure 1.16).

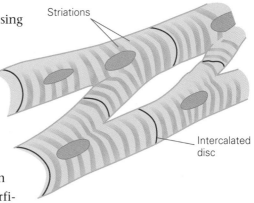

Figure 1.15 Structure of skeletal muscle

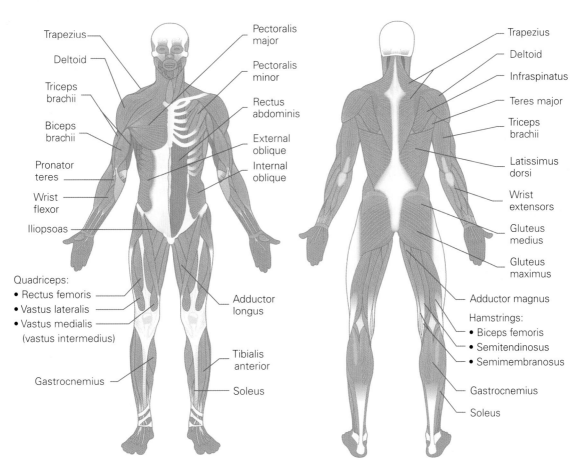

Figure 1.16 Human skeletal muscles

Cardiac muscle is found in the heart. It forces blood into the circulatory blood vessels, such as the aorta and the pulmonary artery. Cardiac muscle cells can only respire aerobically and therefore have the highest concentration of mitochondria. Cardiac muscle has a long rest period so that no summation occurs between contractions. This allows the heart to beat in a rhythmic manner with a rest period between contractions. This rest period prevents fatigue in the cardiac muscle.

Smooth muscle lies internally and has several functions, the main ones being to force food through the digestive system and to squeeze blood through the circulatory system via the artery and arteriole networks.

Table 1.1 Comparison of muscle types

Skeletal	Cardiac	Smooth
Voluntary	Involuntary	Involuntary
Brain sends an impulse for it to contract	Myogenic — creates its own impulse	Activated by its own nerve fibres
Parallel fibres	Intercalating fibres	Arranged in sheets or bundles
Fewer, smaller mitochondria — rapidly fatigue	More, larger mitochondria — resistant to fatigue	More mitochondria than skeletal muscle — resistant to fatigue

Actions of muscles

A joint cannot move by itself — it needs muscles to move the bones into position.

Muscles are attached to bones by tendons. The attachment of the muscle on a bone nearest the midline of the body (proximal end) is referred to as the origin. This is normally a stable, flat bone. The attachment on a bone further away from the midline of the body (distal end) is the insertion; this is the bone that the muscle moves.

When a muscle contracts, it shortens and bulges and the insertion moves closer to the origin. For example, the origin of the biceps brachii is on the scapula and the insertion is on the radius. The biceps is responsible for flexion of the elbow. When the biceps contracts, the radius moves upwards towards the shoulder, thus moving the insertion closer to the origin.

Movement at a joint usually involves several muscles. Each muscle plays a particular role so that movement can take place in an effective and controlled manner. When the muscle contracts, it is responsible for the movement that occurs and is said to be acting as an **agonist** or **prime mover**. There may be more than one agonist acting at a joint, although this depends on the type of movement that is being performed. An **antagonist** muscle is one that works in opposition to the agonist, so when the biceps brachii (the agonist) is contracting, the triceps brachii is lengthening and acting as the antagonist.

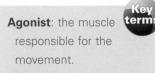

Key terms

Agonist: the muscle responsible for the movement.

Antagonist: the muscle that works in opposition to the agonist, helping to produce a coordinated movement.

When one muscle is acting as an agonist and another is acting as the antagonist, the muscles are said to be working together as an antagonistic pair. In a flexion of the knee movement, the hamstrings are the agonist and the quadriceps are the antagonist.

As well as antagonistic muscle pairs, other muscles contract to make the joint movement stable. These are **fixator** muscles. Fixators are muscles that stabilise the origin so that the agonist can work more efficiently. For example, in the upward phase of an arm curl, the biceps brachii is the agonist, the triceps brachii is the antagonist and the deltoid is the fixator. You can feel tension in the deltoid as it helps to stabilise the shoulder joint.

Top tip

Be careful. The agonist does not automatically become the antagonist when the movement changes, for example from flexion to extension. In the downward phase of the biceps curl, most students think that the biceps is the antagonist, but it is still the agonist. It is now lengthening as it contracts in order to control the lowering of the forearm while it supports the weight.

Joint movements and muscles

It is hard to memorise all the muscles you need to know for your exam so in this section we will isolate each joint and look at the surrounding muscles and the type of movement they are responsible for.

The wrist joint

The wrist is a condyloid joint where the distal ends of the radius and the ulna articulate (meet) with the carpals. The muscles surrounding this joint can produce flexion, extension, abduction and adduction at the wrist (but not rotation). You do not need to know the individual muscle names for AS/A-level — just the collective term for the muscles responsible for flexion and extension, that is, wrist flexors and wrist extensors Figure 1.17 and Table 1.2.

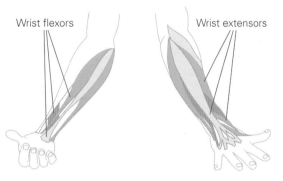

Figure 1.17 The wrist flexors and extensors

Table 1.2 Movement in the wrist joint

Movement	Agonist
Palmarflexion	Wrist flexors
Dorsiflexion	Wrist extensors

The elbow joint

The elbow is a hinge joint, with the distal (far) end of the humerus articulating with the proximal (near) end of the radius and ulna. Only flexion and extension can take place, using the biceps brachii and the triceps brachii (Figure 1.18 and Table 1.3).

Within the elbow joint capsule, the radius articulates with the ulna to form a pivot joint (radio-ulnar joint). Here, pronation and supination occur.

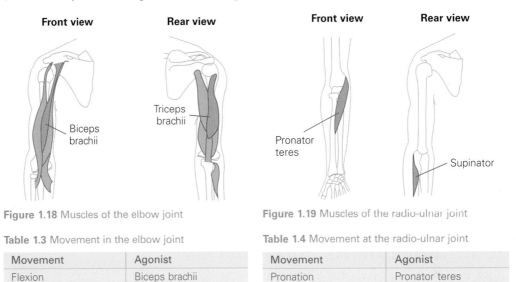

Figure 1.18 Muscles of the elbow joint

Figure 1.19 Muscles of the radio-ulnar joint

Table 1.3 Movement in the elbow joint

Movement	Agonist
Flexion	Biceps brachii
Extension	Triceps brachii

Table 1.4 Movement at the radio-ulnar joint

Movement	Agonist
Pronation	Pronator teres
Supination	Supinator

The shoulder joint

The shoulder is a ball-and-socket joint where the head of the humerus fits into a cavity on the scapula called the glenoid fossa. This type of joint allows the most movement, because of the shallowness of the joint cavity. However, its structure also makes it one of the least stable joints, so it is heavily reliant on ligaments and muscles to increase its stability (Figure 1.20 and Table 1.5).

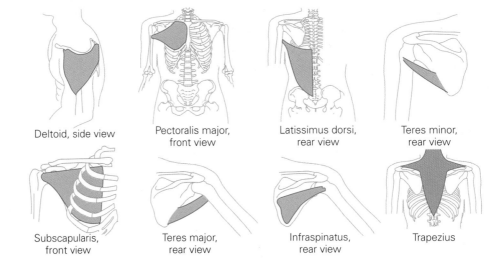

Figure 1.20 Muscles of the shoulder joint

Table 1.5 Movement at the shoulder joint

Movement	Agonist
Flexion	Anterior deltoid
Extension	Posterior deltoid
Abduction	Middle deltoid
Adduction	Latissimus dorsi
Horizontal flexion	Pectoralis major
Horizontal extension	Trapezius
Lateral rotation	Infraspinatus, teres minor
Medial rotation	Subscapularis, teres major

Top tip

You need to know one muscle for each of the movements, so make it easy for yourself and learn each of the different sections of the deltoid, which covers three movements.

The spine

The spine has three types of joint:

- cartilaginous — between the individual vertebrae
- gliding — between the vertebral arches
- pivot — between the atlas and axis vertebrae

Most movement occurs around the gliding joints where there is flexion, extension, lateral flexion (bending to the side) and rotation (looking over your shoulder). In the pivot joint there is rotation (shaking your head).

Key terms

Core stability: the ability to control the position and movement of the trunk during dynamic movements.

The major muscles you need to know for the movements that occur at the spine are the rectus abdominis, erector spinae group, external and internal obliques and sacrospinalis. In addition, the deep trunk muscles, such as the transversus abdominis and multifidus, have an important role in relation to core stability. Core stability is the ability to control the position and movement of the trunk. Muscles deep in the abdomen maintain good posture, which provides a balanced position for all arm and leg movements. The transversus abdominis and multifidus are both important muscles that can be recruited to control the position of the spine during dynamic movements (Figure 1.21 and Table 1.6).

Table 1.6 Movement in the spine

Movement	Agonist
Flexion	Rectus abdominus
Extension	Erector spinae group
Lateral flexion	Internal and external obliques
Rotation	Internal and external obliques

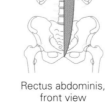

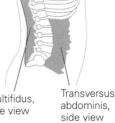

External abdominal oblique, side view — Erector spinae — Sacrospinalis, rear view — Rectus abdominis, front view — Multifidus, side view — Transversus abdominis, side view

Figure 1.21 Muscles of the spine

The hip joint

The hip is a ball-and-socket joint where the head of the femur fits into the acetabulum of the pelvis. The joint cavity for the hip is much deeper than that for the shoulder, thus making the hip more stable but less mobile. The addition of strong ligaments surrounding the hip joint decreases its mobility even more, but at the same time this makes dislocation very difficult (Figure 1.22 and Table 1.7).

Table 1.7 Movement at the hip

Movement	Agonist
Flexion	Iliopsoas
Extension	Gluteus maximus
Abduction	Gluteus medius, gluteus minimus
Adduction	Adductor group
Lateral rotation	Gluteus maximus
Medial rotation	Gluteus medius, gluteus minimus

The muscles that you need to know for the hip joint are the iliopsoas, the gluteus maximus, medius and minimus, and the adductor longus, brevis and magnus.

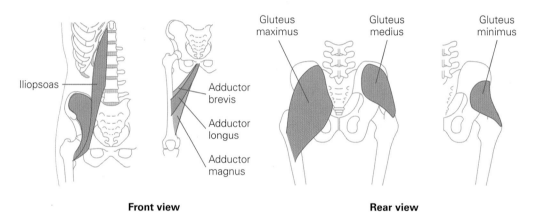

Figure 1.22 Muscles of the hip joint

The knee joint

The knee is classed as a hinge joint and so should only be able to flex and extend (Table 1.8). However, this is not strictly true as some rotation is allowed to facilitate full extension and locking of the knee. The femur articulates with the tibia (not the fibula). Strong ligaments are present in order to prevent any sideways movement. Muscles controlling the knee are shown in Figure 1.23.

Top tip

Make sure you know the names of the three hamstrings and the four quadriceps muscles. The collective term will not earn you a mark in the exam.

Table 1.8 Movement at the knee joint

Movement	Agonist
Flexion	Hamstrings: biceps femoris, semitendinosus, semimembranosus
Extension	Quadriceps: rectus femoris, vastus lateralis, vastus intermedius, vastus medialis

The knee has two huge muscle groups: the quadriceps and the hamstrings. You need to be able to name the muscles in these two groups. The quadriceps comprise:

- rectus femoris
- vastus lateralis
- vastus medialis
- vastus intermedius

The hamstrings are:

- biceps femoris
- semi-membranosus
- semi-tendinosus

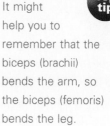

It might help you to remember that the biceps (brachii) bends the arm, so the biceps (femoris) bends the leg.

Vastus lateralis

Biceps femoris

Vastus intermedius

Rectus femoris

Vastus medialis

Semi-membranosus

Semi-tendinosus

Front view   **Rear view**   **Rear view**

Figure 1.23 Muscles of the knee joint

The ankle joint

The ankle is a hinge joint where the articulating bones are the tibia, fibula and talus. The three main muscles that control movement in this joint are the gastrocnemius, the soleus (calf muscles) and the tibialis anterior (shin muscles) (Figure 1.24 and Table 1.9).

Table 1.9 Movement at the ankle joint

Movement	Agonist
Plantarflexion	Gastrocnemius, soleus
Dorsiflexion	Tibialis anterior

Table 1.10 summarises all the joints, articulating bones, movements and agonist muscles required for the AS exam.

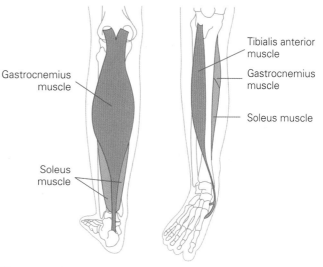

Gastrocnemius muscle

Soleus muscle

Tibialis anterior muscle

Gastrocnemius muscle

Soleus muscle

Figure 1.24 Muscles of the ankle joint

Table 1.10

Synovial joint	Example	Articulating bones	Movement	Agonist
Ball and socket	Hip	Acetabulum of the pelvis and femur	Flexion Extension Lateral rotation Medial rotation Abduction Adduction	Iliopsoas Gluteus maximus Gluteus maximus Gluteus medius/minimus Gluteus medius/minimus Adductors (longus, brevis and magnus)
	Shoulder	Glenoid fossa of the scapula and humerus	Flexion Extension Abduction Adduction Outward rotation Inward rotation Horizontal flexion Horizontal extension	Anterior deltoid Posterior deltoid Middle deltoid Latissimus dorsi Infraspinatus Subscapularis Pectoralis major Trapezius
Hinge	Elbow	Radius, ulna, humerus	Flexion Extension	Biceps brachii Triceps brachii
	Knee	Tibia, femur and patella	Flexion Extension	Biceps femoris Rectus femoris
	Ankle	Tibia, fibula and talus	Plantarflexion Dorsiflexion	Gastrocnemius Tibialis anterior
Pivot	Radio-ulnar	Radius and ulna	Pronation Supination	Pronator teres Supinator
Gliding	Spine	Vertebral arches	Flexion Extension Lateral flexion Rotation (to the opposite side)	Rectus abdominus Erector spinae group External obliques Internal obliques
Condyloid	Wrist	Carpals, radius, ulna	Palmarflexion Dorsiflexion	Wrist flexors Wrist extensors

Types of muscular contraction

A muscle can contract in three different ways, depending on the muscle action that is required:

- concentric contraction
- eccentric contraction
- isometric contraction

Concentric contraction is when the muscle shortens under tension. For example, during the upward phase of an arm curl, the biceps brachii performs a concentric contraction as it shortens to produce flexion of the elbow.

Eccentric contraction is when the muscle lengthens under tension (and does not relax). When a muscle contracts eccentrically, it acts as a brake to help control the movement of the body part during negative work. For example, when landing from a standing jump, the quadriceps muscles are performing negative work as they are supporting the weight of the body during landing. The knee joint is in the flexed position but the quadriceps muscles are unable to relax as the weight of the body ensures that they lengthen under tension.

Isometric contraction is when the muscle contracts without lengthening or shortening. The result is that no movement occurs. An isometric contraction occurs when a muscle acts as a fixator or against a resistance.

Using the biceps curl as an example (Figure 1.25):

- During the upward phase, the biceps brachii contracts to produce flexion of the elbow joint. In this situation it is performing a concentric contraction.
- During the downward phase, if you put your hand on the biceps brachii you will still feel tension. This means that the muscle is not relaxing but is performing an eccentric contraction, where it lengthens under tension.
- If the weight is held still at a 90° angle, the biceps brachii is under tension although there is no movement. This is an isometric contraction.

Concentric contraction: when a muscle shortens under tension.
Eccentric contraction: when a muscle lengthens under tension.
Isometric contraction: when a muscle is under tension but there is no visible movement.

Eccentric contraction is the type most misunderstood. Remember that it is a contraction, so the muscle cannot be relaxing; it is lengthening under tension.

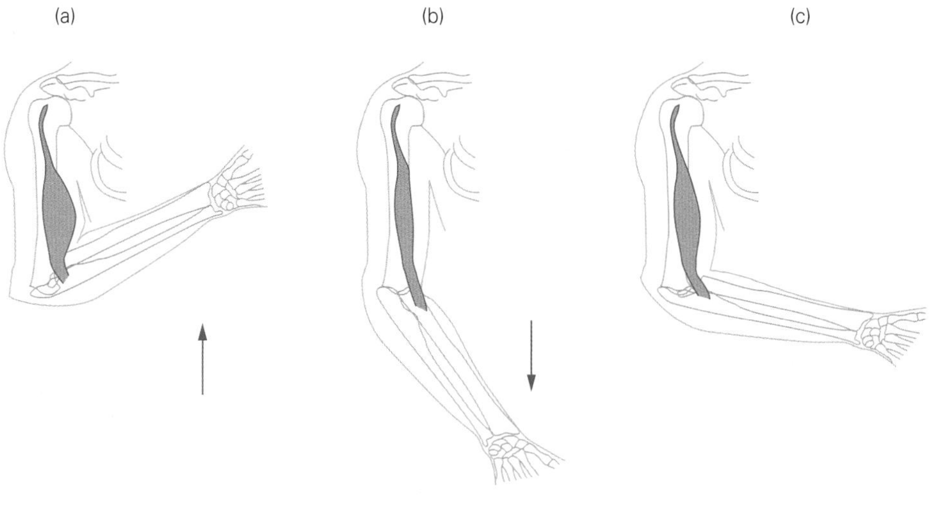

(a)   (b)   (c)

Figure 1.25 A biceps curl: (a) concentric contraction, (b) eccentric contraction, (c) isometric contraction

Tasks to tackle 1.3

Answer the following questions for the movements involved in a press-up.

1 During the downward phase:
- What type of movement happens at the elbow joint?
- Which muscle contracts?
- What type of contraction occurs?

2 During the upward phase:
- What type of movement happens at the elbow joint?
- Which muscle contracts?
- What type of contraction occurs?

3 If the press-up is held in the downward phase:
- Which muscle feels as if it contracts?
- What type of contraction occurs?

Tasks to tackle 1.4

Copy and complete the movement analysis table for the hockey player in Figure 1.26.

Figure 1.26

Joint	Joint type	Articulating bones	Movement	Agonist muscle	Antagonist muscle	Type of contraction
Right elbow						
Right shoulder						
Spine						
Right hip						
Left knee						
Left ankle						

Impact of exercise on the skeletal system

Taking part in physical activity is important for a healthy lifestyle. Physical activity inevitably has an impact on the skeletal and muscular systems. Some activities have a positive impact while others — for example, contact sports and physical activities that are high-impact or involve repetitive actions — can have a negative impact.

Low-impact aerobic activity

Low-impact aerobic activity generally has a positive impact. Osteoporosis (weakening of the bone) is a condition caused by the loss of calcium in the body, in a process called demineralisation. Participation in low-impact activities can reverse this trend. The bones become stronger due to increased calcium deposits and the strength of the muscles, tendons and ligaments increases. Low-impact activity also avoids over-use injuries by varying the line of stress on bones.

> **Key term**
>
> **Osteoporosis**: a reduction in bone mass due to a decrease in bone mineral density. It causes bones to become fragile and to fracture easily.

Osteoarthritis is a deterioration of the joint cartilage and the development of bony spurs on the bones at the edge of the joints. It usually affects the knees, hips, hands, feet and spine. Low-impact aerobic activities can help mild osteoarthritis by increasing blood flow, thus nourishing the cartilage and bone and strengthening the joints, causing them to be more stable.

Strength training and core stability

This type of training can cause hypertrophy of the muscles (the muscles become bigger and stronger). The increase in muscle strength leads to an increase in joint stability. For example, core stability exercises can increase the strength of the rotator cuff muscles, which increases stability in the shoulder joint as well as reducing the likelihood of problems with the lumbar vertebrae. Increasing the strength in the quadriceps muscles helps to stabilise tracking and knee function. Strengthening exercises can also help with mild osteoarthritis by decreasing joint stiffness and strengthening the muscles around a joint, to give protection and absorb shock.

However, strength training involves a lot of eccentric muscle contractions, which can cause muscle damage when pushed to maximum. For example, in a squat, the quadriceps muscles contract concentrically during the upward phase to straighten the knee but eccentrically during the downward (bending) phase. This means that the muscles cannot relax throughout the squat. Overdoing the number of squats can cause muscle damage.

High-impact activity

High-impact activities involve contact, such as a tackle in rugby, or impact through landing, for example in the triple jump. Such activities can cause damage to the growth plate. This is the softer part of young people's bones where growth occurs. Growth plates are found at the ends of bones and are the weakest sections of the skeleton. They are susceptible to injury. Immediate treatment is required in the event of injury as it can affect how the bone grows.

Medial or cruciate ligament damage to the knee can result from side impact, such as a sliding tackle in football. Heavy impact to the shoulder joint can cause dislocation due to the shallow joint cavity.

Flexibility training

Flexibility training involves stretching muscles and connective tissue. With regular and repeated stretching, the soft tissue can elongate and this may be beneficial in avoiding injury. Tendons, ligaments and particularly muscle tissue surrounding a joint increase their resting length due to greater elasticity. This increases the range of movement around the joint. However, extreme flexibility can stretch ligaments and lead to a lack of stability.

Tasks to tackle 1.5

Think of three elite sportsmen or women who have experienced injuries that have kept them out of their sport for some of the season. What caused these injuries? Does their physical activity involve high-impact work, contact or repetitive actions?

Activities involving repetitive movements or over-use

Repetitive stress injuries occur when too much stress is placed on part of the body. The result is inflammation of the bursa, wearing down of the articular/hyaline cartilage in joints and muscle strain or tissue damage. Tennis players, for example, often have elbow or shoulder injuries caused by over-use as they repeat the same movements over and over again. Over-use injuries in children and teenagers usually occur at the growth plates. The most common repetitive stress injuries occur at the elbows, shoulders, knees and heels.

Speed and agility training

This allows muscles to retain more elasticity/elastin, which means they can contract with more speed and power.

Types of muscle fibre

Three main types of muscle fibre can be identified:
- type I, slow oxidative
- type IIa, fast oxidative glycolytic
- type IIb, fast glycolytic

Our skeletal muscles contain a mixture of all three types of fibre but not in equal proportions. The mix is mainly genetically determined. The fibres are grouped into motor units. Only one type of fibre can be found in one particular unit.

The relative proportion of each fibre type varies in the same muscles of different people. For example, elite endurance athletes have a greater proportion of slow-twitch fibres in the leg muscles while elite sprinters have a greater proportion of fast-twitch fibres. Postural muscles tend to have a greater proportion of slow-twitch fibres as they are involved in maintaining body position over long periods of time.

All three fibre types have specific characteristics that allow them to perform their role successfully (see Table 1.11).

Table 1.11 Muscle fibre characteristics

Characteristic	Type I	Type IIa	Type IIb
Contraction speed	Slow	Fast	Fast
Size	Small	Medium	Large
Force produced	Low	Medium	High
Fatiguability	Low	Medium	High
Number of mitochondria	Many	Many	Few
Myoglobin concentration	High	High	Low
Glycogen store	Low	Medium	High
Capillaries	Many	Many	Few
Aerobic capacity	High	Medium	Low
Anaerobic capacity	Low	High	High
Elasticity	Low	High	High

The effect of training on fibre type

Fibre type is mainly genetically determined. However, it is possible to increase the size of muscle fibres through training. This increase in size (hypertrophy) is caused by an increase in the number and size of myofibrils per fibre, with a consequent increase in the amount of protein, namely myosin. As a result there will be greater strength in the muscle.

Top tip

Questions on different fibre types often ask for structural and/or functional characteristics. Make sure you can distinguish between them and give examples. Remember, structure is the make-up of the fibre; function is what the fibre does.

Physiological effects of a warm-up

A warm-up is not just about avoiding injury — it can lead to an improvement in performance. Warming up prepares the body for exercise simply because warm muscles are stronger and have more endurance. Warming up allows for greater speed and accuracy in a game or sporting situation. It has the following physiological effects:

- It releases adrenaline, which increases heart rate and dilates the capillaries. In addition, the vasomotor centre ensures that vasodilation occurs, so that more blood flows (due to the increase in cardiac output) to the working muscles. This allows more oxygen to be delivered to the skeletal muscles.
- Muscle temperature increases. This enables oxygen to dissociate more easily from haemoglobin and increases enzyme activity, making energy readily available.
- An increase in the speed of nerve impulse conduction increases alertness.

- Greater elasticity of the muscle fibres occurs through the increase in muscle temperature. This leads to an increase in the speed and force of contraction.
- Efficient movement at joints occurs through an increased production of synovial fluid.
- A reduction in muscle viscosity improves the coordination between antagonistic pairs, which increases the speed and strength of contraction.
- An increase in enzyme activity in the warmer muscle fibres increases the speed and strength of muscle contraction.

Tasks to tackle 1.6

Identify the predominant fibre type that would be found in the following elite performers (copy and complete the table):

Elite athlete	Predominant fibre type
Marathon runner	
100 metres sprinter	
Centre in netball	
Speed cyclist	
Endurance swimmer	

The cool-down

Having just finished a hard training session or competitive match, your immediate inclination may be to sit down and have a rest. But think again! It is important to perform a cool-down at the end of any physical activity as it helps to return the body to its pre-exercise state more quickly.

A cool-down consists of some form of light exercise to keep the heart rate elevated. This keeps blood flow high and allows oxygen to be flushed through the muscles, oxidising and removing any lactic acid that remains. Performing light exercise also allows the skeletal muscle pump to keep working and prevents blood from pooling in the veins. If we stop exercising suddenly, the amount of blood going back to the heart drops dramatically. This is because there is little or no muscle action to maintain the skeletal muscle pump. Consequently, stroke volume drops and there is a reduction in blood pressure. The performer will begin to feel dizzy and light-headed.

Light exercise should be followed by some static stretches.

Practice makes perfect

1 (a) Identify the prime mover/agonist involved in the ankle joint and the type
of contraction performed during the take-off phase of a standing long jump. *(2 marks)*

(b) Using the same muscle identified in (a), state what type of contraction
is performed during the landing phase and why. *(2 marks)*

2 Copy and complete the movement analysis table. *(6 marks)*

Joint	Joint type	Articulating bones	Movement produced	Agonist
Ankle		Talus, tibia and fibula	Plantarflexion	
Knee	Hinge		Extension	
	Ball and socket			Gluteus maximus

(6 marks)

3 Muscles are arranged as antagonistic pairs. Using flexion of the knee joint
as an example, explain the meaning of **antagonistic pair**. *(4 marks)*

4 Identify the predominant fibre type you would expect to find in the gastrocnemius
muscle of a 100 m sprinter. Give two structural and two functional characteristics
of this type of fibre. *(5 marks)*

5 Give two effects of a warm-up on the strength and speed of muscular contraction. *(2 marks)*

6 Activities involving repetitive movements have an impact on the skeletal and
muscular systems. Identify such an activity and explain the implications of
placing too much stress on a part of the body. *(3 marks)*

Chapter 2 *Anatomy and physiology*

Motion and movement

What you need to know

By the end of this chapter you should be able to:

- define Newton's laws of motion
- describe the three types of motion — linear, angular and general motion
- describe the effect of the size of force, direction of force and the position of application of force on a body
- define centre of mass and explain the effects of changing the position of the centre of mass and the area of support on sports techniques
- apply your knowledge of motion, force and balance to typical sporting actions

Newton's laws of motion

Newton's first law of motion

A body continues in its state of rest or motion in a straight line, unless compelled to change that state by external forces exerted upon it.

This is the law of inertia. In simple terms, it means that a body or an object, such as a ball, will remain in its state of motion (i.e. moving in a straight line) or remain stationary unless there is a force to change this.

Newton's second law of motion

The rate of momentum of a body (or the acceleration for a body of constant mass) is proportional to the force causing it and the change that takes place in the direction in which the force acts.

This is the law of acceleration. More simply, to generate a greater acceleration, the performer must generate a greater force.

Table 2.1 Application of Newton's laws

Newton's law	Application
Law of inertia	A ball (the body) will remain on the penalty spot (in a state of rest) unless an external force is exerted upon it (i.e. it is kicked by a player)
Law of acceleration	When a player kicks (force applied) the ball during the game, the acceleration of the ball (rate of change of momentum) is proportional to the size of the force. So, the harder the ball is kicked the further and faster it will go.
Law of reaction	When a footballer jumps up (action) to win a header, a force is exerted on the ground in order to gain height. At the same time the ground exerts an upward force (equal and opposite reaction) upon the player.

Newton's third law of motion

To every action there is an equal and opposite reaction.

This is the law of reaction. When a ball is kicked, the ball exerts an equal and opposite force on the kicking foot.

Table 2.1 applies these laws to football.

Tasks to tackle 2.1

Copy and complete the table, giving an example of how each of the laws can be applied to a sport of your choice.

Newton's law	Application
Law of inertia	
Law of acceleration	
Law of reaction	

Motion

There are three main types of motion:

Linear motion

This is motion of a body or body part in a straight or curved line. For example, a 100 m sprinter runs from the start to the finish in a straight line, and in the shot put the shot travels in a curved line from its release to landing.

George Side Blonsky/Alamy

The shot travels in a curved line — an example of linear motion

Angular motion

This is movement around a fixed point or axis. This suggests circular or rotational movement. An example of angular motion is a somersault. The arms and the legs as they move in a running action are also in angular motion as they rotate about their axis.

General motion

This is a combination of linear and angular motion. The run-up in the javelin throw is an example of general motion. The body moves in a straight line on the approach but during the throwing action the arm moves in a circular motion.

Force

A force can be described as a 'push or pull'. It can cause a body at rest to move, or cause a moving body to stop, slow down, speed up or change direction.

A force can be measured in terms of:

- size or magnitude. This depends on the size and number of muscle fibres used.
- direction. If a force is applied through the middle of an object, it will move in the same direction as the force (Figure 2.1).
- the position of application. This is an important factor in sport. Applying a force straight through the centre results in movement in a straight line (linear motion). Applying a force off-centre results in spin (angular motion) (Figure 2.2).

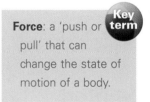

Force: a 'push or pull' that can change the state of motion of a body.

Figure 2.1 A force applied through the middle of an object will move the object in the same direction as the force

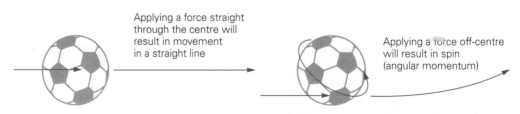

Applying a force straight through the centre will result in movement in a straight line

Applying a force off-centre will result in spin (angular momentum)

Figure 2.2 The effect of applying a force off-centre

OCR AS Physical Education

A force can be either internal or external. Internal forces are provided by concentric and occasionally eccentric muscle contraction. External forces include:

- gravity — the force that draws all bodies towards the centre of the Earth
- air resistance, which opposes the motion of objects through the air
- friction — the resistance to motion caused by contact between two surfaces
- reaction — for every action force there must be an equal and opposite reaction force

Tasks to tackle 2.2

- Screw up a piece of A4 paper into a tight ball.
- Draw three circles on a piece of paper to represent three balls, and under each one draw an up-turned hand.
- Throw the paper ball vertically into the air so that it does not spin. Mark the centre of mass (C) on the first circle and then show both the point of application of the force (P) and the direction in which the force is acting (D).
- Now throw the ball up again and this time give it some back spin. On the second circle, draw the point of application of the force and the direction in which the force is acting.
- Now throw the ball up one more time. This time, try to make it spin forwards. Again (using the third circle), draw the point of application of the force and the direction in which the force is acting.

Centre of mass

The centre of mass is the point of concentration of mass or, more simply, the point of balance. In the human body, the centre of mass cannot be defined so easily due to the body's irregular shape. In addition, the body is constantly moving, so the centre of mass changes. For example, raising your arms in the air raises your centre of mass in order to keep the body balanced. In general, the centre of mass for someone in a standing position is in the lower abdomen (Figure 2.3).

A balanced position depends on:

- the centre of mass being over the base of support
- the line of gravity running through the middle of the base of support
- the number of contact points — the more contact points, the more stable the person is. For example, a headstand has more contact points than a handstand, so is a more balanced position.
- the mass of the performer — the greater the mass, the more stability there is

Figure 2.3 The centre of mass

Centre of mass: the point of balance.
Line of gravity: the line extending vertically downwards from the centre of mass.

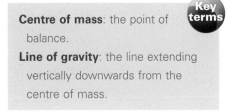

To be in a balanced position, the centre of mass needs to be in line with the base of support. If you lower your centre of mass, your stability increases but if your centre of mass starts to move near the edge of the base of support, then you will start to overbalance. A sprinter in the 'set' position has her centre of mass at the edge of the area of support. As she moves on hearing the starting pistol, she lifts her hands off the ground and becomes off-balanced. This allows her to fall forward and helps to create the speed required to leave the blocks as quickly as possible.

The centre of mass changes as a sprinter pushes off

Tasks to tackle 2.3

Stand against a wall with your back and the back of your heels touching it. Now try to touch your toes.
(a) Can you do this? Give reasons why/why not.

Now kneel on the floor with your bottom touching your heels. Place both elbows in front of your knees and keep your hands flat on the floor.

Place a pen or pencil on the floor level with the tips of your fingers.

Transfer your weight back onto your knees and then with your hands behind your back see if you can pick up the pen with your teeth. (You are allowed to lift your bottom up into the air but you cannot move out of the kneeling position.)
(b) Can you do this? Give reasons why/why not.

Practice makes perfect

1 The effect of a force when applied to a performer can determine the type of motion produced. Using an example from physical education, show how you would produce:
(a) linear motion
(b) angular motion *(4 marks)*

2 Using an example from physical education or sport, explain how the size of force, direction of force and position of application of force can affect performance. *(3 marks)*

3 Explain how an athlete can use his/her knowledge of balance to achieve an effective sprint start. *(3 marks)*

4 Using examples from sport, explain how knowledge of Newton's laws of motion could improve performance. *(3 marks)*

5 It is important to understand the influence of the centre of mass when performing a balance. Identify a named gymnastic balance and describe the factors that affect its performance. *(4 marks)*

Response of the heart to physical activity

What you need to know

By the end of this chapter you should be able to:
- describe the link between the cardiac cycle and the conduction system of the heart
- define stroke volume, heart rate and cardiac output and give resting values
- describe the relationship between stroke volume, heart rate and cardiac output
- explain the changes to stroke volume, heart rate and cardiac output that take place during both low- and high-intensity exercise
- explain neural, hormonal and intrinsic control of heart rate
- evaluate the impact of different types of physical activity on the heart (to include an understanding of coronary heart disease, angina and heart attack)

The structure of the heart

The heart is a muscular, cone-shaped organ and is approximately the size of a clenched fist. It is located in the chest, between the lungs, and is protected by the ribcage. The main purpose of the heart is to pump blood around the body.

Chambers of the heart

The heart is divided into two parts by a muscular wall called the septum (Figure 3.1). Each part contains an atrium and a ventricle. The atria are smaller than the ventricles because all they do is push blood into the ventricles. This does not require much force so they have thinner muscular walls. The ventricles have much thicker muscular walls, because they need to contract with greater force to push blood out of the heart. The left side of the heart has the thickest walls as it needs to pump blood all around the body, whereas the right side pumps deoxygenated blood to the lungs, which are in close proximity to the heart.

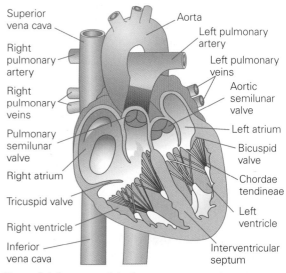

Figure 3.1 Structure of the heart

Blood vessels of the heart

The **vena cava** carries deoxygenated blood from the body to the right atrium. The **pulmonary artery** carries deoxygenated blood from the right ventricle to the lungs. The **pulmonary vein** delivers oxygenated blood from the lungs to the left atrium. The **aorta** carries oxygenated blood from the left ventricle to the body (Figure 3.2).

For the heart to work effectively, it requires a good blood supply. This is provided by the coronary artery, which carries oxygenated blood. Deoxygenated blood drains into the right atrium through a collection of veins called the coronary sinus.

Valves of the heart

There are four main valves in the heart that regulate blood flow by ensuring it moves in only one direction. They open to allow blood to pass through and then close to prevent back-flow. The tricuspid valve is located between the right atrium and the right ventricle. The bicuspid valve lies between the left atrium and the left ventricle. The semilunar valves are located between the right ventricle and the pulmonary artery and between the left ventricle and the aorta.

The conduction system

Blood flows through the heart in a controlled manner, in through the atria and out through the ventricles. Contraction of heart muscle is described as being **myogenic** (it creates its own impulse). An electrical impulse originates in the sinoatrial node (pacemaker) of the heart (Figure 3.3). This electrical impulse then spreads through the heart in what is often described as a wave of excitation (similar to a Mexican wave).

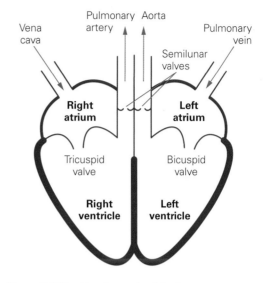

Figure 3.2 The blood vessels of the heart

Tasks to tackle 3.1

Outline the journey taken by a red blood cell from the gastrocnemius in the calf, where it is carrying deoxygenated blood, until it leaves the aorta transporting oxygenated blood.

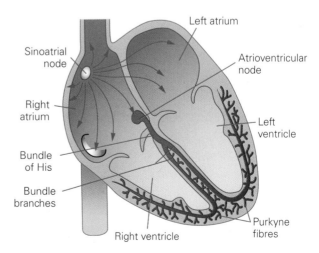

Figure 3.3 The conduction system of the heart

From the sinoatrial node, the electrical impulse spreads through the walls of the atria, causing them to contract and forcing blood into the ventricles. The impulse then passes through the atrioventricular node, found in the atrioventricular septum. The atrioventricular node delays the transmission of the cardiac impulse for approximately 0.1 seconds to enable the atria to contract fully before ventricular contraction begins. The electrical impulse then spreads down through some specialised fibres, which form the bundle of His. This is located in the septum separating the two ventricles. The bundle of His branches out into two bundle branches and then into smaller bundles called Purkyne (or Purkinje) fibres, which spread throughout the ventricles, causing them to contract.

> **Top tip**
>
> Questions often relate the conduction system and the cardiac cycle, so do not learn them as two separate systems.

The cardiac cycle

The cardiac cycle describes the emptying and filling of the heart. It involves a number of stages. The diastole phase is when the chambers are relaxing and filling with blood. The systole phase is when the heart contracts and forces blood either around the heart or out of the heart to the lungs and the body. Each complete cardiac cycle takes approximately 0.8 seconds. The diastole phase lasts 0.5 seconds and the systole phase lasts for 0.3 seconds. The cardiac cycle is summarised in Table 3.1.

> **Key terms**
>
> **Diastole**: the relaxation phase of the heart.
> **Systole**: the contraction phase of the heart.
> **Stroke volume**: the amount of blood pumped out by the left ventricle per beat.

Table 3.1 The cardiac cycle

Stage	Action	Result
Atrial systole	Atrial walls contract	Blood is forced through the bicuspid and tricuspid valves into the ventricles.
Atrial diastole	Atrial walls relax	Blood enters the right atrium via the vena cava and the left atrium via the pulmonary vein but cannot pass into the ventricles as the tricuspid and bicuspid valves are closed.
Ventricular systole	Ventricular walls contract	Pressure of blood opens the semilunar valves and blood is ejected into the pulmonary artery to the lungs and into the aorta to the body. The tricuspid and bicuspid valves close.
Ventricular diastole	Ventricular walls relax	Blood enters from the atria (passive ventricular filling, not due to atrial contraction). The semilunar valves are closed.

Link between the cardiac cycle and the conduction system

The cardiac cycle describes the flow of blood through the heart during one heartbeat. Because the heart generates its own electrical impulses, this flow of blood is controlled via the conduction system.

Cardiac dynamics

Stroke volume

Stroke volume is the amount of blood pumped out by the left ventricle in each contraction. The average resting stroke volume is approximately 70 ml.

Stroke volume is determined by:

- venous return — the volume of blood returning to the heart via the veins. If venous return increases, stroke volume will also increase (i.e. if more blood enters the heart then more blood is pumped out).
- the elasticity of the cardiac fibres — this is concerned with the degree of stretch of cardiac tissue during the diastole phase of the cardiac cycle. The more the cardiac fibres stretch, the greater the force of contraction. A greater force of contraction can increase stroke volume. This is called **Starling's law.**
- the contractility of the cardiac tissue (myocardium) — the greater the contractility of the cardiac tissue, the greater the force of contraction. This results in an increase in stroke volume and an increase in the ejection fraction (the percentage of blood pumped out of the left ventricle per beat). An average ejection fraction is 60% but it can increase by up to 85% following a period of training.

$$\text{ejection fraction} = \frac{\text{stroke volume}}{\text{end diastolic volume}} \times 100$$

Key terms

Cardiac output: the amount of blood pumped out of the left ventricle per minute.

Ejection fraction: the percentage of blood pumped out of the left ventricle per beat.

Starling's law: when stroke volume increases in response to an increase in the volume of blood filling the left ventricle (end diastolic volume). The increased volume of blood stretches the ventricular wall, causing cardiac muscle to contract more forcefully.

Venous return: blood returning to the heart via the veins.

Heart rate

Heart rate is the number of times the heart beats per minute. The average resting heart rate is approximately 72 beats per minute. The fitter an individual, the lower the heart rate. For example, Miguel Indurain, an elite cyclist, had a resting heart rate of only 28 beats per minute.

Cardiac output

Cardiac output is the amount of blood pumped out by the left ventricle per minute. It is equal to stroke volume multiplied by heart rate.

$$\text{cardiac output } (Q) = \text{stroke volume} \times \text{heart rate}$$
$$Q = 70 \times 72$$
$$Q = 5040 \text{ ml (5.04 litres)}$$

If heart rate or stroke volume increases, then cardiac output will also increase.

Heart rate range in response to exercise

Heart rate increases with exercise but how much it increases depends on the intensity of the exercise. Heart rate increases in direct proportion to exercise intensity until it reaches a maximum. Maximum heart rate can be approximated by subtracting the performer's age from 220. For example, a 17-year-old will have a maximum heart rate of around 203 beats per minute.

Figures 3.4 and 3.5 illustrate the changes in heart rate during maximal exercise such as sprinting and submaximal exercise such as jogging.

In Figures 3.4 and 3.5:

a = the **anticipatory rise** due to the hormonal action of adrenaline, which stimulates the sinoatrial node to make the heart beat faster and stronger

b = a sharp rise in heart rate at the beginning of exercise due mainly to anaerobic work

c = the heart rate continuing to rise due to maximal workloads stressing the anaerobic system

d = a steady state as the athlete is able to meet the oxygen demand required for the activity (reaching a plateau)

e = a rapid decline in heart rate as soon as the exercise stops, because there is a decrease in the demand for oxygen by the working muscles

f = a slow recovery as the body systems return to resting levels (but the heart rate remains elevated to rid the body of waste products such as lactic acid)

Always label your graphs clearly.

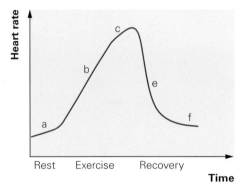

Figure 3.4 Response of heart rate to maximal exercise

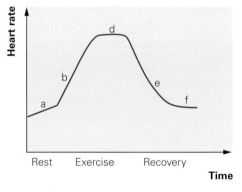

Figure 3.5 Response of heart rate to submaximal exercise

Cardiac output in response to exercise

Regular aerobic training results in hypertrophy of the cardiac muscle — the heart gets physically bigger. This has an important effect on stroke volume and heart rate, and therefore on cardiac output. A bigger heart means that more blood can be pumped out of the left ventricle per beat (i.e. stroke volume increases). In more complex language, the end diastolic volume of the ventricle increases. If the ventricle can contract with more force and thus push out more blood, the resting heart rate will decrease. This is known as **bradycardia**.

This increase in stroke volume and decrease in resting heart rate means that cardiac output at rest remains unchanged. However, this is not the case during exercise. An increase in heart rate coupled with an increase in stroke volume results in an increase in cardiac output. Cardiac output increases as the intensity of exercise increases until maximum exercise capacity is achieved and a plateau is reached (Figure 3.6).

Bradycardia: a decrease in resting heart rate to below 60 beats per minute.

Key term

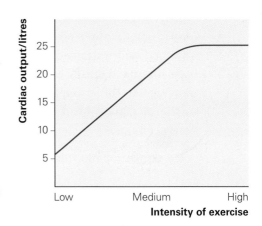

Figure 3.6 Cardiac output versus exercise intensity

Tasks to tackle 3.2

Measuring the response of heart rate to varying intensities of workload

1 Work in pairs and get the passive partner to take and record heart rate values.

2 Note your heart rate while you are resting for a 10-second count.

3 Record your heart rate immediately before the exercise commences for a 10-second count.

4 Commence your choice of submaximal exercise for a period of 3 minutes.

5 Take heart rate values for a 10-second pulse count:
- at the end of the 3 minutes of exercise
- every minute during the recovery phase until your heart rate has returned to its resting value prior to exercise

6 Once your heart rate has returned to its resting value, repeat the investigation but increase the workload to medium intensity.

7 Repeat the investigation at high intensity.

8 Collate your results in a table similar to the one below.

Intensity of workload	Resting heart rate	Heart rate prior to exercise	Heart rate at end of exercise	Heart rate during recovery					
				1	2	3	4	5	6
Low									
Medium									
High									

9 Represent your results graphically.

Table 3.2 shows the differences in cardiac output (to the nearest litre) in a trained and untrained individual both at rest and during exercise. The individual in this example is aged 18 so the maximum heart rate is 202 beats per minute.

$$Q = \text{stroke volume} \times \text{heart rate}$$

Table 3.2 Effect of training on cardiac output

	Stroke volume/ml	Heart rate	Q/litres
Untrained, at rest	70	72	5
Untrained, during exercise	120	202	24
Trained, at rest	85	60	5
Trained, during exercise	170	202	34

This increase in cardiac output has huge benefits for the trained individual as he/she can transport more blood and therefore more oxygen to the working muscles. In addition, when the body starts to exercise, the distribution of blood flow changes. This means that a much higher proportion of blood passes to the working muscles and less passes to non-essential organs such as the intestine. The amount of blood passing to the kidneys and the brain remains unaltered.

Stroke volume in response to exercise

Stroke volume increases as exercise intensity increases but only up to 40–60% of maximum effort. Once a performer reaches this point, stroke volume levels out (Figure 3.7). One explanation is that the increased heart rate near maximum effort results in a shorter diastolic phase. The ventricles have less time to fill up with blood, so they cannot pump as much out.

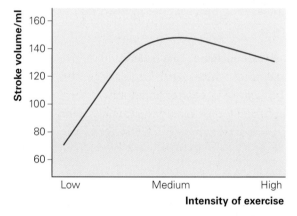

Figure 3.7 Stroke volume as a function of exercise intensity

Control of heart rate

Heart rate increases during exercise to ensure that the working muscles receive more oxygen. The heart generates its own impulses from the sinoatrial node but the rate at which these cardiac impulses are fired is controlled by two main mechanisms:

- neural
- hormonal

Neural control mechanism

The autonomic nervous system comprises the sympathetic system and the parasympathetic system. The sympathetic system stimulates the heart to beat faster; the parasympathetic system returns the heart to its resting level. The cardiac control centre located in the medulla oblongata of the brain coordinates these two systems. The cardiac control centre is stimulated by chemoreceptors, baroreceptors and proprioceptors.

During exercise, chemoreceptors detect increases in carbon dioxide and lactic acid and decreases in oxygen. The role of blood carbon dioxide is important in controlling heart rate. Baroreceptors detect increases in blood pressure; proprioceptors detect increases in muscle movement. These receptors send impulses to the cardiac control centre, which then sends an impulse through the sympathetic nervous system or cardiac accelerator nerve to the sinoatrial node to increase heart rate.

When exercise stops, carbon dioxide levels, blood pressure and muscle movement all decrease. This is detected by the receptors, which send impulses to the cardiac control centre. An impulse is then sent through the parasympathetic system or paravagus nerve, which stimulates the sinoatrial node and heart rate decreases. This process is summarised in Figure 3.8.

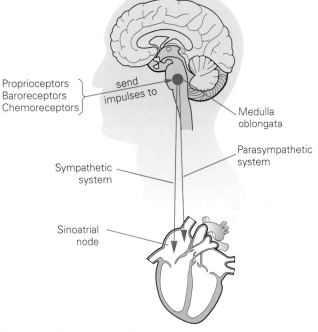

Figure 3.8 Neural control of heart rate

Don't be vague. Tell the examiner what the receptors detect — for example, chemoreceptors detect increases in carbon dioxide.

Hormonal control mechanism

Adrenaline and noradrenaline are stress hormones that are released by the adrenal glands. Exercise causes a stress-induced adrenaline response. This results in:

- stimulation of the sinoatrial node, which results in an increase in both the speed and force of contraction
- an increase in blood pressure due to the constriction of blood vessels
- an increase in blood glucose levels — glucose is used by the muscles for energy

Intrinsic control

During exercise, the heart gets warmer, so heart rate increases. Similarly, a drop in temperature reduces heart rate. In addition, venous return increases during exercise, which stretches the cardiac muscle, stimulating the SA node and in turn increasing heart rate and the force of contraction. As a result, stroke volume increases.

Questions on neural control of the heart are often written in relation to an increase in carbon dioxide.

Effects of training on the heart

If you perform continuous, fartlek or aerobic interval training over a period of time, physiological adaptations take place that make the initial training sessions appear very easy. This is because VO$_2$ max improves due to changes made by the body. Some of these changes affect the heart and it becomes much more efficient:

> **Key term**
>
> **VO$_2$ max**: the maximum amount of oxygen that can be taken in and used by the body in 1 minute.

- **Athlete's heart** is a common term for an enlarged heart caused by repeated strenuous exercise. Due to the demands of exercise, the chambers of the heart enlarge, which allows them to fill with more blood during the diastolic phase of the cardiac cycle. This results in an increase in the volume of blood that can be pumped out per beat, so the heart has to contract less frequently.
- **Hypertrophy** of the myocardium means that the heart muscle gets bigger and stronger. This results in bradycardia (a decrease in resting heart rate) and an increase in stroke volume.
- Maximum cardiac output increases but cardiac output at rest and during submaximal exercise remains the same.
- Increased capillarisation of the heart muscle increases the efficiency of oxygen diffusion into the myocardium.
- Increased contractility — resistance or strength training causes an increase in the force of heart contractions due to a thickening of the ventricular myocardium. This increases stroke volume and ejection fraction, as a higher percentage of blood is pumped.

Lack of physical activity is one of the major risk factors associated with heart disease. Exercise helps the heart to become stronger, enabling it to pump more blood around the body.

Heart conditions related to a lack of exercise include:
- coronary heart disease
- angina
- heart attack

Coronary heart disease

Coronary heart disease is caused by an accumulation of fatty material, calcium and scar tissue (plaque) in the arterial walls that supply the heart muscle (myocardium) with oxygen. This plaque narrows the arteries, so the heart cannot get enough blood and therefore oxygen.

Studies show that regular physical activity, coupled with a diet low in high-fat foods, is the best way of preventing heart disease. Medical experts recommend that individuals should be physically active for around 30 minutes each day. Moderate aerobic exercise can reduce cholesterol and lipid levels, including low-density lipoprotein (LDL — the bad cholesterol). Aerobic exercise can also increase levels of high-density lipoprotein (HDL — the good cholesterol), which is associated with a decrease in coronary heart disease.

Resistance training has been shown to lower heart rate and blood pressure after exercise. This will reduce the risk of heart disease.

Angina

Angina is a symptom of coronary heart disease. It manifests as a chest pain when the muscles do not receive enough blood. Exercises that train and strengthen the chest muscles will help to protect against angina.

Heart attack

A heart attack occurs when part of the heart muscle dies because it has been starved of oxygen as a result of coronary heart disease. Regular aerobic exercise such as brisk walking, jogging, swimming and cycling can help to prevent heart attack.

Practice makes perfect

1 The action of the heart (cardiac cycle) involves the contraction and relaxation of the heart muscle. Describe the flow of blood through the phases of the cardiac cycle. *(6 marks)*

2 A fit 18-year-old student reaches level 14 in the multistage fitness test. Sketch and label a graph to show the changes in heart rate before, during and after this test. *(4 marks)*

3 Define the terms **stroke volume**, **heart rate** and **cardiac output**. What happens to these quantities during exercise? *(4 marks)*

4 How does an increase in the level of carbon dioxide in the blood affect the heart? *(4 marks)*

5 An active lifestyle can help in the prevention of cardiovascular diseases. Name one such disease and explain how exercise can have an impact on its prevention. *(3 marks)*

Response of the vascular system to physical activity

What you need to know

By the end of this chapter you should be able to:

- explain how venous return is maintained and how it can impact on performance
- explain the vascular shunt (how cardiac output is distributed during both rest and exercise)
- explain how blood flow is controlled (vasomotor centre)
- describe how oxygen and carbon dioxide are transported in the vascular system and explain how effective transportation of both oxygen and carbon dioxide helps participation in physical activities
- describe how smoking affects the transportation of oxygen
- define blood pressure and give resting values
- explain the changes that occur in blood pressure during exercise
- describe the effect on the vascular system of a warm-up and cool-down
- evaluate the impact of physical activity on the vascular system (to include an understanding of arteriosclerosis and atherosclerosis)

The vascular system is made up of blood vessels that carry blood through the body. These blood vessels deliver oxygen and nutrients to the body tissues and take away waste products such as carbon dioxide. Together with the heart and lungs, the blood vessels ensure that the muscles have an adequate supply of oxygen during exercise in order to cope with the increased demand for energy.

The structure of the vascular system is not examined but it is important to have knowledge of this structure to help you understand the rest of this chapter.

Blood vessels

The vascular system consists of five different types of blood vessel that carry the blood from the heart, distribute it around the body and then return it to the heart. Arteries carry blood away from the heart. The heart beat pushes blood through the arteries by surges of pressure and the elastic arterial walls expand with each surge, which can be felt as a pulse in the arteries near the surface of the skin. The arteries then branch off and divide into smaller vessels called arterioles, which in turn divide into microscopic vessels called capillaries. These have a single cell layer of endothelium cells and are only wide enough to allow one red blood cell to pass through at a given time. This slows the blood flow, which allows time for the exchange of substances with the tissues to take place by diffusion. There is a dense capillary network surrounding the tissues and this creates a large surface area for diffusion to take place. Blood then flows from the capillaries to the venules, which increase in size and eventually form veins, which return the blood under low pressure to the heart.

To summarise, the order in which the blood flows through the vascular system is:

heart → arteries → arterioles → capillaries → venules → veins → heart

Structure of the blood vessels

Arteries, arterioles, venules and veins all have a similar structure (Figure 4.1). Their walls consist of three layers:

- The **tunica externa** (adventitia) is the outer layer, which contains collagen fibres. This wall needs to be elastic in order to stretch and withstand large fluctuations in blood volume.
- The **tunica media** is the middle layer, which is made up of elastic fibres and smooth muscle. The elastic fibres stretch when blood is forced into the arteries during ventricular systole. When they recoil they smooth out the flow of blood and push it along the arteries. The smooth muscle can contract in the walls of the smaller arteries and arterioles, which ensures that the amount of blood flowing to different organs varies according to demand.
- The **tunica interna** is made up of thin epithelial cells that are smooth and reduce friction between the blood and the vessel walls.

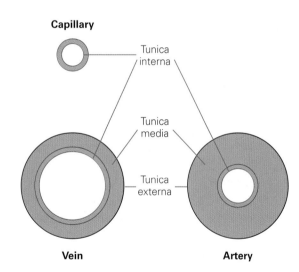

Figure 4.1 Structure of blood vessels

All blood vessels have features that adapt them to their particular functions. These are summarised in Table 4.1.

Table 4.1 Blood vessel adaptations

Feature	Artery	Capillary	Vein
Tunica externa (outer layer)	Present	Absent	Present
Tunica media (middle layer)	Thick with many elastic fibres	Absent	Thinner and less elastic than in an artery
Tunica interna (inner layer)	Present	Present	Present
Size of lumen	Small	Microscopic	Large
Valves	Absent	Absent	Present

Transportation of blood around the body

There are two types of circulation (Figure 4.2):

- the **pulmonary** circulation takes deoxygenated blood from the heart to the lungs and oxygenated blood back to the heart
- the **systemic** circulation carries oxygenated blood to the body from the heart and returns deoxygenated blood from the body to the heart

The venous return mechanism

Venous return is the transport of blood to the right side of the heart via the veins. Up to 70% of the total blood volume is contained in the veins at rest. This provides a large reservoir of blood, which is returned rapidly to the heart when needed.

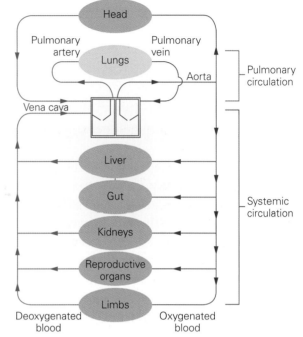

Figure 4.2 Circulation of blood

The heart can only pump out as much blood as it receives, so cardiac output is dependent on venous return. A rapid increase in venous return enables a significant increase in stroke volume and therefore cardiac output. Veins have a large lumen and offer little resistance to blood flow. Blood pressure is low by the time blood enters the veins. This means that active mechanisms are needed to help venous return. These include:

- the **skeletal muscle pump** (Figure 4.3). When muscles contract and relax, they change shape. This change in shape means that the muscles press on nearby veins, causing a pumping effect and squeezing blood towards the heart.

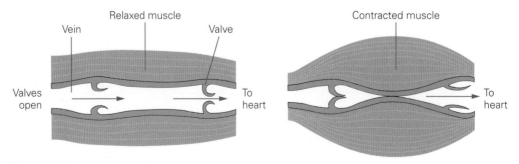

Figure 4.3 The skeletal muscle pump

- the **respiratory pump**. When muscles contract and relax during the inspiration and expiration process, pressure changes occur in the thoracic and abdominal cavities. These pressure changes compress the nearby veins and assist the flow of blood back to the heart.
- **valves**. It is important that blood in the veins only flows in one direction. The valves ensure that this happens. Once the blood has passed through the valves, they close to prevent the blood flowing back.
- **smooth muscle**. There is a thin layer of smooth muscle in the walls of the veins. This helps to squeeze blood back towards the heart.

Venous return must be maintained during exercise to ensure that the skeletal muscles receive enough oxygen to meet the demands of the activity. At rest, the valves and the smooth muscle in veins are sufficient to maintain venous return. During exercise, the demand for oxygen is greater and the heart beats faster, so the vascular system has to help out too. The skeletal muscle pump and the respiratory pump ensure venous return is maintained. This is possible during exercise because the skeletal muscles are constantly contracting and the breathing rate is elevated. These mechanisms need to be maintained immediately after exercise. Performing an active cool-down keeps the skeletal muscle pump and respiratory pump working, and thus prevents the blood from pooling.

The vascular shunt

During exercise, blood flow to the skeletal muscles increases to meet the increase in oxygen demand. This redirection of blood flow to the areas where it is most needed is known as shunting, or the **vascular shunt** mechanism (Figure 4.4).

Key term

Vascular shunt mechanism: the redistribution of cardiac output.

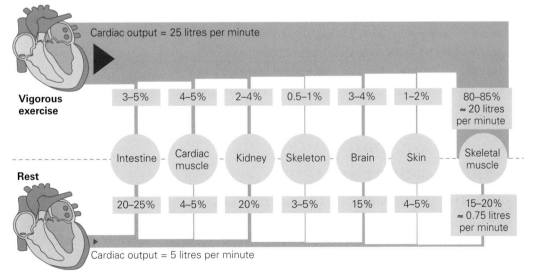

Figure 4.4 The vascular shunt

The control of blood flow

The **vasomotor centre** is located in the medulla oblongata of the brain. It controls both blood pressure and blood flow. During exercise, chemical changes such as increases in carbon dioxide and lactic acid are detected by chemoreceptors. Higher blood pressure is detected by baroreceptors. These receptors stimulate the vasomotor centre, which redistributes blood flow through vasodilation and vasoconstriction.

Vasodilation increases blood flow; **vasoconstriction** decreases blood flow. During exercise, the working muscles require more oxygen, so vasodilation occurs in the arterioles supplying the skeletal muscles, increasing blood flow and bringing in the much-needed oxygen. At the same time, vasoconstriction occurs in the arterioles supplying non-essential organs, such as the intestines and the liver.

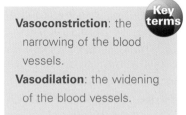

Key terms

Vasoconstriction: the narrowing of the blood vessels.
Vasodilation: the widening of the blood vessels.

Redirection of blood flow also occurs through stimulation of the sympathetic nerves located in the tunica media of the blood vessel. When stimulation by the sympathetic nerves decreases, vasodilation occurs and when sympathetic stimulation increases, vasoconstriction occurs.

Precapillary sphincters also aid blood redistribution. These are tiny rings of muscle located at the opening of capillaries. When they contract, blood flow is restricted through the capillaries and when they relax, blood flow is increased. During exercise, the precapillary sphincters of the capillary networks supplying skeletal muscle relax. This increases blood flow, which in turn helps to saturate the tissues with oxygen.

Redistribution of blood is important to:

- increase the supply of oxygen to the working muscles
- remove waste products such as carbon dioxide and lactic acid from the muscles
- ensure more blood goes to the skin during exercise to regulate body temperature and get rid of heat through radiation, evaporation and sweating
- direct more blood to the heart, because it is a muscle that requires extra oxygen during exercise

Oxygen and carbon dioxide in the vascular system

Oxygen plays a major role in energy production. A reduction in the amount of oxygen in the body has a detrimental impact on performance. During exercise, when oxygen diffuses into the capillaries supplying the skeletal muscles, 3% dissolves in plasma and 97% combines with haemoglobin to form oxyhaemoglobin. At the tissues, oxygen dissociates from haemoglobin because of the lower pressure of oxygen that exists there. In the muscle, oxygen is stored by myoglobin. This has a high affinity for oxygen and stores the oxygen until it is needed by the mitochondria. The mitochondria are the sites in the muscle where aerobic respiration takes place.

Myoglobin: a protein that stores oxygen in the muscle.

Carbon dioxide is transported around the body in the following ways:

- 70% is transported in the blood as hydrogen carbonate (bicarbonate) ions. The carbon dioxide produced by the muscles as a waste product diffuses into the bloodstream where it combines with water to form carbonic acid. Carbonic acid is a weak acid that dissociates into hydrogen carbonate ions.
- 23% combines with haemoglobin to form carbaminohaemoglobin.
- 7% dissolves in plasma.

An increase in the level of carbon dioxide results in an increase in blood and tissue acidity. This is detected by chemoreceptors, which send impulses to the medulla. Heart rate, breathing rate and transport increase so that more carbon dioxide is exhaled and the arterial blood levels of both oxygen and carbon dioxide are maintained.

Smoking and the transportation of oxygen

Smoking has a huge impact on the transportation of oxygen. Oxygen combines with haemoglobin and is transported as oxyhaemoglobin. Smokers inhale high levels of carbon monoxide, which has a greater affinity for haemoglobin than oxygen (200–300 times greater). This means that the level of carbon monoxide absorbed in the blood from the lungs increases, while the level of oxygen decreases. Higher levels of carbon monoxide in the blood reduce the amount of oxygen released from the blood to the muscles, which impacts on performance.

Smoke inhalation also increases the resistance of the airways (often through the swelling of mucous membranes) and therefore reduces the amount of oxygen absorbed into the blood.

Blood pressure and blood flow

Blood pressure is the force exerted by the blood against the blood vessel wall and is often referred to as:

blood flow × resistance

Ejection of the blood by the ventricles contracting creates a high-pressure pulse of blood, which is known as systolic pressure. The lower pressure as the ventricles relax is the diastolic pressure.

Blood pressure is measured at the brachial artery (in the upper arm) using a sphygmomanometer. A typical reading at rest is 120/80 mmHg (millimetres of mercury). The first figure (120) is the systolic pressure; the lower figure (in this case 80) is the diastolic pressure.

Response of the vascular system to physical activity

Blood pressure varies in the different blood vessels and depends largely on the distance of the blood vessel from the heart (Figure 4.5):

- artery — high and in pulses
- arteriole — not quite as high
- capillary — pressure drops throughout the capillary network
- vein — low

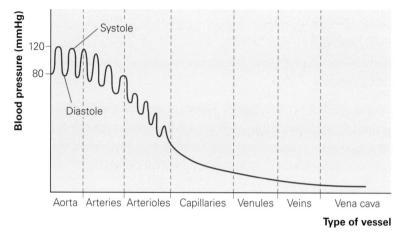

Figure 4.5 Blood pressure as a function of vessel type

Exercise and its effects on blood pressure

Changes in blood pressure occur during exercise and these depend on the type and intensity of the exercise. During aerobic exercise, systolic pressure increases due to an increase in cardiac output and the vasoconstriction of arterioles, which occurs during the redirection of blood flow to the working muscles. When exercise reaches a steady state and the heart rate plateaus, systolic pressure decreases due to vasodilation of the arterioles leading to the working muscles. This reduces resistance exerted by the blood vessel because the lumen is now wider, and lowers mean blood pressure (the average value of systolic and diastolic pressures) to just above resting levels. Diastolic pressure remains constant during aerobic exercise.

Tasks to tackle 4.1

Copy and complete the table below to show what happens to the systolic pressure of an 18-year-old PE student on a 40-minute training run.

	Before exercise	During exercise	Recovery
Blood pressure changes			

During isometric work, diastolic pressure increases due to increased resistance in the blood vessels. This is because, during isometric work, the muscle remains contracted, causing constant compression on the blood vessels, which results in an additional resistance to blood flow in the muscles and therefore an increase in pressure.

Hypertension

Hypertension is high blood pressure. It occurs when constricted arterial blood vessels increase the resistance to blood flow. This causes an increase in blood pressure against the vessel walls. The heart then has to work harder to pump blood through these narrowed arteries. Without medical intervention, damage to the heart and blood vessels is likely, which can increase the risk of stroke, heart attack and even heart failure.

Control of blood pressure

The vasomotor centre controls blood pressure. Baroreceptors located in the aortic and carotid arteries detect increases and decreases in blood pressure and send an impulse to the vasomotor centre located in the medulla oblongata (Figure 4.6).

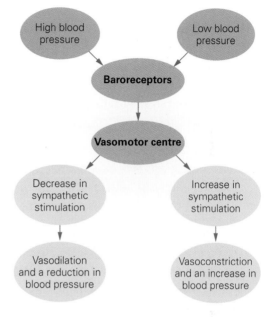

Figure 4.6 Control of blood pressure

Effects of warming up and cooling down on the vascular system

A warm-up helps to prepare the body for exercise. The vasomotor centre ensures that vasodilation occurs, so more blood flows (due to the increase in cardiac output) to the working muscles. This increases the amount of oxygen transported to the working muscles.

The warm-up increases the temperature of the body and muscles. This results in an increase in the transportation of enzymes necessary for energy systems and muscle contraction.

The increase in muscle and body temperature decreases blood viscosity. This improves blood flow to the working muscles. The increase in temperature also enables oxygen to dissociate from haemoglobin more quickly.

A warm-up decreases the onset of blood lactate accumulation (OBLA).

Cooling down involves activity (such as a gentle jog) that keeps the heart rate elevated and allows the body to take in extra oxygen, which can reduce recovery time. An active cool-down keeps the respiratory and skeletal muscle pumps working. This prevents blood from pooling in the veins and maintains venous return.

The capillaries remain dilated so that the muscles can be flushed with oxygenated blood. This increases the removal of lactic acid and carbon dioxide.

The impact of physical activity on the vascular system

Regular endurance activity can have an important impact on the vascular system. The arterial walls become more elastic, which means they can cope with higher fluctuations in blood pressure. There is also an increase in the number of capillaries surrounding the lungs and the muscles, and a small increase in red blood cells, all of which improve oxygen transportation.

Research shows that regular aerobic activity can help prevent vascular diseases such as arteriosclerosis and atherosclerosis.

Arteriosclerosis

Arteriosclerosis is commonly referred to as 'hardening of the arteries'. It can contribute to strokes and heart attacks. The walls of the arteries thicken, harden and lose their elasticity. Lack of physical activity is a risk factor for this condition.

Atherosclerosis

Atherosclerosis is a type of arteriosclerosis. It is a common disorder of the arteries in which fat and cholesterol collect along the walls of the arteries. The fat and cholesterol form a hard substance called plaque, which causes the arteries to become narrow and less flexible. This makes it increasingly difficult for the blood to flow.

Practice makes perfect

1 Explain how oxygen is transported in the blood. *(2 marks)*

2 Why would a warm-up be of benefit to the vascular system of a sports performer? *(2 marks)*

3 As you begin to exercise, more blood has to be distributed to the working muscles as the demand for oxygen increases. This redirection of blood flow is the vascular shunt. Explain how this increase in blood flow is achieved. *(4 marks)*

4 Sketch a graph to show the changes in blood pressure as blood passes through the vascular system. *(3 marks)*

5 What effect does smoking have on the transportation of oxygen? *(3 marks)*

6 Why is a cool-down after exercise important for the vascular system? *(2 marks)*

Chapter 5

Response of the respiratory system to physical activity

Anatomy and physiology

What you need to know

By the end of this chapter you should be able to:
- describe the mechanics of breathing at rest and name the muscles involved
- explain the changes in the mechanics of breathing during physical activity and name the additional muscles involved
- describe how the respiratory centre controls breathing
- describe the process of gaseous exchange between the alveoli and the blood and between the blood and the muscle cells
- explain the changes in gaseous exchange as a result of participation in physical activity
- explain the increased diffusion gradient and the accelerated dissociation of oxyhaemoglobin
- explain the effects of altitude training on the respiratory system
- describe how physical activity can have an impact on the respiratory system (to include an understanding of smoking and asthma)

The body needs a continuous supply of oxygen to produce energy. When we use oxygen to break down food to release energy, carbon dioxide is produced as a waste product and the body must remove this. Respiration, therefore, is the taking in of oxygen and the removal of carbon dioxide. It includes:
- ventilation — getting the air into and out of the lungs
- external respiration — gaseous exchange between the lungs and the blood
- transport of gases
- internal respiration — exchange of gases between the blood in the capillaries and the body cells
- cellular respiration — the metabolic reactions and processes that take place in a cell to obtain energy from fuels such as glucose (this is covered at A2)

The structure of the respiratory system

The lungs are found in the thorax. They are protected by the ribcage and separated from the abdomen by the diaphragm, which is a large skeletal muscle. Each lung is surrounded by a pleura, a double membrane containing lubricating pleural fluid (see Figure 5.1). The pleural fluid reduces friction. The right lung is slightly larger than the left and has three lobes; the left lung has two lobes.

Response of the respiratory system to physical activity

Air is drawn into the body through the nose, where it is warmed, humidified and filtered by a thick mucous membrane. It then passes through the pharynx and on to the larynx (voice box). The epiglottis covers the opening of the larynx to prevent food from entering the lungs. The air moves on to the trachea (windpipe). This is approximately 10 cm long and is held open by rings of cartilage. Mucus and ciliated cells line the trachea and filter the air. The trachea divides into the right and left bronchi. Air moves through the bronchi, which subdivide into secondary bronchi feeding each lobe of the lung. These get progressively thinner and branch into bronchioles, which lead into the alveolar air sacs.

The alveoli (Figure 5.2) are responsible for the exchange of gases between the lungs and the blood. Their structure is designed to help gaseous exchange. A dense capillary network supplies them with oxygen. Their walls are extremely thin (only one cell thick) and together they create a huge surface area (about the size of a tennis court in total) to allow for a greater uptake of oxygen.

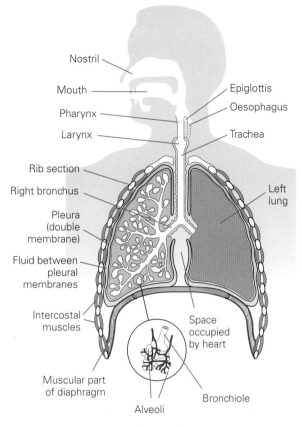

Figure 5.1 The structure of the respiratory system

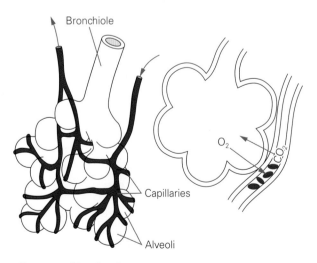

Figure 5.2 The alveoli

Tasks to tackle 5.1

Rearrange the following words to show the correct order of the passage of air:

larynx nose → trachea → pharynx → alveoli → bronchioles → bronchi

The mechanics of breathing

Air moves from areas of high pressure to areas of low pressure. The greater the pressure difference, the faster air flows. This means that in order to get air into the lungs (inspiration), the pressure needs to be lower inside the lungs than in the air we are breathing. To get air out (expiration), the pressure needs to be higher in the lungs than in the air we are breathing.

Inspiration

Inspiration increases the volume of the thoracic cavity through contraction of the muscles surrounding the lungs. The diaphragm contracts and flattens while the external intercostals contract and pull the ribs up and out (Figure 5.3 (a)). This reduces the pressure of air in the lungs.

Expiration

Expiration decreases the volume of the thoracic cavity. The diaphragm and external intercostals relax. This increases the pressure of air in the lungs, forcing air out (Figure 5.3 (b)). At rest, expiration is a passive process.

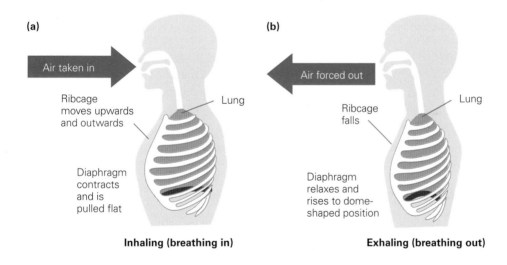

Figure 5.3 The mechanics of breathing

Breathing during exercise

During exercise, more muscles are involved because air needs to be forced in and out of the lungs much more quickly. The extra inspiratory muscles are the sternocleidomastoid, which lifts the sternum, and the scalenes and pectoralis minor, which help to lift the ribs. The extra expiratory muscles are the internal intercostals, which pull the ribs down and in and the abdominal muscles, which push the diaphragm up.

Top tip
'Intercostals' is not normally an acceptable answer. You have to be more specific — *external* intercostals for inspiration and *internal* intercostals for expiration.

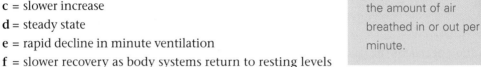

Changes in pulmonary ventilation

Pulmonary ventilation is the technical term for breathing. It is the movement of air into and out of the lungs. At rest we inspire and expire approximately 0.5 litres of air per breath. Changes in pulmonary ventilation occur during exercise. As you would expect, the more demanding the physical activity the more breathing increases to meet the extra oxygen demand This is illustrated in Figures 5.4 and 5.5.

a = anticipatory rise

b = sharp rise in minute ventilation

c = slower increase

d = steady state

e = rapid decline in minute ventilation

f = slower recovery as body systems return to resting levels

> **Key term**
>
> **Minute ventilation**: the amount of air breathed in or out per minute.

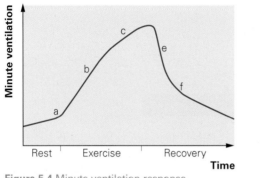

Figure 5.4 Minute ventilation response to maximal exercise

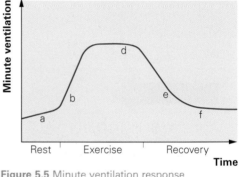

Figure 5.5 Minute ventilation response to submaximal exercise

Control of ventilation

The nervous system can increase or decrease the rate, depth and rhythm of breathing. The respiratory centre located in the medulla oblongata of the brain controls breathing. An increased concentration of carbon dioxide in the blood stimulates the respiratory centre to increase respiratory rate.

The respiratory centre has two main areas. The inspiratory centre is responsible for inspiration and expiration. The expiratory centre stimulates the expiratory muscles during exercise, when stretch receptors detect changes in the rate and depth of breathing.

The inspiratory centre sends out impulses via the phrenic and intercostal nerves to the inspiratory muscles. When the stimulus stops, expiration occurs.

During exercise, conditions in the body change. These changes are detected by:

- chemoreceptors, which detect changes in pH — blood acidity increases as a result of an increase in the plasma concentration of carbon dioxide and lactic acid production
- baroreceptors, which detect an increase in blood pressure
- proprioceptors, which detect movement

OCR AS Physical Education

An impulse is sent to the respiratory centre and then down the phrenic nerve to the inspiratory muscles. As a result the rate, depth and rhythm of breathing increase.

During exercise, the lungs are stretched more. Stretch receptors prevent over-inflation of the lungs by sending impulses to the expiratory centre and then down the intercostal nerve to the expiratory muscles so that expiration occurs.

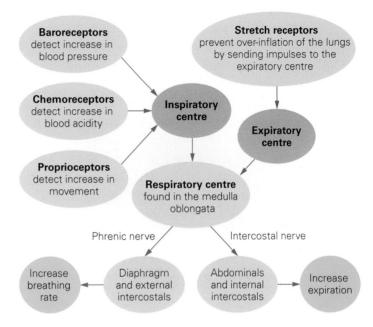

Top tip

A question on control of ventilation may refer to how an increase in carbon dioxide can affect breathing.

Figure 5.6 Control of ventilation

Gaseous exchange at the lungs

Gaseous exchange at the lungs (external respiration) is concerned with the replenishment of oxygen in the blood and the removal of carbon dioxide. Partial pressure is often used when describing the gaseous exchange process. All gases exert a pressure. Oxygen makes up a part of air (approximately 21% — see Table 5.1), so it exerts a partial pressure. Since gases flow from areas of high pressure to areas of low pressure, it is important that, as oxygen moves from the alveoli to the blood and then to the muscle, the partial pressure of oxygen of each is successively lower.

The partial pressure of oxygen in the alveoli (105 mmHg) is higher than the partial pressure of oxygen in the capillary blood vessels (40 mmHg). This is because the working muscles remove oxygen, so its concentration in the blood is lower and therefore so is its partial

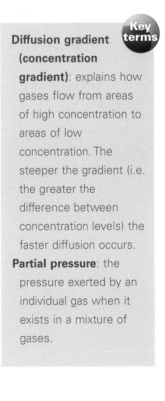

Key terms

Diffusion gradient (concentration gradient): explains how gases flow from areas of high concentration to areas of low concentration. The steeper the gradient (i.e. the greater the difference between concentration levels) the faster diffusion occurs.

Partial pressure: the pressure exerted by an individual gas when it exists in a mixture of gases.

Table 5.1 Percentages of gases in inspired and expired air

	Inspired air (%)	Expired air at rest (%)	Expired air during exercise (%)
Oxygen	21	16.4	15
Carbon dioxide	0.03	4.0	6
Nitrogen	79	79.6	79
Water vapour	Varies	Saturated	Saturated

pressure. The difference between any two pressures is referred to as the diffusion (concentration) gradient and the steeper this gradient, the faster the diffusion. Oxygen diffuses from the alveoli into the blood until the pressure is equal in both.

The movement of carbon dioxide occurs in the same way but in the reverse order, from the muscle to the blood to the alveoli. The partial pressure of carbon dioxide in the blood entering the alveolar capillaries is higher (45 mmHg) than that in the alveoli (40 mmHg), so carbon dioxide diffuses from the blood into the alveoli until the pressure is equal in both.

> **Top tip**
>
> Remember that the diffusion of gases at the alveoli is helped by the alveolar structure. Alveoli are only one cell thick, so there is a short diffusion pathway; they have a vast surface area, which facilitates diffusion; and they are surrounded by a vast network of capillaries.

Gaseous exchange at the tissues (internal respiration)

For diffusion to occur, the partial pressure of oxygen must be lower in the tissues than in the blood. The partial pressure of oxygen in the capillary membranes surrounding the muscle is 40 mmHg and in the blood it is 105 mmHg. This allows oxygen to diffuse from the blood into the muscle until equilibrium is reached.

Conversely, the partial pressure of carbon dioxide is lower in the blood (40 mmHg) than in the tissues (45 mmHg), so again diffusion occurs and carbon dioxide moves into the blood to be transported to the lungs.

The oxyhaemoglobin dissociation curve

During exercise, oxygen diffuses into the capillaries supplying the skeletal muscles. Three percent dissolves in plasma and 97% combines with haemoglobin to form oxyhaemoglobin. Fully saturated haemoglobin carries four oxygen molecules. Haemoglobin is fully saturated when the partial pressure of oxygen in the blood is high, for example in the alveolar capillaries of the lungs. At the tissues, oxygen dissociates from haemoglobin because of the lower partial pressure of oxygen that exists there.

The relationship of oxygen and haemoglobin is often represented by the oxyhaemoglobin dissociation curve (Figure 5.7).

At the partial pressure of oxygen in the lungs, haemoglobin is almost completely saturated with oxygen. In the tissues, the partial pressure of oxygen is lower and therefore the haemoglobin gives up some of its oxygen to the tissues.

Under certain conditions, haemoglobin gives up some of its oxygen more readily and the S-shaped curve shifts to the right (Figure 5.8). This is important during exercise when there is a greater demand for oxygen. These conditions are:

- an increase in temperature of the blood and muscle
- a decrease in the partial pressure of oxygen in the muscle during exercise, increasing the oxygen diffusion gradient
- an increase in partial pressure of carbon dioxide during exercise, which increases the carbon dioxide diffusion gradient
- an increase in acidity caused by an increase in carbon dioxide levels in the blood during exercise, lowering the pH (the Bohr effect)

Bohr effect: the reduction in the affinity of haemoglobin for oxygen due to an increase in blood carbon dioxide and a decrease in pH.

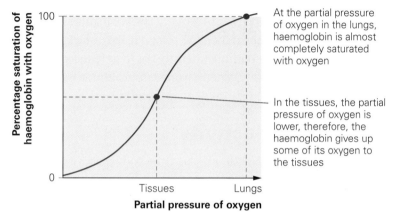

At the partial pressure of oxygen in the lungs, haemoglobin is almost completely saturated with oxygen

In the tissues, the partial pressure of oxygen is lower, therefore, the haemoglobin gives up some of its oxygen to the tissues

Figure 5.7 The oxyhaemoglobin dissociation curve

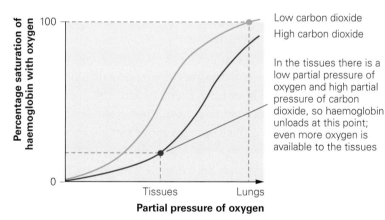

Low carbon dioxide

High carbon dioxide

In the tissues there is a low partial pressure of oxygen and high partial pressure of carbon dioxide, so haemoglobin unloads at this point; even more oxygen is available to the tissues

Figure 5.8 The Bohr shift

Effects of altitude training

An adequate supply of oxygen to the working muscles is essential for performance. At high altitude there is less air and therefore less oxygen. The partial pressure of oxygen decreases as altitude increases, usually by up to 50% at an altitude of 5000 metres compared with sea level. This lower partial pressure of oxygen has an effect on respiration, decreasing its efficiency. This means that the muscles do not receive as much oxygen because haemoglobin cannot be fully saturated, and this affects performance. There is an earlier onset of fatigue. The body can adapt to high altitude eventually by increasing the levels of red blood cells and haemoglobin.

Training at high altitude has the following advantages:

- It increases the number of red blood cells.
- It increases concentration of haemoglobin.
- It enhances oxygen transport.

However, altitude training can be expensive in terms of costs of flights and accomodation and can lead to altitude sickness. It may be difficult to train due to the lack of oxygen. When the performer first trains at altitude, the training intensity has to be reduced due to the decreased availability of oxygen (detraining). Any benefits gained from altitude training are quickly lost on return to sea level.

Impact of physical activity

Endurance training improves lung function because the body makes adaptations.

Small increases in lung volumes occur due to an increase in the efficiency of the respiratory muscles, namely the diaphragm and the external intercostals.

The exchange of gases at the alveoli becomes more efficient due to an increase in the surface area of the alveoli. There is also an increase in the density of capillaries surrounding the alveoli. This means that more oxygen can get to the working muscles and waste products such as carbon dioxide are dealt with more efficiently.

The transport of respiratory gases becomes more efficient. Blood volume increases due mainly to an increase in blood plasma volume but there is also a slight increase in the number of red blood cells, which leads to an increase in haemoglobin. This allows more oxygen to be taken to the working muscles and more carbon dioxide to be removed.

There is an improvement in the uptake of oxygen by the muscles due to an increase in myoglobin content and mitochondrial density in the muscle cells. This leads to an increase in VO_2 max of up to 20%. Having more oxygen available for the working muscles also affects the arterial venous oxygen difference (difference in oxygen content between the arteries and the veins).

Asthma

Asthma is a chronic disease in which the walls of the airways constrict and become inflamed. During an asthma attack, less air gets to the lungs, which causes wheezing, shortness of breath and chest tightness. Asthma sufferers are often allergic to certain substances, or can react to environment stimuli such as cold air, warm air, stress or exercise.

Asthma sufferers should be able to take part in most physical activities and regular physical activity can help to manage the disease. For example, aerobic exercise increases lung capacity.

Swimming is a good activity because the warm, humid environment is unlikely to trigger asthma symptoms. Scuba diving is the only sport not recommended. If you suffer from asthma, consult your doctor before undertaking any vigorous exercise.

Smoking

Smoking has a great impact on the transportation of oxygen because it reduces the amount of oxygen available in the body. This is because smoking increases the level of carbon monoxide in the lungs. Haemoglobin has a much higher affinity for carbon monoxide than it does for oxygen, so there is a reduction in the amount of oxygen that diffuses and binds to the haemoglobin in the red blood cells. In addition, smoke inhalation increases the resistance of the airways by causing long-term swelling of the mucous membranes, and therefore reduces the amount of oxygen absorbed into the blood.

Research shows that regular aerobic exercise has a beneficial effect in helping an individual to stop smoking. It induces biochemical changes in the body that increase mental alertness and decrease stress levels. Regular, sustained aerobic exercise increases endorphin levels in the brain, which helps to produce a state of relaxation and wellbeing. Such emotions can help an individual who is trying to stop smoking.

Practice makes perfect

1 Describe the mechanism of breathing at rest and explain how it changes during exercise. *(5 marks)*

2 During exercise the volume of air that is ventilated increases to meet the increase in demand for oxygen. Explain how the amount of air ventilated by the body is controlled. *(4 marks)*

3 Identify two active muscle groups that cause increased lung capacity during a long rally in tennis. *(2 marks)*

4 Performance in sporting activity is influenced by gas exchange and oxygen delivery. Explain how oxygen diffuses from the lungs into the blood and how it is transported to the tissues. *(4 marks)*

5 Peak performance in certain activities may be affected by altitude. Describe the effects of altitude on the exchange of gases at the alveoli and why this may influence performance. *(4 marks)*

Chapter 6

Acquiring movement skills

Skill and ability

What you need to know

By the end of this chapter you should:
- know the difference between skill and ability
- know how abilities develop into skills
- be able to classify skills according to distinct criteria

If you watch football on television, you will have heard the commentator remark on a particular player's great ability, especially when that player executes a skill in an effective way. The terms skill and ability are used frequently in sport, sometimes with confusion between the two, so we need to establish the differences between the two terms.

Ability

Abilities are the building blocks of skill. There is no such thing as general ability, but rather a group of abilities that are specific to a skill. For example, a sprint start in athletics requires the abilities of

> **Key term**
> **Ability**: an innate characteristic that lays the foundation of skill.

power, gross body coordination and speed. Abilities are therefore varied and numerous, and they combine in groups to be the foundation for the development of specific sporting skills.

Ability in sport is an innate characteristic required for performing movement. We might be born with good coordination, for example, which could help us to develop passing skills after periods of practice. We inherit natural abilities from our parents and while these abilities can be enhanced, the fact remains that you have either got them or you haven't!

Abilities are enduring. You are born with them and they tend to remain with you. A player born with natural strength will retain that ability for life and be able to call upon it when required, especially if weight training enhances that natural strength.

Examples of abilities include:

- explosive strength
- static balance
- speed
- agility
- gross body coordination
- dynamic strength
- dynamic balance
- power
- visual acuity
- manual dexterity
- stamina
- perceptual ability
- gross motor ability
- hand–eye coordination
- psychomotor ability

You are probably familiar with most of these abilities but some may be new to you. Visual acuity is the ability to scan the playing arena in order to pick up information. Manual dexterity is the ability to coordinate actions with the hands. The term dynamic refers to active movement, so dynamic balance is needed on the move, as in a gymnastic floor sequence, while static balance is needed during a handstand.

Perceptual ability is particularly important. It is the ability to sense and interpret information. For example, a netball player may have the ability to assess how far away another player is before deciding how hard to project the ball when making a pass. Psychomotor ability is the ability to deal with information once you have sensed it. In other words, it involves the ability to make decisions based on information received. Having sensed how far away your team-mate is in netball, you might then decide on the best type of pass to use.

Gross motor ability is the characteristic required to perform large muscle-group movements, such as the strength needed to make a rugby tackle using the deltoid and latissimus dorsi muscles in the shoulder.

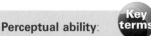

Key terms

Perceptual ability: the ability to sense and interpret information.

Psychomotor ability: the ability to assess a stimulus and respond with the correct action.

Skill: a learned, efficient movement performed with a purpose and to a consistently high standard.

Skill

Skill differs from ability in that it is not innate. Skill is learned, and developed from ability after a period of practice. To produce a skilled performance, the player must practise, to enhance the underlying abilities. Think of some skilful performances in sport, such as a magnificent free kick in football that bends around the defensive wall, or an exquisite performance on the ice by an Olympic skater.

Characteristics of a skilful performance

Skilled performances:

- are **learned**. On the basis of existing abilities, the practising of skills and drills in some form of training will help to produce a skilful movement.
- are **consistent**. A skilled player is able to perform the task to the same high level time after time. For example, a penalty taker in hockey might score nine penalty flicks out of ten during the season.
- are **goal-directed**. A player will practise skills with an aim in mind. He/she might want to improve shooting skills in order to score more goals.
- are **aesthetic**. They look good. A top-class dance routine is pleasing to watch.
- follow a **technical** model. A skilful performance will closely match a correct demonstration of the skill.
- are **controlled**. The skilful performer is in charge, controlling the rate and timing of the skill.
- are **efficient**. The skill is performed without any wasted energy.
- are **smooth**. The movement appears to flow.

The sports lecturer and author Barbara Knapp summed up the characteristics of skilful performance when she defined skill in sport as:

> ...the learned ability to bring about predetermined results with maximum certainty, often with the minimum outlay of time, energy or both.

You should learn this definition because it includes many of the characteristics of skilful performance.

A skilful performance has two elements:

- a **cognitive** part
- a **motor** part

The cognitive part of the skill requires thought before action. The motor part requires control and efficient movement. A football player about to make a pass must first look to see which other players are in a good position to receive the pass before the ball is kicked.

Top tip

Exam questions often ask you to name three characteristics of skill. Make sure that you name three *different* characteristics because the examiner will mark the first three only. The terms goal-directed, consistent and learned would get the marks but the terms smooth, fluent and efficient might be considered too similar to score separate marks.

Tasks to tackle 6.1

Draw a simple diagram or table to show the main characteristics of skill and ability.

Top tip

The following mnemonic might help you to remember the characteristics of skill for exam purposes:

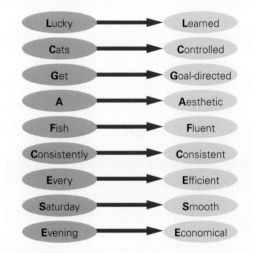

Lucky	Learned
Cats	Controlled
Get	Goal-directed
A	Aesthetic
Fish	Fluent
Consistently	Consistent
Every	Efficient
Saturday	Smooth
Evening	Economical

The relationship between skill and ability

The abilities we are born with are the foundations of skills but they need to be developed before a high skill level is reached. Sporting abilities are enhanced in childhood by:

- simple play — running and catching games played by primary school children
- early coaching — basic and introductory level coaching schemes under the control of national governing bodies
- experiencing a variety of situations — for example games, individual sports and swimming

Children copy role models and are therefore more likely to pursue sports if they see their parents involved in sporting activities. Having access to good sporting facilities will further encourage this interest.

Abilities develop into **fundamental** or foundation skills. These are the basic movements from which more advanced (**sport-specific**) skills develop. They include running, throwing, catching, kicking, balancing and jumping. Specific skills such as a javelin throw or a tennis serve are attained with practice. For example, someone born with the abilities of power, coordination and manual dexterity could enhance these abilities into the foundation skills of catching and throwing, and these could be developed into the sport-specific skill of a netball pass.

The relationship between skill and ability is explained in Figure 6.1.

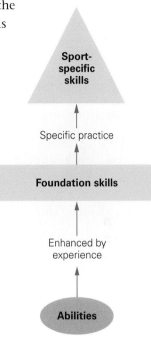

Figure 6.1 The skill–ability relationship

Tasks to tackle 6.2

Name a skill from a sport of your choice, the abilities that underpin it and the fundamental skills from which it could have been developed. For example, a netball pass is built on the abilities of hand–eye coordination and manual dexterity, and developed from the fundamental skills of catching and throwing.

Skills classification

Skills are classified so that coaches can decide on the best ways to practise them. They are usually classified on a sliding scale called a **continuum**, which shows the extent to which a skill meets certain criteria. The continuum can also reveal how a skill varies depending on the situation. The criteria used to classify skills are detailed below.

Muscular involvement

A **fine** skill has small, delicate muscle movements, such as the finger control required in a pistol shot at a target. A **gross** skill uses large muscle group movements, such as the movement of the biceps and triceps during a badminton drop shot. Most skills in sport are gross skills. A rugby tackle uses the deltoid muscle in the shoulder and is also a gross skill. The rugby tackle is further towards the gross end of the continuum than the badminton drop shot.

Figure 6.2 The muscular involvement continuum

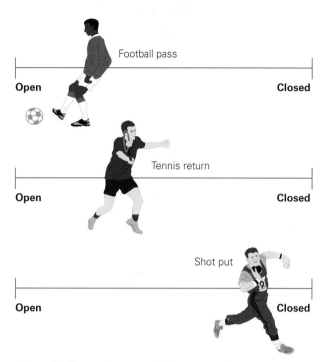

Figure 6.3 The environmental influence continuum

Figure 6.4 The continuity continuum

Environmental influence

An **open** skill is one that is affected by the sporting environment, which includes conditional elements such as the weather, as well as the positions of other players and the pressure exerted by opponents. The performer has to make decisions. Open skills are usually externally paced. Examples include a football pass, when the ball carrier has to decide which team-mate to pass to, or a tennis return that depends on the opponent's shot. In either case, the player has to adapt to the actions of others and make a decision on where to place the ball.

A **closed** skill involves less decision-making because it takes place in a more predictable environment and the performer knows exactly what he/she should be doing. An example is the shot put, which is always performed in a circle of the same size. The performer can use the same routine without much adaptation. A closed skill is self-paced: the rate at which it is executed is up to the performer. It can become a habit and tends not to be affected by the environment.

The environmental decisions continuum is shown in Figure 6.3. Note how the football pass and the tennis return are both open but the football pass is more open than the tennis return. The continuum therefore shows the range between skills and, in the case of open or closed skills, by how much the coach needs to vary training so that a degree of adaptation is included in practice.

Continuity

A **discrete** skill has a short time span and a distinct beginning and end. An example is a tennis serve, where the action is short, sharp and clearly defined. A **continuous** skill has no clear beginning or end. The end of one part of the movement links into the next. An example is the leg movement in cycling or jogging. A **serial** skill is a set of discrete movements, linked together in a particular order to form a more continuous task. Serial skills therefore occupy the middle ground on a continuum, indicating that there are discrete elements that form a more continuous task. Examples include the leap, jump, turn and kick that might be linked together to form a dance routine, and the hop, step and jump that must be performed in a specific order in the triple jump in athletics. In both cases, each discrete movement can be practised separately.

Pacing

A **self-paced** skill is one during which the performer controls the rate of execution. The performer can decide how to execute the (usually closed) skill before doing so. Such pre-decision-making is called **pro-action**. For example, when a penalty is taken in football, the player can decide to place the ball in the corner of the goal or 'blast' it past the goal-keeper.

An **externally paced** skill is one during which the rate of execution is outside the control of the performer, who may have to react to external conditions. It is usually an open skill. In sailing, for instance, the speed of the wind dictates the pace of the boat and the yachtsman or woman has to react accordingly. In an invasion game such as netball, the timing of the pass might depend on the pressure exerted by the opponents.

Difficulty

A **complex** skill involves a high level of decision-making and has a large cognitive or thinking element to it. Examples include a passing sequence in netball or a set of tackles in rugby league. Players need to concentrate on the task and pay attention to numerous variables.

For a **simple** skill, such as a forward roll in gymnastics, the performer has a limited amount of information to process and the skill has a smaller cognitive element. The performer can concentrate on the task and focus on its successful completion.

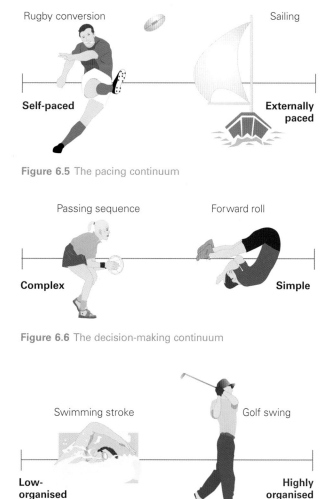

Figure 6.5 The pacing continuum

Figure 6.6 The decision-making continuum

Figure 6.7 The organisation continuum

Organisation

A **low-organised** skill can be broken down into parts, or subroutines. The subroutines of the task can be identified as independent actions. For example, when teaching a swimming stroke, the arm and leg actions can be taught separately using a float. A **highly organised** skill is hard to break down since it is fast and ballistic in its execution. The parts that make up the task are integrated closely in the action. A golf swing is an example.

Tasks to tackle 6.3

Using the named skill from Tasks to Tackle 6.2 (page 61), classify the skill as gross or fine, open or closed, discrete, serial or continuous, externally paced or self-paced, complex or simple, and highly organised or low-organised. Give reasons for each classification.

Top tip

When answering questions on skill classification be careful not to fall into the trap of describing the skill instead of explaining why it is classified as it is. For example, a football pass is open because the sporting environment influences it and decisions are needed. Use a diagram of the skill classification continuum to show that you know the difference between types of skill, and make sure that you label it and name the skills to get the mark.

Practice makes perfect

1 Explain why there is no such thing as a general ability in sport. *(2 marks)*

2 Explain why a continuum is needed to classify skills in sport. *(2 marks)*

3 Explain why a football pass can be described as an open skill. *(3 marks)*

4 Use an example from sport to explain what is meant by a serial skill. *(3 marks)*

What you need to know

By the end of this chapter you should be able to:

- discuss the factors that need to be considered before a skill is taught
- understand the different practice and teaching methods available to a sports coach
- suggest when and how a coach could use these practice methods
- suggest advantages and disadvantages of these practice methods

Coaching sports skills

The students' learning environment can be enhanced if the coach or teacher takes into account the factors that affect learning in sport and the classification of the skill. The planning of coaching sessions is important for effective learning and should take into account the nature of the task and the characteristics of the students being coached.

In terms of the nature of the task, the coach must be aware of the appropriate skills classification. Open skills should be practised with variety, in different situations, so that the performer has to adapt to take account of the changing nature of the skill. Closed skills can be practised continuously and repetitively to promote learning and habitual response. Externally paced skills can be practised under pressure, so that the player has to adapt. Self-paced skills can be practised repetitively as a whole, in the player's own time. Gross skills may require contact and therefore a safety element to practice, while fine skills can be broken down to focus on technique and performed in a calmer environment. Highly organised and discrete skills are difficult to break down and should be practised in their entirety. Low-organised and serial tasks are more easily broken down and can be practised in parts.

The coach must also be aware of the characteristics of the students. If the students are well motivated and fit, a hard practice session with limited breaks could ensue. If the students are beginners, the coach may want to slow down the rate of practice and use rest intervals to emphasise certain points. The students' abilities should also be considered — it is no good doing complicated passing drills with students who have little coordination.

Tasks to tackle 7.1

Make a checklist of issues to consider before coaching a skill. Use the headings 'Task' and 'Performer'.

Top tip

Sometimes questions are very specific and ask you to discuss issues concerning the *task* that you might consider before coaching a skill. Make sure you don't mention the *performer*.

Key terms

Distributed practice: allowing rest intervals between practice sessions.

Fixed practice: repetition of a drill.

Massed practice: training sessions with no rest interval.

Part practice: the skill is divided into subroutines in order to focus on specific cues during practice.

Varied practice: using different drills and methods in training sessions.

Whole practice: skills are practised in their entirety, with subroutines intact.

Whole practice may be better for more experienced performers

Types of practice

The types of practice that the coach can choose to use are:

- whole practice
- whole–part–whole practice
- pure part practice
- progressive part practice
- massed practice
- distributed practice
- fixed practice
- varied practice

Whole practice

Whole practice means that the skill is performed in its entirety, with all its subroutines. Whole practice promotes fluency and understanding because the links between each subroutine are established. For example, in a tennis serve the toss of the ball and the timing of the strike must be coordinated.

Whole practice is used when the skill is:

- highly organised and cannot be broken down into its parts
- discrete, with a clear beginning and end
- simple and the information can be easily recalled

The coach chooses this type of practice to enable the performer to develop a feel for the whole task and to provide a more realistic method of practice. Consistency in the execution of the skill is achieved, so that the image of the skill is stored in the memory as a motor programme.

The problem with whole practice is that it may require learners to undertake a task that is too advanced for them, with too much information for them to process at once.

Whole–part–whole practice

Whole–part–whole practice can be used to highlight a weakness in performance, or when a beginner is performing a complex task, or a task that is hard to break down. The task is performed in its entirety and the weaknesses are identified. The weaker parts are practised separately and are then integrated back into the whole task.

The whole–part–whole method of practice is useful when there is a particular point in technique that needs improvement and the skill is fluent and fast. For example, a particular point in the technique of a golf swing could be improved by focusing on one aspect before integrating this aspect back into the whole task.

Although it is time-consuming, this method is good for error correction, especially if the athlete is a more advanced performer.

Part methods of practice

Part practice is when a skill is split into subroutines and each part is practised separately. The parts are then reassembled to make the whole skill. Part practice is used when the skill is low in its organisation. There are two types of part practice:

- pure
- progressive

Pure part practice can be used when a skill is easily broken down into its subroutines. For example, a swimming stroke can be broken down into the leg action, the arm action, body position and breathing. Each of these can be practised independently (Figure 7.1).

Pure part practice is good for beginners, as it means that they are not given too much information at once and can concentrate on improving one aspect of the task at a time.

This method is also advantageous when there is an element of danger. By focusing on only part of the skill, the danger might be eliminated. For example, a trampolinist has to learn to do a basic move before trying something more complicated.

Photodisc/Cadmium

The whole–part–whole method can be used when the skill is fluent and fast

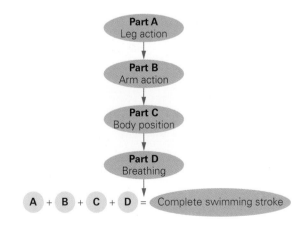

Figure 7.1 Learning a swimming stroke by the pure part method

The disadvantages of pure part practice are that it is time-consuming and essential links between each subroutine of the skill may be neglected. For example, in breaststroke there is a link between the end of the leg kick and the start of the arm pull, called the glide phase. In pure part practice, this link may be neglected.

Progressive part practice attempts to solve one of the problems associated with pure part practice by maintaining the links between subroutines. The individual component parts of the task are practised separately and in the correct order, but at each stage the tasks are progressively linked to promote a fluid performance. Gradual progress is made.

Progressive part practice can be used:

- for serial skills in which each discrete element can be added in turn — for example, a dancer can add successive elements to complete a routine in this manner
- for beginners, so that they can make gradual progress
- for skills that are complex, so that the performer can concentrate on one part of the task at a time
- to reduce dangerous elements of a skill — by learning the early parts of the task before attempting the more difficult parts, risks are eliminated

For example, in the development of a dance routine the dancer might begin with the first two parts of the routine, say the turn and the kick, and practise these together. The third part of the skill, the leap, can be added to the routine later. The remaining parts of the sequence can be added until the whole routine is completed (Figure 7.2).

The drawbacks of progressive part practice are that it is time-consuming and there may be negative transfer between each part of the skill as it is learned.

Massed practice

Massed practice is when no rest intervals are given between each component of the training session. It is used when a coach wants to promote a high level of fitness.

Massed practice has the advantage of promoting over-learning, so that the performer can cope with the demands of a real game. In rugby, for example, a coach who has put the players through their paces for an hour without a break, perhaps doing a pre-planned, structured routine, can be confident that they will cope with a 40-minute half game play.

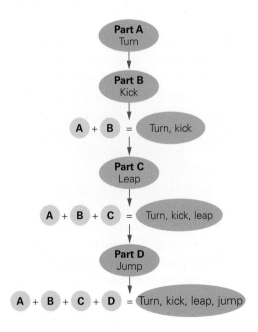

Figure 7.2 Learning a dance routine using the progressive part method

OCR AS Physical Education

This form of practice is appropriate for:

- simple skills that demand little attention, so the performer can still focus on the task after numerous attempts
- discrete skills with a clear beginning and end. These are usually short and sharp and can be undertaken easily without a rest, for example a professional footballer practising advanced shooting skills.

Massed practice is best for performers with a higher level of skill who want to fine-tune their technique. The skill can become habitual and can be stored in the memory in the form of a motor programme.

One problem with massed practice is that there is no opportunity for input or feedback from the coach during breaks, and the coach is unable to bring the players together during the session to correct faults. Massed practice may also cause fatigue, leading to a dip in performance levels towards the end of the session.

Distributed practice

Distributed practice is when a rest interval is given to allow recuperation. Feedback, coaching and advice on technique can be given during the interval. It is suitable for:

- beginners, who can focus on an early part of a task and may need to rest before moving on to the next part
- performers who are unfit or need to rest
- performers who need encouragement from the coach to improve motivation

It is appropriate for serial skills and complex skills, so that one aspect of the task can be learned before the next part is outlined in the rest interval. For example, a netball coach might give a beginner some basic drills to start with and then offer a rest before the next, more difficult, task is outlined and then attempted. It can also be used to improve safety, as any dangerous elements can be discussed during the break.

Distributed practice is time-consuming but it does ensure that skills are learned thoroughly.

Fixed practice

Fixed practice uses repetition of the same activity to promote over-learning. This ensures that more advanced performers maintain consistency in their performance and that their responses are habitual.

It is appropriate for closed skills that do not require adaptation to the environment, self-paced skills, and simple skills that have a discrete element to them. For example, a national league hockey player might practise penalty flicks or short corners repeatedly so that these skills are performed automatically in a game situation.

Tasks to tackle 7.2

Choose a skill from a sport of your choice. Classify the skill and suggest which type of practice you would use to coach it. Give reasons for your choice.

Problems of boredom and fatigue can occur if this type of practice is used too much, so it is important for the coach to make sure that the performer is well motivated.

Varied practice

Varied practice involves using different methods to achieve a learning goal, or performing a task in different situations. It aims to provide the performer with the ability to adapt a skill to a range of possible circumstances.

This method is appropriate for open skills, where the sporting environment tends to change. For example, when practising passing techniques in a team game, there will be a variety of drills that suit different situations within the game, such as attacking and defending.

When the skill is externally paced, varied practice may be used because players need to be able to adapt their performance under pressure. For example, when a full court press is used to try to force a mistake by the defensive team in basketball, the attacking team must respond to the added pressure.

Varied practice is often used for beginners, because it allows them to progress when more difficult elements of the task are added to those they are already familiar with. Novice players developing their passing skills may use different drills and small-sided games to help them learn to adapt to the presence of opponents. Varied practice is therefore good for developing experience and may help each player to develop core concepts or schemata for the skill (see pp. 100–101 for more information on schema theory). Variety can also be used to motivate performers.

Varied practice is time-consuming and there can be negative transfer between different tasks.

> **Top tip**
> Questions on types of practice always require practical examples. Make sure that you can justify your choice of any type of practice by quoting specific examples.

Guidance

Various methods of guidance are used in conjunction with practice to help the performer become familiar with patterns of movement. There are four main methods:

- visual
- verbal
- manual
- mechanical

Visual guidance involves presenting the performer with an accurate picture of the required skill patterns. This may come in the form of a demonstration from the coach, or it could be from a DVD presentation, from a book or from a chart similar to those used by football managers to highlight players' positions and formations.

> **Key terms**
> **Manual guidance**: physical support to help a performer in the early stages of learning.
> **Mechanical guidance**: using a device to help a beginner.
> **Verbal guidance**: an explanation of technique.
> **Visual guidance**: a demonstration of technique.

Visual guidance is useful for novices, who may need to see the skill performed before they try to copy it. This gives an initial understanding of the requirements. It can also be used to correct weaknesses in technique, as highlighted by the coach.

When using visual guidance it is important that:

- the demonstration is accurate, so that the performer does not gain a false impression
- the coach does not give too much information, as this could cause confusion
- the learner is capable of performing the task accurately

Verbal guidance occurs when the coach gives a full explanation of the coaching points and requirements of the task. The coach should help the performer to gain an understanding of why certain movements are performed.

Verbal guidance can be used for:

- beginners, to help them form a mental picture of the task and to explain the basics of the skill
- for more advanced players, who want to fine-tune their performance
- in team games, to develop tactics and strategies
- giving feedback to a player at the end of the match

Verbal guidance is best used in conjunction with visual guidance. For example, a tennis coach might demonstrate a 'slice' serve and explain that this particular serve is used to move the opponent to the side of the court to pave the way for a winning shot into the empty space.

Verbal guidance should be given in small chunks, because the athlete will be unable to act on a great deal of information given at one time, and in simple language, so that the performer understands all the information given.

Manual and mechanical guidance are physical, hands-on methods used to help the novice performer. Manual guidance involves physical support for the performer. Examples include support for a gymnast doing a handstand, or physically moving the arm of a novice tennis player to achieve the right movement pattern when performing a return shot. Mechanical guidance is the use of a device to support the performer, such as a harness on the trampoline or an armband in swimming. Both these types of guidance can provide early confidence for the learner. He/she will gain an early feel for the skill and be able to accomplish the task with success.

Manual and mechanical guidance can be used in dangerous situations to promote safety. However, these physical types of guidance should be used only in the early stages of learning, otherwise the performer may become dependent on the support and reluctant to perform the skill without it. The performer could also lose motivation if he/she feels unable to undertake the task unaided.

Top tip

You may be asked for the advantages and disadvantages of certain types of practice or guidance, or about which type of practice or guidance you would use with either a novice or an expert. Remember that if such a question is worth 4 marks, you will score 2 marks for any two advantages and 2 marks for any two disadvantages. In other words, make sure that you answer both parts of the question.

Sports players gain an inner feel for the movement patterns of a task and use an inner sense called kinaesthesis to help them recognise the movements in the muscles. This inner sense can be hindered if too much physical help is offered. Kinaesthesis is discussed in more detail on p. 75.

Mental practice

The best improvements in performance are made when physical practice is combined with mental rehearsal. The performer goes over the task in his/her mind, concentrating on the successful aspects of performance. Mental practice should be done in a quiet, calm environment, just before a major event or after a training session with the coach. Figure 7.3 illustrates the relative benefits of physical, mental and combined practice.

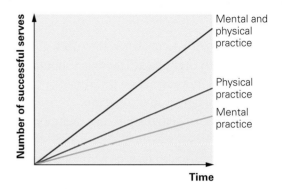

Figure 7.3 Benefits of combined practice

Mental rehearsal activates receptors in the muscle spindles, even though no movement takes place, and the athlete gains a sensation of the task. Mental rehearsal improves reaction times and confidence. Motivation levels may also increase as the athlete develops a desire to succeed.

Mental practice is becoming popular with sports coaches and players but the technique should be used in different ways for beginners and more experienced athletes. With a beginner the coach could combine mental practice with distributed practice, doing short sessions of mental rehearsal during rest intervals, going over techniques that have just been practised physically. More advanced performers can use quiet times to go over an imminent event in their mind, concentrating on a successful performance. Fine details, strengths to concentrate on and opposition weaknesses may have been highlighted by the coach during training and can be focused on by the performer in preparation for a big match.

Practice makes perfect

1 Why is the organisation of a skill important when considering which type of practice to use when teaching that skill? *(2 marks)*

2 What is the **whole method of practice**? What are the advantages and disadvantages of teaching a skill using the whole method compared with the part method? *(4 marks)*

3 What is meant by the term **mental rehearsal**? What benefits does mental rehearsal have for the sports performer? *(4 marks)*

Chapter 8

Information processing

What you need to know

By the end of this chapter you should be able to:

- analyse the methods and processes by which information is collected and coded from the sporting environment
- explain how this information is stored in the memory
- explain the advantages of reacting quickly to information from the sporting environment

Ways to process information

In Chapter 6 it was noted that skills can be divided into a cognitive part and a motor part. The cognitive part is concerned with thinking about and processing information before we use it. So information processing occurs in the early stages of movement and looks at the ways that information is dealt with initially, an essential process before actions take place.

There are three stages to information processing:

- **Stimulus identification**. The player needs to pick out the important cues from the environment. For example, in cricket a fielder needs to pick out the flight and speed of the ball when the batsman hits it towards him before he can make a catch.
- **Response selection**. The second stage of information processing is decision-making. Once the stimulus has been identified, the performer must decide what to do with the information. The fielder has to decide how to make the catch — whether to move to the left or to the right and at what speed — based on the information he has gathered.
- The final stage is **response programming**. Having made a decision, the fielder has to instruct his muscles to make the required movement so that the action of making the catch can be performed. The brain sends a message to the muscles telling them to contract. The motor part of the skill can now take place.

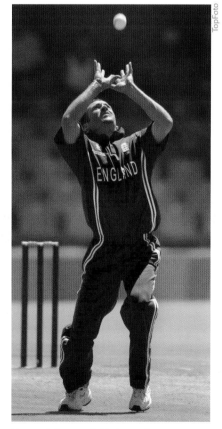

TopFoto

Howzat! Successful information processing brings rewards in sport

Information processing models

The mechanics of information processing in sport can be analysed in detail by reference to models of information processing. The models represent the mechanisms involved in the brain when information is dealt with as a flow chart — a logical sequence of events expressed visually. The two models you need to study are the **Welford** and **Whiting** models (Figures 8.1 and 8.2).

Key term

Information processing: the methods used to deal with information collected by the senses.

Information processing terminology

The **display** is the sporting environment from which all information is gathered. It includes all the information available to the performer — whether relevant or irrelevant. For example, in tennis the display could include the essential items such as the ball and the position of the opponent as well as peripheral information such as the umpire and the crowd watching the game. At times the player might be tempted to pay attention to the crowd and not to hitting the ball, causing him/her to make errors.

Information is picked up from the display using the **senses.** All the senses are used in sport. For example, vision is used to track the flight of a

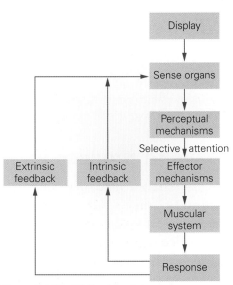

Figure 8.1 The Welford model

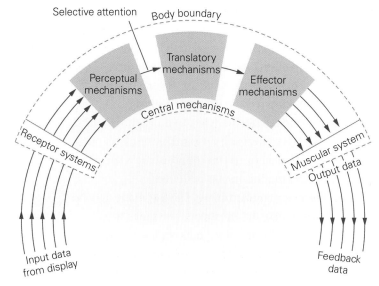

Figure 8.2 The Whiting model

ball and hearing or audition is used in team games — a player might hear the call of a team-mate, or pay attention to the referee's whistle. A sense of balance or equilibrium ensures that there is stability in the player before he/she makes a move. Balance is an essential requirement for gymnasts performing on the balance beam. Sports players are said to have a good sense of touch if they are able to weight a pass delicately into the path of a team-mate. The final sense used in sport is an inner sense. It tells the player how much tension is present in the muscles when they contract, and the angle at which the joints are placed. This inner sense is called **kinaesthesis** and it tells the athlete about body movements. A javelin thrower would know without looking that her arm is behind and held straight and high just prior to the release of the javelin.

With all the information present in sport and the variety of senses used to collect it, some sorting out is necessary to prevent the performer from becoming confused. Have you ever been trying to concentrate on watching a game on television, only to be disturbed by your brother or sister asking you a question? It is difficult to focus on two things at the same time, never mind a multitude of things. It is the same when you are playing. It is impossible to pay attention to *all* the information contained in the display without becoming confused and probably taking much too long to think about your next move. In the next stage of information processing — the **perceptual mechanisms** — the wealth of information picked up by the senses is filtered by **selective attention**. The relevant information is filtered from the irrelevant information so that the player is left with just the stimulus, or important information, to concentrate on. Irrelevant information (noise) is disregarded.

Once such relevant information has been filtered and **coded**, it is marked as important and any subsequent decisions can be based on the relevant information alone. **Decision-making** then takes place in the perceptual mechanisms. A right-handed tennis player, having determined that the ball is coming to the left-hand side, would decide to hit a backhand. In the Welford model, decision-making is included in the perceptual mechanisms but in the Whiting version it is given a separate identity — the **translatory mechanisms**. The Whiting model shows a reduced number of arrows going from the perceptual mechanisms to the translatory mechanisms, indicating that selective attention reduces the volume of information from the display so that any decision is based on the stimulus alone. In the translatory mechanisms the information received is adapted and compared with movement programmes stored in the long-term memory

When a decision has been made, it has to be communicated to the muscles so that movement can be initiated. The **effector mechanism** is the network of nerves that transport the decision from the brain to the muscles. In Whiting's model there are again several arrows going

> **Key term**
>
> **Selective attention**: filtering of relevant information from irrelevant information.

> **Top tip**
>
> Information processing involves definitions and specific terminology that you must be familiar with. Learn all these new terms off by heart. You might be asked to explain what you understand by any of the features of the information processing models, so make sure that you know them all and that you can define each feature and illustrate it with an example.

from the effector mechanism to the muscles, indicating that more than one set of muscles are used. These muscles are triggered into action by the effector mechanism. It is now possible for **muscular contractions** to take place. These muscular contractions facilitate movement so that the motor part of the skill, the actual **response**, can take place.

The performer can be helped by **feedback** — information given after the response to promote movement correction. Two types of feedback are shown in Welford's model. **Intrinsic** feedback comes from within the player, who might know when he/she has over-hit a shot. **Extrinsic** feedback is given by the coach.

Feedback

Feedback is an integral part of information processing, which can help to provide confidence and motivation for the performer. Feedback has a vital role to play in correcting errors and improving performance.

If you have played in a game and felt you had done particularly well, one of the first things you might have done afterwards is to speak to your coach, or your friends who were watching, and ask them how they thought you played. If you watch a performance on television, it is usual for the event to be analysed by a panel of experts, often with the aid of a variety of statistics. The reason that feedback is so popular in sport is that it tends to improve performance. Players who receive feedback perform better than those who don't.

Feedback: information received to help modify performance.

The different types of feedback are shown in Table 8.1.

Table 8.1 Types of feedback

Type	Definition	Phase of learning (see Chapter 11)	Example
Positive	Information about correct technique given to encourage and motivate the player	Cognitive	Praise from the coach to a novice after a good shot
Negative	Information about incorrect technique given to eliminate errors	Associative autonomous	A basketball player being told by a team-mate that a pass was too slow
Intrinsic	Feedback from within the player	Autonomous	A tennis player knowing that she has over-hit a return
Extrinsic	Feedback from an outside source	Cognitive autonomous	Tactical advice from the coach, telling a rugby player not to hold on to the ball for too long before passing
Knowledge of results	Basic information to determine success or failure	Cognitive	A netball player noting that a shot has just missed the goal
Knowledge of performance	More detailed information about technique	Autonomous associative	A netball player being told why the shot missed goal
Concurrent	Feedback given during the performance	Autonomous	The team captain summarising the opponent's strengths
Terminal	Feedback given after a performance	Cognitive autonomous	The coach summarising the performance after a game

Different types of feedback can occur at the same time. After a game, a coach's summary of a performance could be extrinsic, terminal and negative.

Making feedback effective

Feedback should be given to the performer as soon as possible after the event so that it has maximum impact. It should be target-related and given in language that is understandable and not too technical, especially for beginners. Information given during a game is best broken down into simple chunks. A player will have a lot to think about during the game and will not be able to remember much information.

The coach should be careful to give feedback appropriately. A novice performer will have different needs from a more experienced player. Novices need encouragement, so positive feedback should be given to provide motivation. Experienced players can use negative feedback to eliminate errors. A starting point for the beginner could be knowledge of results, and as he/she gains experience, knowledge of performance can be used to fine-tune technique. A beginner who has not yet developed a feel for the game may best use extrinsic feedback as guidelines; more experienced players will realise their own errors using intrinsic feedback.

> **Tasks to tackle 8.2**
>
> What types of feedback would you use for a beginner in sport?

Memory

Once information has been processed, it can be stored so that it can be used again in similar sporting situations. The memory system stores and codes the results of the information processing mechanisms. It consists of a number of stores and ways of moving information between the stores. The **short-term sensory store** is a temporary storage facility. It works quickly, taking only a fraction of second to hold and code all the information from the sporting environment. The information from the display is collected using the senses and then almost immediately this wealth of information is filtered using the process of **selective attention**. It is necessary to filter the information from the display to avoid information overload.

The relevant information or stimulus is sent to the **short-term memory**. This has a limited capacity and can only deal with about seven items of information at any one time. The short-term memory is often called the working memory because it has many functions. It receives the relevant information from the sensory store and uses this information to initiate movement. It then passes this information to the **long-term memory** (Figure 8.3) Information can remain in the short-term memory for about 30 seconds before it is either lost or moved to the long-term memory.

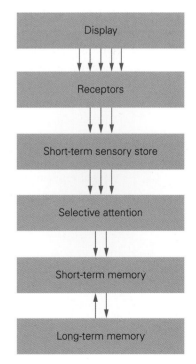

Figure 8.3 The memory system

Once the information has been logged into the long-term memory, it remains there for a long time. The long-term memory has an unlimited capacity and can store a lifetime's information. You might well have learned how to ride a bike when you were at primary school and this is a skill that you will not forget, even if you rarely cycle. The information is stored in the long-term memory in the form of a motor programme — a method of storing the components of a task in a logical sequence.

There is a two-way relationship between the short-term memory and the long-term memory. They work in tandem so that information can be moved from the short-term to the long-term memory for storage and then retrieved at an appropriate time in the future.

Coding information in the long-term memory

It is important for the coach to be aware of the two-way relationship between the long-term and the short-term memory systems, so that movement patterns can be stored in the long-term memory and used by the performer when needed. The coach can enhance the process of storing motor programmes in the long-term memory by making the player practise the task repeatedly. During such practice the coach should offer praise and reinforcement to the player, because we tend to remember pleasant experiences. We also tend to remember unpleasant experiences. For instance, if you are injured making a bad tackle, you will remember it. For the same reason, the coach might use punishment to emphasise what not to do.

Skills are more likely to be remembered if they are associated with other items already stored in the memory. If you are trying to learn an overarm volleyball serve and you already know how to serve in tennis, the coach might let you start by thinking about the tennis serve.

Tasks to tackle 8.3

List the features of the short-term and the long-term memory.

People can often recall where they were and what they were doing when some major event took place. If the coach makes sessions unusual in some way, the learner will recall the information by associating the session with the learned task. Coaching sessions should be fun and enjoyable.

Mental rehearsal involves going over the task in your mind. It stimulates the brain and the associated muscles and so helps to store information in the long-term memory. The coach should ensure that demonstrations are clear and accurate, so that players do not recall inaccurate information.

Information can be remembered more easily if it is broken down into small, bite-sized pieces and given in stages, a process called **chunking**.

Reaction, movement and response

It is a great advantage to the athlete if information collected and stored in the memory can be dealt with quickly. It takes only fractions of a second to go through all the mechanisms required to process information but if those mechanisms can be speeded up even more, then that extra fraction of time enables the performer to read the situation and gives a little more time to select the appropriate action.

Before reacting to a stimulus the performer needs to:

- receive information from the display via the senses
- code this information into relevant and irrelevant items using selective attention
- make a decision based on the relevant information — select the response
- initiate the response by sending impulses to the muscles

In relative terms, coding the information and making a decision take longer than receiving the information and initiating the response but all four activities take place just prior to actual movement. Therefore **reaction time** involves no movement. It is the time taken from the presentation of the stimulus to the onset of the movement. **Movement time** is the time it takes to complete the task from start to finish. The **response time** is the time taken from the presentation of the stimulus to the completion of the task — it is the sum of the reaction time and the movement time. Figure 8.4 shows the relationship between response time, reaction time and movement time.

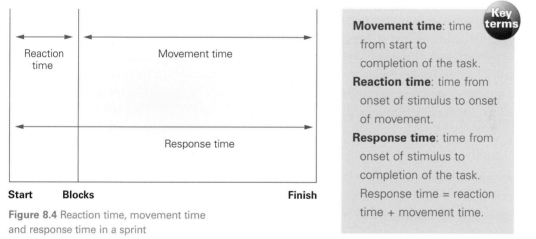

Figure 8.4 Reaction time, movement time and response time in a sprint

In the 100 metres sprint, the reaction time is the time from hearing the gun to the point just before leaving the blocks. Movement time is the time from leaving the blocks to hitting the tape at the finishing line. The response time is the time from hearing the gun to hitting the tape.

Influences on reaction time

The time it takes to react, and therefore to respond, to a stimulus is influenced by a number of factors.

The number of stimuli

The more choices available, the slower the reaction will be. A simple reaction time can be very fast because it involves only one choice to one stimulus. For example, the only response of an athlete to hearing the starting gun is to push away from the blocks and run as fast as possible. A choice reaction time involves more decision making and usually takes more time. For example, a midfield hockey player must choose which player to pass to from a number of available team-mates. However, the relationship between reaction time and the number of choices is not linear. The *rate of* increase in reaction time decreases with increasing choice. Hicks's law describes the relationship between the number of choices and reaction time (Figure 8.5).

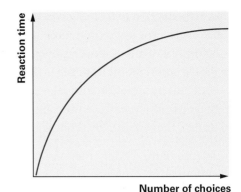

Figure 8.5 Hicks's law

Hicks's law states that, although having more choices makes performance slower, the rate of increase in reaction time decreases as the number of choices increases. For example, a goalkeeper faced with two attackers who are clean through on goal might rush out and pressure the player with the ball. This increases the ball carrier's choices. He has to go around the goalkeeper, pass to his team-mate or shoot, and making the decision will cause him to hesitate. On the other hand, footballers are told by the coach not to dive in at the feet of an opponent with the ball in midfield but rather to hold their position and see what the attacking player does before making a move. This is because the attacking player already has a number of options to choose from and adding one more will increase reaction time only by a small amount, according to Hicks's law.

Experience

A player's experience will affect the reaction time. Experienced players can anticipate the bounce of a ball and get there first. Have you ever played squash against a more experienced player? You might have found yourself chasing the ball around the court while your wily opponent always seemed to be in the middle of the court, exactly where the ball landed. Anticipation, or the ability to pre-judge a stimulus, is a major influence on reaction time.

The ability to anticipate comes with experience. Guessing what your opponent is going to do is easier if you can get a feel for the way the pitch or court is playing. For example tennis players need to get a feel of the court if they are changing from the clay courts of the French Open championships in Paris to the grass courts of Wimbledon. This process is called **effector anticipation**.

Anticipation can be improved by gaining prior knowledge of the opponents from your coach, or by watching the opponents before you play them. This prior knowledge is called **perceptual anticipation**. Players can also gain information on their opponents during the game by looking at the way they shape up to make a play, the stance or the grip on the ball.

Picking up such cues from the environment is called **receptor anticipation**. Whichever method is used to aid anticipation, the performer should remember that it is a gamble. If you anticipate correctly, reaction times and response times will be reduced and there will be more time to play your shots and concentrate on detailed aspects of the performance. You will also suffer less from fatigue. However, if your gamble is wrong and you make the wrong guess, reaction times and response times will increase dramatically and you may not have time to make the play.

Gender and age
Studies have shown that men tend to react faster than women but women retain their ability to react quickly until much later in life. Ageing slows the reactions of both men and women.

Performance-enhancing drugs
Performance-enhancing drugs can affect reaction time. The infamous start made by Ben Johnson in the 100 metres at the 1988 Seoul Olympics was made under the influence of performance-enhancing steroids.

Stimulus intensity
The intensity of the stimulus can affect reaction time. Athletes tend to react faster to a stimulus that is loud or bright, such as the loud bleep at the start of a swimming race, or the brightly coloured cricket ball that is played with during night matches.

Fitness
Increased fitness levels lead to improved reaction times.

Improving reaction time
Two theoretical concepts that explain reaction time are the single-channel hypothesis and the psychological refractory period.

The **single-channel hypothesis** suggests that a stimulus is processed along a single nerve track and that the brain can only process one stimulus at a time — think about the capillary network, which allows only a single blood cell to pass through at any one time. The single-channel hypothesis implies that any subsequent stimulus must wait for the one before it to be processed before it can be dealt with, rather like a queue of cars waiting at a road junction. The single-channel hypothesis is illustrated in Figure 8.6.

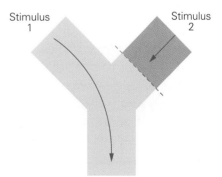

Figure 8.6 The single-channel hypothesis

The **psychological refractory period** (Figure 8.7, p. 82) is based on the single-channel hypothesis. It too suggests that only one stimulus can be processed at a time, and if a second stimulus is presented to the performer before the original one is processed, then an unavoidable delay will occur. This delay is known as the psychological refractory period (PRP). The PRP occurs because the second stimulus must wait for the first one to be processed, even though the first stimulus is no longer valid. An example of this phenomenon is the ball hitting the net in tennis and being deflected in a different direction. A dummy pass in rugby is an attempt to present a first stimulus to the opponent, who begins to follow the flight of the imaginary pass. When the player keeps the ball and runs with it, the opponent is momentarily confused and the reaction is delayed. Experienced players often use the PRP to their advantage by using dummies or body language to present two stimuli to their opponents in quick succession, so that there is no time to deal with the first stimulus before the second is presented.

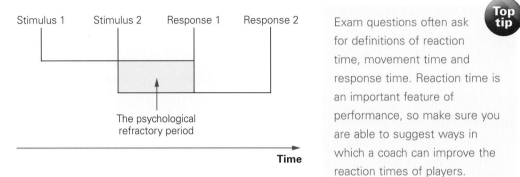

Top tip

Exam questions often ask for definitions of reaction time, movement time and response time. Reaction time is an important feature of performance, so make sure you are able to suggest ways in which a coach can improve the reaction times of players.

Figure 8.7 The psychological refractory period

Practice makes perfect

1 How could a sports coach ensure that information is stored in the long-term memory of a sports performer? *(4 marks)*

2 Define the terms **reaction time**, **movement time** and **response time** in terms of sport. Show how fast reactions can benefit a sports performer. *(4 marks)*

3 What are the factors that can influence the reaction time of a sports performer? *(4 marks)*

Chapter 9

Motor control

What you need to know

By the end of this chapter you should be able to:

- describe the mechanisms used to develop and control sporting actions
- explain the influences on the mechanisms used to control movement
- identify the differences between open-loop and closed-loop control ·

Open-loop and closed-loop control

Imagine a golfer at the first tee of a golf course. He thinks about how he is going to approach the fairway with his first shot. In a fraction of a second, his swing is completed and he watches uncomfortably as the ball sails to the right and lands in the rough. As he makes his way to the spot where the ball has landed, he considers why and how he made the error in sending the ball to the right and resolves to correct the error at the next hole.

Now imagine a skier on the slopes in Austria, about to set off down a challenging run that will test her skiing ability. She thinks carefully about how she is going to tackle the run. On the way down, she starts to overbalance. Almost automatically, using her skiing experience, she corrects the error and completes the run successfully.

These examples are similar in that both performers are competing at a high standard and the performer uses internal feedback to correct errors. However, there is also an important difference. On the ski slope, the error is corrected *during* the performance, so that the skill is adjusted before the completion of the task. On the golf course the error is corrected *after* the task has taken place, so that it can be adjusted next time. The difference in how the skills are corrected serves to highlight the difference between open-loop control and closed-loop control.

In **open-loop control** the performer does not refer to feedback while the skill is being carried out because there is not time to do so. The skill is fast and ballistic in its execution, such as a golf swing. The player may have a memory trace of the performance but he/she has to wait until the task is over before comparing the action to the memory trace and adjusting the movement next time the skill is performed. For example, a tennis player might hit the first serve out and although he is aware of what went wrong he is unable to correct the error

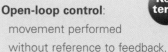

Open-loop control: movement performed without reference to feedback.

Key term

during the fraction of a second it takes to hit the first serve. The error is adjusted in time for the second serve a few moments later by retaining an image of the first serve in the memory. Open-loop control therefore does not utilise feedback during the execution of the task but uses feedback next time the skill is performed.

During **closed-loop control**, the performer has time to utilise feedback during the performance. Using a combination of past experience and intrinsic feedback, any errors that occur can be corrected during play. An error such as an overbalance can be detected by the inner sense of kinaesthesis. Corrective messages are sent from the brain to the working muscles almost automatically, and the movement is adjusted.

Closed-loop control can be thought of as a continual process. It is a self-checking mechanism that can help experienced players to correct errors subconsciously and make their performance smooth and efficient.

> **Key term**
>
> **Closed-loop control**: when feedback is used to adjust performance.

Closed-loop control can also operate at another level. Consider the novice gymnast trying to learn a simple move on the balance beam. Progress across the beam may be slow and appear to be uncoordinated. The gymnast may lose her balance and have to check progress frequently while the movement is being executed.

In this example, closed-loop control is being used during the performance but the feedback is not automatic. At a lower level of performance the feedback is conscious and essential. Any error in the performance such as the overbalance is detected and can be compared with an early image or trace of the required skill that the performer may have been given by the coach in the form of a demonstration. Any noticeable errors are relayed via the brain to the muscles and the performer has to stop and think about how to use this feedback to correct the error. The feedback takes time to process and progress is slow.

The lower level of performance is often called level 3 of motor control. Automatic use of closed-loop control by more experienced performers is referred to as level 2 of motor control. Open-loop control that does not require feedback is referred to as level 1 of motor control.

> **Top tip**
>
> Make sure you know the essential differences between open-loop control and closed-loop control. Open-loop control does not use feedback while the skill is being executed. Closed-loop control is a more continuous process that depends on feedback.

> **Top tip**
>
> You need to know examples of when open-loop control is used, such as for short, fast skills like a golf swing, and that closed-loop control is used for longer tasks such as downhill skiing.

Motor programme theory

Imagine that you are an experienced athlete and that you have been practising the skill of a shot put for many years. When you compete at a major event, the performance of the shot put is the same as it has been during all those years of practice, because it is a closed skill and is not affected much by changes in the environment. A motor programme controls your movements.

A motor programme is a set of movements, stored in the long-term memory, which specify the components of a skill. A motor programme is formed by specific and continued practice. As a skill is practised, images are built up in the long-term memory and the effective actions are stored while the incorrect and negative aspects of performance are eliminated. Internal and external feedback help to check errors and amend performance continually. The net result is the storage of a perfect image that can be called upon for future use.

The use of a motor programme to control movements has obvious advantages. The player, having perfected the task with practice, is in the autonomous phase of learning and therefore has almost automatic control of movement. The performer is able to concentrate on the finer aspects of the task and pay attention to detail. Movements are smooth and efficient and reaction times are fast. An expert basketball player is able to score from a free throw at the edge of the key after a foul because he/she has practised this skill many times.

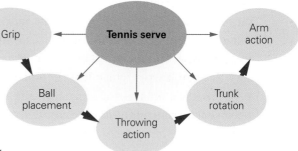

Figure 9.1 Tennis serve motor programme

Key terms

Subroutines: the parts of a skill that can be practised in isolation.

Motor programme: a set of movements, stored in the long-term memory, that specify the components of a task or skill.

Tasks to tackle 9.1

How is a motor programme developed in the long-term memory?

Motor programmes are stored in the long-term memory to be retrieved when required. They are stored in the form of an image that contains both the required task (sometimes called the executive) and the subroutines that make up the executive. For example, the skill of a tennis serve is made up of the subroutines of the ball toss, the hit, the trunk rotation and the correct footwork.

Top tip

You should know the advantages of developing a motor programme in terms of efficiency, and how motor programmes are developed using mental and physical practice and feedback.

Tasks to tackle 9.2

Make a list of the subroutines associated with a named skill from a sport of your choice.

Motor programmes can be developed from an early age by practice. These basic motor programmes become the foundation for more complex ones at a later stage. In Chapter 6 we noted how foundation skills such as throwing are developed by early practice. The motor programmes for these foundation skills might become an essential part of a more complex task, such as a tennis serve, which uses the ball toss (a throwing action) as an essential subroutine.

The problem with motor programmes is that they cannot be used for open skills because open-skill movements need to be adjusted according to changes in the environment.

Practice makes perfect

1 Explain the differences between open-loop and closed-loop methods of controlling skills in sport. *(5 marks)*

2 What are the advantages of having motor programmes stored in the long-term memory when performing sports skills in a competitive situation? *(3 marks)*

Chapter 10

Acquiring movement skills

Motivation and arousal

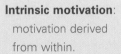

What you need to know

By the end of this chapter you should be able to:
- distinguish between different forms of motivation
- understand how motivation affects performance
- establish how coaches can use motivation to help promote better performance

Motivation

Motivation is defined as the external influences and internal mechanisms that arouse and direct our behaviour. This implies that motivation is a powerful tool that can be used to shape the behaviour of an athlete. Motivation affects the amount of effort that a player puts into the game and players with a strong will to win are usually more successful. Players who are motivated will persist with the task, even when the odds are against them. A team that is a goal down with only a few minutes left to play will benefit from players who are well motivated, because they will keep trying until the end of the game to score a last-minute goal.

Motivation also affects performance relative to ability. A coach might motivate novice performers by offering rewards and incentives, such as a 'player of the week' award. A beginner who feels he/she is doing well in an activity will increase in confidence and will want to continue to improve.

More experienced players may be motivated by their own success. The knowledge that they have had a good game is enough. The motivation will still be there for the next game.

This more permanent type of motivation is called **intrinsic motivation**. Intrinsic motivation comes from within the performer and is characterised by feelings of pride and satisfaction from completing or succeeding in a task. A feeling of enjoyment may be derived both during and when reflecting on the performance. Examples of intrinsic motivation include the thrill of scoring a goal, the satisfaction of winning a major competition and the pride you feel on reaching the top of a mountain after a difficult walk. The feeling of wellbeing derived from such motivation ensures that the performer maintains the desire to continue with the activity. Hence intrinsic motivation is long-lasting.

> **Key terms**
>
> **Intrinsic motivation**: motivation derived from within.
>
> **Motivation**: the internal mechanisms and external stimuli that arouse and direct behaviour.

Extrinsic motivation is more temporary. It includes both tangible and intangible rewards from an outside source. Intangible rewards are non-physical, such as the praise and encouragement given by the coach to a beginner who has performed well on the early part of a task, or to a championship athlete after a record-breaking performance. There may not be a trophy, but the applause from the crowd brings satisfaction. Tangible rewards include the medals and trophies that are awarded to players at the end of the season, or for player of the match. Other examples include the certificates given to young swimmers as they progress through the early swimming grades, or the money on offer to professional players when they sign a new contract.

> **Key term**
>
> **Extrinsic motivation:** motivation derived from an outside source.

Both extrinsic and intrinsic methods of motivation can be used to help sports performers of all grades, but the coach should use these two types of motivation carefully and appropriately. Extrinsic rewards are a good way of attracting newcomers to an activity, and young performers in particular are delighted to receive certificates or medals for any early success that they achieve. However, although extrinsic rewards may provide the foundation for future participation, they should not be used all the time. The continued use of praise and rewards may mean that a player participates for the 'trophy', rather than for the pleasure of taking part. In this way the overuse of extrinsic motivation may undermine intrinsic motivation. The coach should offer praise and reinforcement whenever possible, especially to beginners, but remember to limit the use of extrinsic rewards as the player gains experience.

Intrinsic motivation is desirable because it is a more permanent way of maintaining interest in an activity. The coach should gradually decrease the extrinsic rewards and replace them with intrinsic motivators. Setting personal goals for the performer and then giving ownership of those goals to the performer can promote intrinsic motivation.

Other ways for a coach to motivate players include making training sessions fun. A variety of activities and some 5- or 6-a-side games could be introduced. The coach could also adjust the training environment to suit the players — for example, small groups may be planned so that players of similar ability train together. The coach could inspire players by pointing out role models. These need not be established star players but should include players of good ability, perhaps from within the club, who are well respected. The achievements of such lesser role models can appear to be within reach of novice players rather than being impossible to achieve.

> **Top tip**
>
> Exam questions on goal setting are nearly always related to the type of goals that can be set by coaches and the factors that should be considered when those goals are set. Make sure that you have a thorough knowledge of both these concepts.

As players gain experience, more demanding goals can be set. An athlete who has reached a personal best should be praised for the achievement and then set another higher target to meet. The coach should stress that goals achieved are due to the ability and effort of the player. In other words, success should be attributed to internal factors. Personal improvements can be emphasised as a reason for individual or team success. The coach should ensure that tasks set at the start of a training programme are within the capabilities of the performer. By allowing success, the coach provides confidence and a desire to continue training.

> **Tasks to tackle 10.1**
>
> What strategies could a coach use to provide motivation to players?

The greatest benefits from motivation can be gained by rewarding specific behaviour. An improvement in a particular technique that has been worked on in recent weeks could be praised. It could be emphasised that a better performance is a direct result of the improvement.

The coach should consider the personality of the performer before deciding on the best way to offer motivation. Extrovert individuals enjoy the limelight and can be praised openly. Others might prefer to be praised quietly, away from other people. Motivational praise should be given as soon as possible after a performance. A young player receiving the player of the match award at the team meeting immediately after the game will feel proud.

Arousal and performance

Arousal is defined as the performer's level of readiness to perform. It is an energised state that prepares the body for action. However, too much or too little arousal can have a detrimental effect on performance.

The approach of a major competition or game, a large audience, frustrating circumstances such as being fouled, or a fear of failure could cause an increase in arousal levels. The effect of arousal on performance is explained by a number of theories, the first of which is **drive theory**.

> **Arousal**: the degree of activation and readiness required to perform a task.
>
> **Key term**

Drive theory

Drive theory states that performance improves as arousal increases. There is a linear relationship between arousal and performance (Figure 10.1).

Drive theory is summarised by the formula:

$$P = D \times H$$

that is, performance is equal to drive multiplied by habit.

The 'drive' part of the formula suggests that we are initially motivated by the challenge of meeting the task or by the 'big game' and that the increased effort we put in brings us more success and a stronger drive to continue performing.

The 'habit' part indicates that success provides reinforcement, and we carry on repeating the successful responses so that the performance becomes habitual.

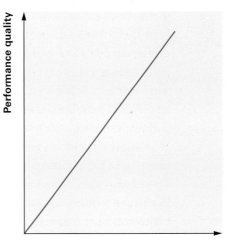

Figure 10.1 Drive theory

At high levels of arousal, the performer takes in less information from the environment and may only focus on the dominant response or most intense stimulus. Only expert players who can deal with pressure, or those performing simple skills that do not require a lot of thinking, can continue to show improvement at high levels of arousal. Therefore, drive theory may not be applicable to novice performers at high levels of arousal.

Drive reduction theory

Drive reduction theory suggests that, rather than a continual improvement in performance, as portrayed in the drive theory, motivation is high at the start of the learning process but performance can begin to deteriorate once the task has been mastered.

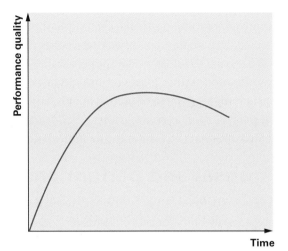

Success achieved on the task satisfies the initial drive but the performer may then lose motivation and become bored with doing the same task. To maintain motivation, the performer must be offered a new challenge or the existing skill must be extended, so that there is something new to focus on.

Figure 10.2 Drive reduction theory

The inverted U theory

Like drive theory, this theory examines the relationship between arousal and performance, but it offers a more realistic approach.

The inverted U theory suggests that an increase in arousal levels initially improves performance but only up to a maximum point, which occurs at moderate arousal levels. Any further increases in arousal levels beyond this optimum point cause performance to deteriorate. At high levels of arousal, the performer can process only limited amounts of information and the perceptual field from which information is gathered narrows.

According to the inverted U theory, the performer can suffer from both under-arousal, when motivation levels are not high enough to energise performance, and over-arousal, when an influx of even limited information can cause confusion.

However, a moderate level of arousal may not always be the most productive. The best level of arousal for optimum performance can vary according to the task and the personality and expertise of the performer. Novices operate best at low levels of arousal. They must be calm because they need to focus attention on the task and will be easily distracted by extra pressure. Expert performers are used to more pressure and can do well at higher levels of arousal. Introverts have naturally high levels of adrenaline and need only a little stimulation to increase arousal. They therefore need to keep arousal levels low. Extroverts, on the other hand, have naturally low levels of adrenaline and can cope with an adrenaline rush. The amount of stimulation required to increase adrenaline levels and arousal is measured by the reticular activating system in the brain.

Simple skills can be performed at high levels of arousal because only a limited amount of information is required. Tasks that require little decision making can be attempted at high arousal levels because fewer items of information are processed in the brain. A simple task such as a forward roll can therefore be attempted at high arousal. More complex skills are better performed at lower levels of arousal because they require a lot of information, and the amount of information that can be used by the performer decreases as arousal levels increase.

Fine skills are best performed at low arousal levels, as more emotional and mental control is required. Gross skills can be performed at higher arousal levels because a lower degree of accuracy is needed. For example, a rugby tackle can be attempted with a higher level of arousal than a pistol shot.

Figure 10.3 shows the inverted U theory and how it can be modified to take account of the skill and the performer.

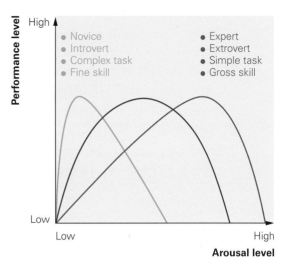

Figure 10.3 Modified inverted U theory

Catastrophe theory

The inverted U theory implies that there is a gradual decline in performance with increase in arousal above the optimum level. Catastrophe theory suggests that rather than a gradual decline, there is a dramatic reduction in performance at a certain arousal level (Figure 10.4). This is caused by a combination of cognitive anxiety, such as worrying about not playing well, and the physical effects of anxiety, such as muscular tension. Even experts can experience this type of disaster.

A change in the situation can be enough to cause an increase in arousal and provoke catastrophe. For example, you might score from a penalty in the first half of a cup game. But say you are called on later in the game to take the final kick of a penalty shoot-out to decide who goes through to the final. The increased pressure might cause you to bungle the kick.

To overcome the catastrophic decline, the performer must try to reduce anxiety levels and

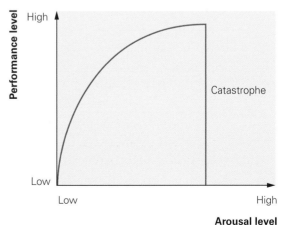

Figure 10.4 Catastrophe theory

return to a level of arousal that was present before the catastrophe occurred. This may not be possible in the middle of a match or performance.

Catastrophe theory is an adapted version of the inverted U theory. It offers a more realistic idea of the reduction in performance caused by anxiety and stress. Once the athlete begins to experience catastrophe, stress levels may increase as he/she begins to believe that he/she is unable to meet the demands of the situation. The increase in stress may cause performance to deteriorate further.

Practice makes perfect

1 Explain how the task and the ability of the performer can affect the relationship between arousal and performance. *(4 marks)*

2 What is meant by the terms **intrinsic motivation** and **extrinsic motivation**? *(2 marks)*

3 Explain the drive reduction theory applied to sports performance. *(3 marks)*

Chapter 11

Theories of learning

What you need to know

By the end of this chapter you should:

- know the three phases that performers pass through as they develop their skills
- be able to present practical examples to show how a coach could help a player to progress from the early to the latter stages of learning
- understand the theoretical concepts that explain how learning sports skills can be achieved

The phases of learning

The psychologists Fitts and Posner proposed that learners pass through three stages as their skills develop. These three stages are known as the phases of learning.

The cognitive phase

This is the first phase of learning experienced by a beginner who tries to work out and understand what is required to perform a new movement. The novice might watch a demonstration of a skill and then try to perform the task with uncoordinated movements. It is a short phase during which a trial-and-error process is used to help develop an early understanding of the parts of the skill. The performer in this phase uses closed-loop control and relies heavily on feedback. Time is needed to think and to check movements. The coach might use manual and mechanical guidance and concentrate on extrinsic and positive feedback to offer encouragement and ensure improvement.

The associative phase

This is often called the practice phase of learning. The learner compares his/her current level of performance with that of a top-level player. Long periods of practice and the use of feedback to correct errors are needed to perfect the skill. Trial and error may again be used to achieve a smoother performance and fine-tune any errors. The feedback during the trial-and-error process may be internal, from within the player, who may now have more idea of the perfect movement. During this phase the player begins to build up a mental framework of the task, with the parts of the skill — its subroutines — coded in the memory. This framework is called a **motor programme**. The performer should now be able to use intrinsic feedback and begin to alter the level of skill, using negative feedback. Verbal and visual guidance could be used.

The autonomous phase

This is the third and final phase of learning. At this stage, movements are perfected to the point where they are almost automatic. The player can concentrate on the finer details of the task and the performance is completed with maximum efficiency. A football player at this level can do a pass almost without thinking about it and can now perfect that pass by weighting it to perfection. This is a phase for experts, who must continue to practise if they want to remain at this top level. Motor programmes are firmly stored in the memory. At this high level of performance the player could benefit from both intrinsic feedback and from advice from the coach (extrinsic feedback). Any guidance is tactical and verbal.

Coaches can use strategies to help players to progress from the early cognitive phase to the final autonomous phase of learning. An understanding of some of the theoretical concepts behind these strategies will further enhance learning. Learning leads to a permanent change in behaviour and movement patterns. However, performance is a temporary response to a situation and can still fluctuate. The psychologist Steve Bull summed it up as follows:

> Learning may be considered to be a more or less permanent change in performance associated with experiences [while] performance may be thought of as a temporary occurrence fluctuating from time to time due to many operating variables.

A professional player in the autonomous phase of learning must practise to maintain his standard

Tasks to tackle 11.1

Suggest what types of practice, feedback and guidance you might use for performers in the cognitive phase, the associative phase and the autonomous phase of learning. Information on feedback can be found on p. 76. Information on practice and guidance can be found on pp. 66–72.

Top tip

Exam questions often refer to the three phases of learning. Make sure that you know a couple of salient points about the cognitive, associative and autonomous phases, backed up by examples, so that you can describe the key characteristics of each phase.

The cognitive theory of learning

The cognitive theory suggests that the performer uses his/her own knowledge, based on experience, to help find solutions to problems. He/she already has an **insight** to help.

A performer learns by thinking about and understanding what is required, rather than simply developing a series of responses to various stimuli. The problem is solved as a whole, using previous knowledge and experience. For example, an athlete in a long-distance race may work out that the best way to beat the other runners who have a faster finish is to set off at a fast pace. If this tactic works, the performer might be motivated to repeat the same response when confronted by a similar problem in the future.

To work out solutions to problems, the performer must develop an understanding of the tactics required. Past experiences may be used to find the correct response. The solution to the problem (referred to in cognitive theory as an **intervening variable**), is arrived at because the athlete understands why he/she is choosing a particular course of action. Athletes may feel more comfortable working things out for themselves rather than being told.

Gestalt (from German 'pattern', 'form') theory supports the cognitive theory of learning by suggesting that problems are best solved using a whole approach, rather than focusing on just part of the task.

> **Key terms**
>
> **Cognitive theory of learning**: learning based on solving problems using past experience, and concentrating on the whole skill.

> **Tasks to tackle 11.2**
>
> Give a practical example for each of the four elements of cognitive theory displayed in Figure 11.1.

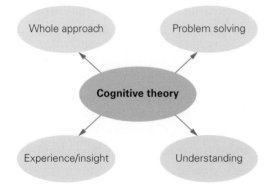

Figure 11.1 The cognitive theory of learning

> **Top tip**
>
> Make sure that you differentiate between the cognitive phase of learning and the cognitive theory of learning. Under the pressure of an exam, it is easy to misinterpret a question and write about the wrong topic.

Top athletes know each other's strengths and weaknesses and use this knowledge in their tactical decision making

The observational theory of learning

Children playing football in the park might celebrate scoring a goal by pulling their shirts off and running around the pitch. They are copying the behaviour of professional players they have seen on television. Sports coaches can use the fact that significant behaviour is often copied by using strategies to ensure that the learner copies desired behaviour.

The performer might also learn behaviour by associating with other people and copying their behaviour. This process can be called social learning.

The psychologist Bandura suggested that behaviour and demonstrations are more likely to be copied if they are consistent, so it is important to give accurate demonstrations each time. Behaviour is more likely to be repeated if it is reinforced with success, particularly if it is a powerful image performed by a role model. Bandura suggested that there are four principles that should be followed (Figure 11.2).

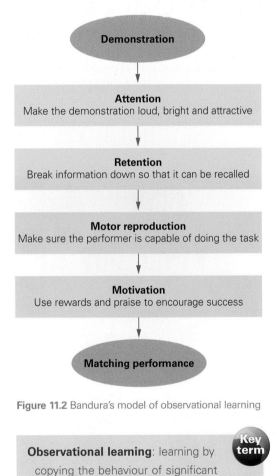

Figure 11.2 Bandura's model of observational learning

Observational learning: learning by copying the behaviour of significant others.

Key term

Attention

The learner must be attracted to the demonstration. The coach should grab the player's attention by making the image powerful, bright and relevant. Cues should be used to highlight key points. The coach is responsible for 'selling' the skill to the performer by pointing out its function. For example, it could be suggested that the reason for learning a new pass in rugby is to allow the ball to be transferred faster to create more time to beat the defence. Reference to an effective pass by a top player might add to the attractiveness of the task.

Retention

Once the player has accepted the idea of a new skill, the coach must make sure that it is remembered. The information should be broken down into bite-size pieces so that it can be processed more easily in the short-term memory, which has a limited capacity. Practice and repetition must take place to ensure that the skill is learned thoroughly.

Motor reproduction

The performer must have the ability to do the task. During early learning the coach should demonstrate basic skills. For example, the basic grip on the ball in rugby must be correct before a pass is attempted. The

Offloading a pass in the tackle is a useful skill when trying to beat the defence

coach should make sure that the player has the necessary coordination and power in the arms and shoulders to make the pass.

Motivation

The learner is more likely to continue to practise and learn if he/she is motivated. The coach can motivate players by offering positive reinforcement in the form of praise or rewards when the demonstrated skill is copied correctly. Most sports governing bodies have award schemes for young players who can demonstrate specific skills successfully.

Transfer of learning

The theory of transfer explains that the learning and performance of one skill can be affected by the learning and performance of another.

There are six types of transfer. An understanding of the different types of transfer can be useful to both the coach and the player.

Proactive transfer is when a skill learned previously is used to help one being currently developed. For example, a netball player might use a netball pass to help in the initial stages of playing basketball. She is

Top tip

There are a lot of technical terms associated with the theories of learning. Make a checklist as you revise and make sure you know them all.

Key term

Transfer of learning: the effect of the learning and performance of one skill on the learning and performance of another.

using a skill she already has to affect the performance of a new task. **Retroactive transfer** is when a skill being learned currently interferes with a skill already learned. When the netball player returns to netball training after playing basketball, there may be some effect on her netball pass.

In **positive transfer** the learning of one skill is aided by the learning of another because of similarities in execution. The skills must have a similar shape and form, so they are built on similar abilities. For example, a tennis player might be able to use the subroutines of the tennis serve to help in learning an overarm volleyball serve. Both tasks involve a throwing action, an overhead hit and a trunk rotation, and the subroutines of both tasks are used in a similar way. As the performer develops, feedback could be used to refine the task so that the volleyball serve becomes more technically correct.

Exam questions on the theories of learning require detailed revision. An exam question will typically ask you to say what is meant by a key point and then ask you to apply your understanding of that topic. For example, you might be asked what positive transfer means and how you would ensure that it occurs.

The movement skills involved in the volleyball serve and the tennis serve are similar

Negative transfer also occurs in the initial stages of learning, but in this case the learning and performance of one skill is hindered by the learning and performance of another.

Negative transfer occurs when two tasks have some similarities but are not identical. A strike in rounders and a cricket shot both involve striking actions but a rounders ball is hit one-handed and at waist height. If you attempted a cricket shot in this way you would most likely be bowled out. The subroutines of the tasks are used in different ways.

Negative transfer is an unwelcome phenomenon for sports performers but with a little specific practice and some help from the coach it can be resolved. Remember that the effects of transfer occur in the initial stages of learning. Negative transfer may occur because the player fails to understand the requirements of the task, or because he/she tries to use a skill from one game in a different and inappropriate environment. The coach should point out the specific requirements of the task.

> **Top tip**
>
> Make sure you know the difference between positive and negative transfer and appropriate examples to show the difference between them.

The movement skills involved in hitting a ball in rounders and in cricket are very different

Zero transfer is often confused with negative transfer. For negative transfer to occur there must be some resemblance between the two tasks. In zero transfer there is no such similarity and therefore there are no effects of the learning and performance of one skill on another. Two skills such as swimming and rock climbing are so different that there is no learning effect from one to the other.

In **bilateral transfer** a learned skill is transferred from limb to limb across the body. A good coach will always encourage players to use both sides of the body. A right-handed basketball player needs to be able to do a lay-up shot with either hand. A left-footed football player needs to practise with the right foot, and a rugby player who is better at passing from the right hand should try passing from the left hand.

Positive transfer is most beneficial and there are ways that a coach can encourage it. Simply pointing out the concept of transfer to a player might help. One of the best ways to promote positive transfer is to offer a realistic approach to training and practice. For example, in the early stages of learning to dribble in hockey, the coach may use cones (and no defenders) to make it easy to master the task. In the later stages of learning, the players have to transfer this skill to the real game. The coach should therefore introduce opponents in practice sessions and perhaps do drills that involve the attack against the defence to simulate a real game situation. The more realistic the practice, the more beneficial it is likely to be.

One way to use the concept of positive transfer during training sessions is to make sure that the tasks are performed in a progressive manner, so that the easiest part of the skill is well learned before moving on to a more difficult aspect of the task. For example, when learning a pass, a performer might concentrate on the grip of the ball before progressing to the actual passing technique and then to passing against passive opponents.

The coach can use positive reinforcement to make the most of positive transfer. When a player brings a skill from a previous game and uses that skill to good effect, the coach might praise the player and say, 'We can use that to start with and build on it.'

Schema theory

Schema theory is similar to transfer of learning. It suggests that the same skills can be used in different sports because the performer has developed a general set of concepts that allows skills to be adapted to suit the situation.

> **Key term**
>
> **Schema**: a rule or concept based on experience.

A schema is therefore a rule based on experience. A motor programme that has been developed for a well-learned skill such as a netball pass could be adapted using feedback so that the pass could be used in basketball. There are similar principles behind the execution of a pass in both games. They both involve passing to a target player, they both involve grip of the ball and both require an arm action and a follow-through.

To initiate a pass in either game the player could use the basic concepts of passing stored in the memory in the form of a motor programme and adapt them with some internal feedback to suit a particular situation. In other words, the principles of passing stored in the memory could be used for a basketball *or* netball pass. Further experience could allow the pass to be used in rugby or even water polo so that, rather than a concrete, well-defined skill, the performer has a set of concepts available to suit the situation (Figure 11.3).

A schema is general in the sense that it can be used in different sports, but it is also specific. Passing, for example, is a particular skill.

Feedback is an essential feature of developing a schema because its use in adapting the existing motor programme is important.

The schema is developed in four parts:

- The **initial conditions**. In the first instance the player needs to gather information from the environment, such as the position of other players. For example, a basketball player making a pass needs to take in information from the environment to determine his/her own position on court as well as the position of teammates.
- The **response specifications**. The basketball player now needs to decide what to do. As a result of an awareness of the initial conditions, the player can decide on the best type of pass to use, to which player and how far the ball needs to be projected.

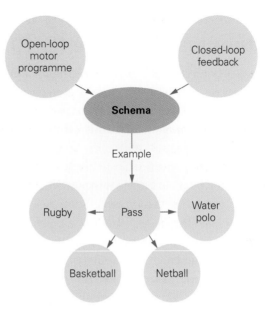

Figure 11.3 Schema theory — the core concepts of the pass can be adapted for use in different sports

- The **sensory consequences**. The player gathers sensory information to help adjust the weighting and timing of the pass. He/she uses vision to sense the best available recipient of the ball. The sense of touch helps gain a feel for the pass.
- The **response outcome**. When the pass has been delivered, the player might receive information on the outcome. Did the pass reach its intended target?

The first two parts of the schema — the initial conditions and the response specifications — initiate the action and are called the **recall schema**. An experienced player will have faced similar situations before and can recall a plan or outline of the skill from memory.

Top tip

You need to learn the four parts of schema theory thoroughly.

The third and fourth parts of the schema — the sensory consequences and the response outcome — are called the **recognition schema**. They require the performer to use sensory information to adapt the task, using feedback gained from the environment. The recognition part of the schema is responsible for controlling the movement.

Schema theory is a useful learning tool for the coach and player. The coach should encourage the development of schemata by expanding the player's experience with a variety of practice and using positive reinforcement when the player uses a schema successfully. Most coaches vary their training sessions for team games, so that, for example, the attack might play against the defence in a variety of situations. Such variety is the best way to build a schema. If a particular player does well on a task, praise and encouragement should be offered.

Operant conditioning and the stimulus–response (S–R) bond

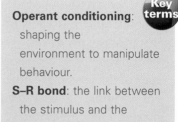

Key terms

Operant conditioning: shaping the environment to manipulate behaviour.

S–R bond: the link between the stimulus and the response.

The S–R bond is the link between a stimulus and a response. In sport we learn by associating the correct response with a stimulus. Hence this theory is known as the **connectionist theory**. In badminton, for example, if an opponent hits the shuttlecock high and short to the middle of the court, the appropriate response is a smash shot. It is an advantage to the badminton player to learn to recognise when the smash is the best course of action and the coach can help to promote such recognition by using the right approach in training. The theory of operant conditioning explains how correct responses to a stimulus can be made stronger if the action is reinforced and the coach manipulates the performer during and after the performance.

Skinner studied rats in captivity. The rats quickly learned to hit a lever, which presented them with food. Skinner called this process of learning to repeat actions for reward **operant conditioning**. Skinner's work showed that we learn by trial and error. If the response is correct then we are motivated to repeat it. If the response is incorrect we should be motivated to change it. For example, a tennis player who hits the first serve into the net will lift the ball higher on the second serve.

Operant conditioning works on the principle that actions are made stronger by repetition. When correct actions are reinforced, a stronger link to the stimulus is developed. Incorrect actions that are not reinforced make a weaker link to the stimulus.

A coach can accelerate the trial-and-error learning process by using strategies to:

- make the adoption of the correct response stronger
- make the neglect of the incorrect response stronger

The tactics used to demote the significance of the incorrect response are as important as the promotion of the correct response.

The strategies used to strengthen the S–R bond and promote adoption of the correct response are as follows:

- Use **positive reinforcement**. This is defined as something that increases the likelihood of the correct response being repeated. Positive reinforcement involves giving something pleasant after the correct response, such as praise and rewards.
- Allow **early success**. The coach should set easy targets at first to ensure success. A marker or a target could be drawn on the court for a player learning to serve in tennis to help get the ball on the right spot. If the player finds the serve difficult, he/she should be allowed to move in towards the net. Initial success develops confidence in the player and offers an incentive to continue.
- Use **mental rehearsal**. Going over the performance in the mind helps to develop an automatic response to the stimulus.

- Practise the **task as a whole**. The coach should allow the performer to practise the skill in its entirety as soon as he/she is able, in order to promote fluency and understanding of how all the subroutines come together.

Incorrect actions can be weakened so that they are eliminated. The coach should do the following:

- Use **negative reinforcement**. If the performer begins to make mistakes, the coach withdraws the praise and encouragement that he/she has been giving for doing the task well. For example, a swimming coach might stop praising a swimmer who has been doing a nice leg action when the leg kick begins to deteriorate with fatigue. The idea is that the swimmer will be motivated to apply more effort in order to regain the praise and encouragement from the coach.
- Use **punishment** when actions are incorrect. Coaches should use punishment carefully to avoid lowering the player's confidence while at the same time trying to prevent repetition of the unwanted response. Forms of punishment include being fined, booked, penalised, dropped from the team or made to do extra training.

Negative reinforcement is often confused with punishment. Negative reinforcement is best remembered as taking something (the incentive) away.

Thorndike suggested three laws to link the stimulus to the response and promote learning:

- The **law of exercise** states that practice will strengthen the S–R bond. Players who practise regularly quickly recognise the appropriate response to a stimulus. Repetition of skills and drills in training sessions can produce movements that are almost automatic responses to the stimulus.
- The **law of effect** states that a satisfier such as praise will strengthen correct responses and that an annoyer such as criticism will weaken incorrect actions. Encouragement and praise are good ways to motivate and generate the drive to keep producing the correct response. Players do not take kindly to criticism and will be motivated to prevent negative comments from the coach by changing incorrect actions.

> **Top tip**
>
> Learn the difference between positive and negative reinforcement. Positive reinforcement is adding a pleasant stimulus such as praise when you get it right and negative reinforcement is taking away that praise when you get it wrong.

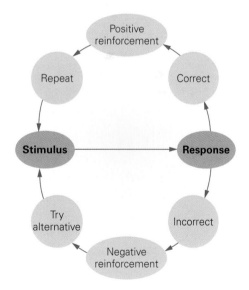

Figure 11.4 Learning by trial and error

> **Top tip**
>
> Learn Thorndike's laws for making the S–R bond stronger.

- The **law of readiness** states that any task set by the coach should be within the capabilities of the player. The task should be challenging so that a sense of achievement is fostered. The performer must be both mentally and physically prepared to do the task. For example, a swimming coach would not expect a beginner to swim long distances or in the deep end. Simple drills in the shallow end would be practised to start with.

Tasks to tackle 11.3

List the differences between positive and negative reinforcement.

Practice makes perfect

1 Transfer of training is the effect of the learning and performance of one skill on the learning and performance of another. Use examples from sport to explain how different types of transfer can help or hinder performance. *(4 marks)*

2 In sport, skills can be learned by establishing a link between the stimulus and the response. How can a coach strengthen the S–R bond? *(4 marks)*

3 What are the four parameters needed when a schema is used to develop skilful movement in sport? *(4 marks)*

Chapter *12*

Physical activity

What you need to know

By the end of this section you should be able to demonstrate knowledge and understanding of the key definitions, characteristics and key benefits of the various concepts listed below and be able to compare and contrast these concepts with one another:

- physical activity as an umbrella term, which might include physical and outdoor recreation, physical and outdoor education and sport
- the meaning of various terms associated with physical activity
- factors leading to increasingly sedentary lifestyles and why more regular participation should be encouraged
- recommendations in terms of frequency, intensity and type of physical activity for an active, healthy lifestyle
- possible barriers to regular participation in physical activity by young people
- physical recreation
- physical education
- outdoor and adventurous activities as outdoor recreation and outdoor education
- sport and sporting attitudes

Physical activity can be described as an umbrella term because it covers a variety of types of participation that you need to be aware of for Unit G451 (e.g. physical recreation, outdoor recreation, physical education, outdoor education and sport).

An activity such as running could come under the umbrella of physical activity in a number of ways. Running or jogging around parks and streets to maintain health and fitness is physical recreation. Running up a mountain would be categorised as outdoor recreation. In school PE lessons or extra-curricular clubs, pupils can be formally taught running techniques to improve their physical skill levels and this would constitute physical education. Running in competition against others, governed by strict rules and with the aim of winning constitutes sport. All these concepts are considered in more detail in this chapter.

Leisure

Characteristics

Leisure can be defined as spare time during which individuals can choose what to do. As a hard-working PE student, your leisure time may be limited because there are a lot of things you *have* to do, such as going to school or college, earning money through a part-time job, doing your homework or coursework and so on. When all your duties have been completed, you might have a little time left to spend as you wish. This is your leisure time and you can spend it in various ways, such as going to the gym, or playing the latest computer game. Many people like to relax and spend their leisure time inactively. Others look for excitement and danger — it is a matter of **personal choice**.

> **Key terms**
>
> **Characteristics**: important features used to help identify a particular concept.
>
> **Objectives**: important aims or functions of a concept for individuals or society in general.

Objectives

When used positively, leisure serves many purposes both for individuals and for society in general (Figure 12.1). For individuals, leisure helps people to **relax** and **unwind**, gives them the opportunity to **socialise** and meet other people, and allows for improvements in **health** and **fitness**. They can develop physical skills and improve their confidence and achieve a sense of self-fulfilment.

For society in general, leisure can encourage **conformity**, **civilise society** and encourage **social and racial mixing**.

It is sometimes difficult to separate individual from social functions of leisure as they often overlap. For example, individual improvements in health and fitness reduce the demands on the NHS for society.

The term 'leisure' covers a variety of types of active participation, for example play, physical recreation and sport. Physical education is a compulsory subject at school and as such lessons cannot be considered leisure time. However, school PE programmes can 'educate for leisure' and provide extra-curricular options for pupils in their free time.

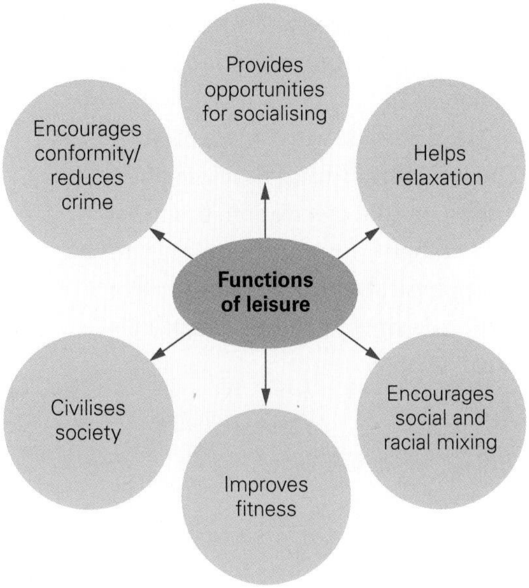

Figure 12.1 Functions of leisure

> **Top tip**
>
> If you are asked, 'What are the values of physical education?', 'development of skills' is too vague an answer to earn any marks. It is important to state clearly the type of skills being developed, for example physical skills, social skills, cognitive skills.

Tasks to tackle 12.1

Do the following examples fit the description of leisure time?

(a) watching sport on television
(b) going to a pub quiz with friends
(c) doing your homework
(d) playing football professionally
(e) going to school or college for AS PE lessons

The leisure continuum (Figure 12.2) illustrates levels of participation, which vary considerably at the two extremes.

Flexible rules	Strict rules
Choice	Obligation
Outcome unimportant	Competitive/outcome important
Spontaneous	Planned
Flexible time	Strict timing
Self-officiated	Officials present

| **Play** | **Physical recreation** | **Outdoor recreation** | **PE** | **OAA** | **Sport** |

Figure 12.2 The leisure continuum

Factors influencing leisure-time activities

A number of factors can affect a person's participation in active leisure (Figure 12.3). These include:

- **socioeconomic status** — i.e. how much time and disposable income someone has
- **stereotyping** — traditional viewpoints may limit participation in leisure-time activities that 'go against the norm', for example female bodybuilding and male dancing
- **disability** — local facilities and availability of specialist coaches are often inadequate for accommodating people with disabilities
- **age** — some activities are seen as being suitable only for the young, for example skate-boarding
- **ethnicity** — some ethnic groups do not place as high a priority on 'active leisure' as they do on educational achievement and religious observances
- **lack of facilities** — while people may have plenty of free time, local facilities are often limited or of poor quality

Barriers to participation are explored in more detail in the section on pp. 144–150.

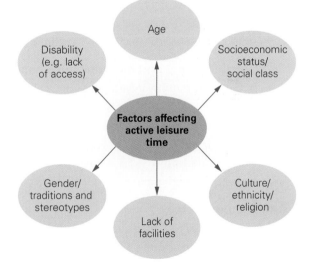

Figure 12.3 Factors affecting active leisure time

Leisure time is not always spent actively. Some people choose to spend it sedentarily (inactively), for example reading, watching television or listening to music. Active leisure time includes a wide range of activities, for example hill walking, swimming and playing netball.

Top tip

Exercising for health

The term exercise has a number of different meanings (check your dictionary). Your understanding of exercise in relation to sport and PE should be along the lines of 'physical activity to maintain a healthy lifestyle'.

The amount of exercise people take and the intensity they work at varies between individuals and their relative involvement in recreation/sport. In today's society, people are increasingly sedentary (inactive) and our health is suffering as a result. Obesity and cardiovascular problems are increasing.

Maintaining a healthy balanced lifestyle

A number of lifestyle factors (i.e. how we live our lives) need to be considered by individuals from an early age if they are to maintain their health and wellbeing for as long as possible.

Sensible eating and maintaining a balanced diet

In today's society, over-eating is a common problem, particularly for individuals who are physically inactive. If too many calories are consumed in relation to calories used, the excess energy is stored as body fat, resulting in obesity for many. Energy intake should balance energy output (the energy balance equation).

It is important to eat a varied, balanced diet containing energy sources (fats and carbohydrates) as well as protein and vitamins to help growth and the repair of body tissues.

Regular exercise

Evolution has adapted the human body for frequent and prolonged activity, so exercise is needed in order to stay fit and keep the body in good working order.

Until a few thousand years ago, humans obtained their food by hunting and gathering. This involved a lot of walking and running, for which the human body is well adapted. Nowadays, some people suffer decreased health and wellbeing as a result of a lack of exercise.

Exercise helps keep the body supple and strong, as well as maintaining stamina and a healthy body weight. Lack of exercise often leads to a gradual loss of muscular strength, stamina and suppleness. Exercise also has important psychological benefits. It can give a sense of achievement and boost self-esteem and self-confidence. It also leads to the secretion of body chemicals called endorphins, which produce feelings of pleasure and contentment.

Today, exercise is important because the circumstances of life are different from those during most human evolution. Few jobs now require physical strength and people frequently travel without any exertion, by car or bus. People have more leisure time than ever before but for large numbers of people it is spent inactively, watching television or playing computer games.

Young people in today's society are generally less healthy because:

- they are much less active
- parents are concerned about the safety of playing outside
- their diets often contain a lot of fast food, which is high in fats and low in fibre and vitamins
- they travel by car or bus rather than cycling or walking
- there is less time for activity during the National Curriculum
- they spend more time watching television and playing computer games

Limiting alcohol consumption

Excessive consumption of alcohol is increasing in the UK, with subsequent concerns about associated health risks, including damage to the stomach, liver and kidneys. This is partly due to an increase in wealth compared with 50–100 years ago. It might also be due to the 'cultural beliefs', particularly among young people, that drinking is 'cool' and getting drunk is a desirable state, resulting in social pressure to drink.

Limiting tobacco consumption

The risks associated with cigarette smoking, such as heart, circulatory and respiratory diseases, are well publicised. Despite this negative publicity and campaigns to raise awareness, cigarette smoking persists at alarmingly high rates and contributes to an unhealthy lifestyle for many people.

A poor diet, lack of regular exercise, drinking excessive amounts of alcohol and smoking are all factors that contribute to an unhealthy lifestyle. For many people, these factors combine to make a much greater contribution to ill health than each factor individually.

Lifelong physical activity

A government policy has been set up to help individuals participate in activities that will enrich their lives, as well as their communities, for a very long time. 'Lifelong Learning', hopefully involving physical activity/sport for many, encourages participation in a wide range of activities that people can continue well into old age, such as

> **Tasks to tackle 12.2**
>
> Give reasons why golf can be classified as a lifelong sporting activity.

swimming, cycling and golf. Such an increase in exercise patterns will have a number of physical, social and mental benefits. It is therefore important to encourage it from an early age.

Traditionally, school PE programmes in the UK have been dominated by team games such as football and netball. Research suggests that such activities are discontinued as people get older. Schools have begun to branch out and now offer a broader range of activities as preparation for active leisure, hopefully encouraging lifelong participation. Sometimes community facilities are used and links are made with local clubs in an attempt to foster from an early age awareness of the opportunities available in the wider community.

Increasing participation in physical activity has many benefits for young and old alike. If the young teenage section of society drops out from sport and recreation, it has a number of important physical and social consequences. Apart from the obvious declines in health and fitness, there are possible behavioural problems. Sport is seen as a way of engaging and involving the youth of society in positive activities that channel their energies, and make them less likely to resort to drugs, alcohol or crime. Involvement in sport can help individuals acquire a variety of physical, mental and social skills necessary to integrate them into wider society and give a sense of usefulness and belonging.

> ## Tasks to tackle 12.3
>
> List three factors that can influence a young person's participation in physical activity.

Ways to increase participation by young people and increase the chances of lifelong participation include:

- providing more appealing PE programmes, for example more options at Key Stage 4
- increasing school–club links
- increasing school–community links
- setting up more outdoor play areas, for example skateboard parks and outdoor basketball courts
- publicising the availability of facilities and activities
- subsidising costs and membership to clubs and leisure centres

Barriers to participation

Possible barriers to regular participation in physical activity by young people include:

- lack of time due to school work or part-time work demands
- lack of money/cost of participation
- poor availability of equipment or facilities in the local area
- geographical location — where you live affects choices and opportunities to participate in certain activities, for example living in an urbanised inner city area limits the amount of space available, and access to the natural environment for outdoor recreation/outdoor education)
- poor PE experience, low status given to PE in school attended
- low skill levels, low self-confidence
- poor availability of coaching in the activities you want to take part in
- pressure from peer groups/friends

Recommendations for a healthy lifestyle

Organisations such as the Health Education Council give recommendations on physical activity for the 'general population' in relation to frequency (i.e. how often), intensity (i.e. how hard) and type of activity.

A minimum of 30 minutes of aerobic exercise such as walking, jogging, cycling or swimming five times per week is commonly recommended for healthy living. The Health Education Authority 1998 made the following recommendations:

- All young people should participate in 1 hour per day of moderate physical activity, at least twice a week. This hour should include activities that help to maintain and enhance muscular strength, flexibility and bone health. It could be accumulated throughout the day during PE, break-time activity, sport, active play or structured exercise.
- Young people who currently do little activity should participate in physical activity of at least 'moderate intensity' for at least half an hour per day.

Top tip

You need to understand the meaning of various terms contained in the specification (e.g. exercise, lifelong participation) and how much physical activity is recommended for sustaining a healthy lifestyle.

Key term

Moderate intensity: physical activity that causes you to breathe harder than normal and to become warmer, for example brisk walking.

Physical recreation

Characteristics

Recreation can be defined as the **active** aspect of leisure. It is entered into **voluntarily** during **free time** and people have a **choice** concerning which activities they take part in. The focus is on **participation** rather than results.

A number of key features help to identify physical recreation. It is **flexible** in relation to rules, time spent on an activity and space used. The atmosphere tends to be **relaxed** — taking part is the main motive. For example, an adult having fun with friends while taking part in a relatively energetic physical activity is engaged in physical recreation.

Top tip

Recreation can be identified by its emphasis on participation as opposed to competitiveness, which is linked more to sport.

Physical recreation is generally non-competitive and takes place in a relaxed atmosphere

Objectives

Recreation provides many benefits, including the opportunity to:

- relax and unwind
- socialise and meet new people
- be creative and do something you are proud of (self-fulfilment)
- improve health and fitness

Such benefits explain why recreation is important to individuals in our society.

Almost everyone has the opportunity to take part in some kind of recreation. Venues can be chosen and agreed by participants who decide when to take part (i.e. what time of day) and how regularly.

A key reason why many people take part in recreational activities is to relax and recuperate from the stresses of everyday life, for example work and family responsibilities. Playing team games helps them to gain social benefits as well as improve fitness. Outdoor pursuit activities may encourage creativity. Achievement of personal goals helps to develop self-esteem.

Recreation can also be said to increase conformity and morality in society as a whole. Social benefits of recreation include:

- community integration through mass participation events
- less strain on the NHS
- social control and crime reduction
- employment opportunities
- economic benefits

Outdoor recreation

The key distinguishing feature of outdoor recreation is that it takes place in the natural environment, for example climbing a mountain or canoeing down a fast-flowing river. The challenge of the natural environment is therefore a key identifying feature of outdoor and adventurous activities (OAA) as outdoor recreation. Freedom of choice in leisure time distinguishes outdoor recreation from OAA as compulsory National Curriculum PE.

Functions of OAA as outdoor recreation

Individuals who choose to participate in outdoor recreational activities such as skiing and rock climbing do so for a number of reasons including:

- to improve health and fitness
- for stress release and relaxation

Top tip

Questions often require an understanding of the benefits of recreation and active leisure for individuals or society in general, and these often overlap.

Tasks to tackle 12.4

Consider the following examples of people taking part in physical recreation:

(a) a group of workmates playing five-a-side football every Thursday night after work

(b) a group of teenagers training regularly to improve fitness at a boxing club after school

List the benefits that individuals and society would receive from such participation.

- as a personal challenge, to develop self-esteem and self-confidence
- to develop an appreciation of the natural environment
- to develop cognitive skills and decision-making
- to develop social skills and work as a team
- to develop survival skills

Physical education

Physical education (PE) can be defined as a formally planned and taught curriculum, designed to increase knowledge and values through physical activity and experience.

PE serves a number of functions (*why* do we teach PE?) that justify its existence as a National Curriculum subject. These include:

- developing **physical skills**, for example coordination, body awareness
- developing **social skills**, for example communication, cooperation, forming friendships
- developing **mental** or **cognitive skills**, for example decision-making, self-control
- improving **health** and **fitness** through activity and knowledge of the benefits of exercise
- developing **self-esteem** and confidence through **success**
- developing **leadership** skills
- helping to prepare young adults for **active leisure** when they leave school, for example via school–club links and taster sessions at local sports centres

PE is delivered mainly to children and young adults (*who* is taught?), in schools and colleges (*where* PE is delivered). It is delivered mainly in lessons, at lunchtimes or after school (*when* PE is experienced) by teachers using a variety of teaching styles and activities (*how* PE is delivered).

Figure 12.4 Objectives of National Curriculum PE

Tasks to tackle 12.5

List and explain four functions of PE as a compulsory National Curriculum subject for children from age 5 to 16.

A triangular model of PE

Shortly after becoming prime minister in July 2007, Gordon Brown stated his aim for all school children to be able to experience 5 hours per week of sport or PE, including sport of a competitive nature.

A pupil's experiences of PE should involve three elements:

- education
- sport
- recreation

Education

Pupils experience National Curriculum PE from the age of 5 to age 16 as a compulsory subject. They are taught a range of activities and physical skills in six areas of activity:

- games
- athletics
- swimming
- gymnastics
- dance
- outdoor and adventurous activities

A number of different roles should be experienced, including those of performer, coach and official.

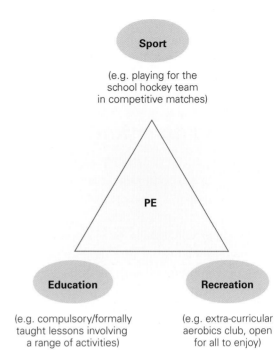

Figure 12.5 A triangular model of PE

Sport
(e.g. playing for the school hockey team in competitive matches)

PE

Education
(e.g. compulsory/formally taught lessons involving a range of activities)

Recreation
(e.g. extra-curricular aerobics club, open for all to enjoy)

Sport

Sport gives pupils an opportunity to experience organised, optional, extra-curricular activities with a competitive element. They might be chosen to play for the school netball team or to compete in an inter-schools swimming gala.

Recreation

Pupils can choose to engage in non-competitive physical activity in extra-curricular time. Many schools and colleges have open-access clubs for this purpose.

These three elements can be combined in a single lesson. For example, during a swimming lesson a coach may instruct pupils about technique (education), a race may be held (sport) and free time may be given at the end of a lesson when the pupils are allowed to choose what they want to do (recreation).

Outdoor education

Outdoor and adventurous activities form one of the six areas of National Curriculum PE. OAA can be defined as 'the achievement of educational objectives via guided and direct experiences in the natural environment'. For example, pupils who are up a mountain and being formally instructed in skills such as map reading and taking a compass bearing are taking part in outdoor education.

Functions of OAA in the National Curriculum

OAA have many purposes, including raising awareness of and respect for others, oneself, the natural environment and danger or risk. Risks should be perceived only (i.e. in a pupil's mind) rather than real (actual danger).

Outdoor activities such as hill walking, caving and canoeing can give personal challenges to individuals, as well as teaching them how to work effectively with each other (teamwork, cooperation). They can provide opportunities to experience the responsibilities of leadership, such as making decisions that affect the rest of the group. Communication skills and an awareness of an individual's strengths and weaknesses may develop.

A sense of adventure and excitement is an important element of the outdoor experience.

Despite their compulsory status as part of National Curriculum PE, OAA in most schools tend to be of relatively low quality. A number of factors may negatively affect a pupil's OAA experience.

- If staff are lacking in specialist qualifications, experience or motivation, the opportunities for a positive and meaningful experience will be reduced.
- Lessons do not allow much time for such activities.
- Access or transport to the natural environment is a problem for many schools.
- Money and resources — the expense of undertaking OAA may be too much for many schools and parents. Specialist equipment may not be readily available.
- Parents and teachers are likely to be deterred by the inherent risks of certain activities such as skiing and mountain climbing. Negative media publicity of injuries to children participating in these activities has fuelled existing concerns.

Key terms

Perceived risk: the risk exists only in a person's mind — the actual situation is safe, for example abseiling down a mountainside with an expert instructor controlling every move.

Real risk: the risk actually exists, for example there is a real risk of an avalanche when skiing.

Top tip

Make sure you can explain the difference between real risk and perceived risk using practical examples.

Figure 12.6 Functions of OAA

Top tip

Outdoor activities need to be specifically linked to the natural environment, for example hill walking and rock climbing. Such activities as part of compulsory National Curriculum PE belong under the overall umbrella of PE, and so involve the same potential set of values (physical skills, health and fitness improvement and social and cognitive development).

It is the element of risk, danger and unpredictability that distinguishes outdoor education from the rest of the PE experience. Teachers should ensure that the natural environment that pupils experience is as predictable as possible, that is, under the control of the participant and not open to unpredictability such as flash floods and rock falls.

Tasks to tackle 12.6

Consider the following activities. If they could fulfil the characteristics of OAA as part of National Curriculum PE, explain how. If not, give reasons why.

(a) cycling   **(b)** hockey   **(c)** running

Top tip

It is important to be able to give a critical evaluation of a pupil's OAA experience in relation to the factors identified above, and to appreciate that in many schools OAA are taught in a limited manner due to such issues, for example orienteering activities may be restricted to the school grounds.

Sport

Characteristics

Sport can be defined as a contrived competitive experience and is identified by a number of key features. It is **goal-orientated** and involves **competitiveness** (i.e. the will to win). It is **serious**, particularly at the elite level. **National governing bodies** look after the interests of, and try to develop the popularity of, particular sports. They also provide strict **rule structures** that are enforced in **competitions** by **officials**. Sport requires high levels of **physical prowess** (skill) and **endeavour** (effort) in order to succeed and gain the **extrinsic rewards**, such as trophies or money, that are on offer.

An element of **chance** is often involved in sport and can mean the difference between winning and losing. **Time and space restrictions** apply and **specialist equipment** may be required. A high level of **commitment** to training is needed to improve performance and fitness.

Key characteristics of sport
Serious/competitive — 'win at all costs' attitude or sportsmanship (*how?*)
Prowess — high skill levels, particularly by 'professionals' (*who?*)
Organised — sport has rules/regulations (*how?*)
Rewards — available for winning (extrinsic) and intrinsic satisfaction (*why?*)
Time and space restrictions apply (*when?/where?*)

Figure 12.7 Key characteristics of sport

Key terms

Prowess: outstanding or superior skill.
Endeavour: maximum effort, trying your hardest.

Tasks to tackle 12.7

Using an example, explain how an outdoor adventurous activity could be classified as sport.

The levels of seriousness, commitment and skill in sporting involvement vary. Some individuals are talented enough to take part professionally (i.e. they earn their living from sport). Others participate in sport as amateurs during their leisure time at a local netball, hockey or cricket club for example.

Sport is therefore different from recreation in that it is competitive, strict rules apply and extrinsic rewards are available.

Table 12.1 Comparison of physical recreation and high-level sport

Physical recreation	High-level sport
Immediate pleasure	Sometimes enjoyable, particularly in victory, but may involve anxiety and pain
Participation provides intrinsic rewards and enjoyment	There may be extrinsic rewards
Length of participation is the individual's own choice	Time constraints on training or length of game
Spontaneity exists	Less spontaneous because of game plans
Level of training is the individual's own choice	Serious training is required
Flexible rules	Strict rules

Top tip

The more you can identify features such as competition, high skill levels and physical exertion, the more likely it is that the activity can be classified as sport.

Top tip

Make sure you can compare sport and recreation.

Functions of sport

Sport serves a number of important functions for individuals, including:

- improved health and fitness
- increased self-esteem and self-confidence
- opportunities for socialising

Participation in sport also has a number of important benefits for society. Some of these are similar to the benefits of recreation, including less strain on the NHS as people's health and fitness increase, and improved social control as people's free time is spent in a positive manner. Sport can help to integrate society through participation by different socioeconomic or ethnic minority groups. The sporting success of national teams creates national pride, for example England becoming rugby union world champions in 2003 and winning the Ashes in cricket in 2005. Economically, sport provides financial and employment benefits. For example, money is invested into provision of sports facilities, and sport provides jobs and regeneration opportunities, as illustrated by the London Olympics for 2012.

Sporting ethics

When participating in sport, performers adopt various codes of behaviour, which can be viewed on a continuum. At one end is **sportsmanship**, which

Tasks to tackle 12.8

How many marks would you award the following answer?

Q Identify four characteristics of sport. *(4 marks)*

A ● improved fitness
  ● increased social control
  ● improved integration in society
  ● more jobs on offer in society

involves treating the opponent with respect and as an equal, fair play and playing within the rules or etiquette of the game. At the other end is **games-manship**, that is, the use of unfair practices to gain an advantage, often against the etiquette of the game, but sometimes without actually breaking the letter of the law, for example wasting time at the end of a game when you are winning.

Such codes of conduct can have positive or negative effects on the sporting contest. On the one hand, sportsmanship can help a game to run smoothly and encourage goodwill among players and spectators. On the other hand, gamesmanship can lead to ill feeling and a contest disintegrating as officials struggle to make decisions and keep control. Anger among players and spectators lowers the status of sport and leads to negative role models.

> **Key term**
>
> **Deviance**: behaviour that is against the norms of society and is considered unacceptable, for example drug taking in sport.

–   +
|——|

Gamesmanship   **Sportsmanship**

Examples of gamesmanship	Examples of sportsmanship
– Playing on despite injury to opponent	+ Kicking the ball out if an opponent is injured
– 'Sledging' — using verbal insults to put an opponent off and affect his/her performance	+ Verbally congratulating the positive performance of an opponent
– Diving intentionally to try to gain a penalty	+ Trying to stay on your feet and score despite a late tackle

Figure 12.8 The gamesmanship–sportsmanship continuum

Deviant behaviour goes beyond gamesmanship. It involves cheating and going against the accepted rules of an activity. Deliberately fouling or injuring an opponent is regarded as deviant behaviour in sport.

Gamesmanship is evident in modern-day professional sports, such as football, and has filtered down to amateur and school sports performers who copy the negative behaviour of their role models.

Practice makes perfect

1 Identify four key characteristics of sport. *(4 marks)*

2 Define the term **outdoor recreation**. *(2 marks)*

3 Explain how an activity such as badminton can be classified as physical recreation, physical education *and* sport. *(3 marks)*

4 Explain the difference between **sportsmanship** and **gamesmanship**, and give some examples to illustrate your answer. *(4 marks)*

5 List three educational values of outdoor and adventurous activities. *(3 marks)*

Chapter *13*

Sport and culture

What you need to know

By the end of this section you should be able to:

- demonstrate knowledge and understanding of surviving ethnic sports and games in the UK
- describe the characteristics of surviving ethnic sports and reasons for their continued existence and popularity
- explain the role of nineteenth-century public schools in promoting and organising sports and games
- explain the relatively recent move from the traditional amateur approach to a more professional approach in sport
- describe key characteristics of the USA
- explain the nature of sport in the USA
- analyse the game of American football with respect to its origins and nature
- describe the key characteristics of Australia
- explain the nature of sport in Australia
- analyse the game of Australian rules football with respect to its origins and the factors influencing its development

Sport as a reflection of UK culture

Characteristics of surviving ethnic sports and games

Some traditional sports and festivals have survived over many years in isolated rural communities, away from the influences of highly populated cities and towns. Relative isolation allows local customs to prevail. The Highland Games is one example of a surviving multi-sports festival and is a representation of Gaelic heritage.

Tossing the caber is one event in the Highland Games

Such ethnic sports have a number of key features, which can also be seen as reasons for their survival. For example, they:

- are usually annual
- offer the opportunity for social gathering
- help to maintain tradition and celebrate the past
- attract tourists, generating welcome income
- occur in rural or isolated areas
- are localised/specific to an area — for example, cheese rolling in Gloucestershire

Certain rituals are characteristic of surviving ethnic sports, with pagan or medieval rituals evident in costumes, singing and dancing. Some rowdiness may be evident.

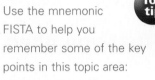

Culture: the outcome of a society's traditions, customs, religion, sport, values, beliefs etc.

Key term

Use the mnemonic FISTA to help you remember some of the key points in this topic area:

- Financial benefits
- Isolation
- Social
- Traditional
- Annual

Top tip

Figure 13.1 Key features of ethnic sports

The characteristics of surviving ethnic sports and games are similar to the reasons for their continued existence, so answers to questions on either of these should be made from the same list of key points (tradition, social gathering etc.)

Top tip

Tasks to tackle 13.1

The following nine words are characteristics of, and reasons for, the continued existence of ethnic sports and games. How many marks would these words score in answer to a question asking you to state the characteristics of surviving ethnic sports such as the Highland Games? Give a brief reason for the mark you award.

1 festival

2 local

3 occasional

4 ritual

5 rural

6 isolated

7 social

8 tourism

9 tradition

The role of nineteenth-century public schools in promoting and organising sports and games

Public schools have a long tradition in Britain, dating back hundreds of years for some — for example, Eton (1440) and Harrow (1571). These schools were highly prestigious and catered for the upper classes in Victorian society, that is, those who could afford to send their sons and who had a high social standing (the 'elite' of society). Our focus here is on the key role such schools played in promoting and organising sport in the nineteenth century.

Large numbers of boys attended the early nineteenth-century public schools. They caused problems in local areas, trespassing, poaching and gambling in their free time, which was largely unsupervised. The authorities disapproved of such activities because they had no moral qualities and they brought the school's reputation into disrepute. The public schools were therefore under pressure from various sources, including the government, to improve the control and behaviour of the boys in their care. The Clarendon Commission report supported the teaching of team games for their educational value.

> **Key terms**
>
> **Games cult**: a fanatical devotion to team games and the benefits they could bring to young men.
>
> **Public school**: a private, independent, fee-paying school.
>
> **Social control**: the process whereby society seeks to ensure conformity to the dominant norms and values of that society.
>
> **The Clarendon Commission**: a report on an investigation of public schools in 1864, which criticised many aspects of public school life and gave advice on how to improve these schools, for example using sport as a key reforming influence.

The public schools, under pressure to improve standards of behaviour, played a key role in the technical development of games such as rugby and football. Boys arriving at school from their villages brought with them numerous versions of mob games and participated in these games regularly in their spare time. Mob games were violent and disorderly; they were played by the working classes and had few rules. The masters realised the potential of these games for channelling the boys' energies and as a way of keeping them on the school grounds. The schools allowed mob games to be played only if they were organised and given rules. Many schools developed their own unique games, mostly due to the architectural features of their own schools — for example, the Eton Wall game.

A feature of the early organisation of games in public schools was that the boys organised the activities themselves. This was called self-government and it gave the boys organisational skills that were useful in later life. The boys set up games committees. The hierarchical structure among the boys allowed the sixth-form prefects to organise the younger boys. This was a form of social control.

It was only later that members of staff were recruited to teach and coach sport. Oxford and Cambridge 'blues' returned to their old schools to assist with sports coaching. By the time this specialist teaching of sport had started, the 'games cult' had become important and headmasters used success on the sports field to impress future parents.

Athleticism combined physical effort with moral integrity or sportsmanship. It led to a craze for team games, which were valued for their character-building qualities. By the late nineteenth century, athleticism had reached cult proportions and was an obsession for many public schools.

Games afternoons were introduced, and inter-house and inter-school fixtures were played regularly and reported in the press. Sports Day became an important public relations exercise to entertain the 'old boys', parents and governors. Headmasters such as Thomas Arnold at Rugby School began to support the use of 'blues' from universities who could provide specialist coaching. In addition, specialist facilities were provided, such as extensive playing fields and swimming pools. Because the boys boarded, a lot of time was devoted to sport, particularly to occupy their free time in the early evening and at weekends. Sport was funded from the boys' fees and support from the governors.

The public school influence on the structure and organisation of sports resulted in the following:

- Games were played regularly.
- Boundaries and player numbers were reduced.
- The equipment and facilities became more sophisticated.
- A division of labour was introduced, with positional roles emerging.
- Tactics and strategies began to be used.
- A competition structure was devised, initially through the inter-house system and later among schools
- Individual school rules gave way to nationally recognised rules (codification).
- Conformity to the rules, fair play and sportsmanship were of key importance, with playing honourably more important than winning.

Tasks to tackle 13.2

Explain how the provision and organisation of late nineteenth-century English public schools promoted sport and games.

The move from amateur to professional approach

Since national governing bodies for sport emerged in the UK, mainly from the mid-nineteenth century onwards, the structure of sport has become complex. Organisations exist to promote and develop sport from mass participation through to sporting excellence.

The UK has a decentralised system of sports administration with little government involvement or interference. Voluntary sports clubs at grassroots level tend to run themselves, with central government providing little in terms of overall sporting policy, though the provision of lottery money may be linked to achieving certain government targets, such as increased school–club links.

Historically, sport in the UK was organised by volunteers, acting as unpaid coaches and unqualified administrators. From small local voluntary clubs to NGBs and major sports associations, large numbers of unpaid staff were involved in the system, giving it an amateur approach due to lack of expertise in an increasingly commercial environment. An overall policy for sports development was lacking and full-time paid administrators were in short supply. This led to inconsistency in effectiveness within and among organisations.

In recent years, however, there has been a period of organisational change in sports organisation and administration, which has led to a more business-like approach. Support and interest from the government increased towards the end of the twentieth century and has continued to grow, particularly since the successful 2012 Olympic bid. The government has set up the Department for Culture, Media and Sport, which has various responsibilities, such as appointing a Minister for Sport and distributing grants to UK Sport and the home country sports councils.

The desire for international sporting success has led to increasing numbers of full-time, paid administrators taking up positions in NGBs, particularly in well-funded sports such as football, cricket and rugby. Funding allocations have been increasingly linked to meeting performance targets, that is, a 'no compromise' approach to sports excellence funding filtering through from organisations such as UK Sport to NGBs and the performers they fund. Many NGBs are now appointing performance directors, with sports excellence and the achievement of world titles and gold medals very much in mind.

The aims of various sports organisations are explored in greater detail in Chapter 14, but it should be noted here that there have been important recent attempts to minimise duplication, overlap and bureaucracy in the work of various sports organisations. For example, at national level, sports excellence is the ultimate responsibility of UK Sport, with Sport England taking on the task of increasing participation in the community. In this reallocation of roles, undertaken in 2007, the Youth Sport Trust has been given the important responsibility of school PE/sport.

Sport as a reflection of US culture

The USA is one of the world's top sporting nations. Sport in the USA is the most technically advanced in the world, and its sports stars are among the richest. In certain sports, for example American football and baseball, the USA is the leading nation, perhaps because it is one of a few nations playing some of these sports at a high level.

The USA cut its colonial links relatively early (in comparison with Australia) and for many years developed in isolation from Europe. Sports were developed and adapted from the old European games to suit the USA's new image as a young, capitalist nation.

Sports currently played in the USA fall into three categories:

- adaptations — modifications to games already in existence, for example American football from rugby

Key terms

Colonialism: a system of direct political, economic and cultural intervention by a powerful country in a weaker one.

NGBs: national governing bodies, such as UK Athletics, which control different sports.

- adoptions — games taken directly from European cultures, for example tennis
- inventions — new sports designed to suit the 'New World' culture, for example basketball

Sport in the USA is now a multi-million dollar industry, committed to the entertainment market and driven by the profit motive.

Population and geographical factors

The population of the USA is approaching 300 million, drawn from a wide variety of cultures. The population density is about 70 per square mile and while some areas are remote and uninhabited, others such as New York and Los Angeles have huge urban sprawls with serious congestion and air pollution problems. These densely populated areas have been the hotbeds in the development of 'urban sports' such as American football, baseball and basketball.

The USA is a very large country with a huge population. Travelling between venues for sport is difficult and this makes media coverage very important. It should be noted, however, that the Americans are more prepared than the British to travel long distances to watch sport — by car, plane or train.

The nature of sport in the USA

Sporting events in the USA reflect the US culture where the win ethic dominates. The mainstream competitive culture has acquired the term Lombardianism, after American football coach Vince Lombardi coined the phrase, 'Winning isn't everything — it's the only thing'. Failure in sport is not an option.

Sport in the USA is big business. At all levels it is driven by commercialism. Private and corporate businesses use sport to promote their products, as well as to achieve goodwill. Commercialism of sport starts early, at high school level. Sport in high school has a high profile and attracts large amounts of sponsorship. Huge crowds are drawn to school sporting events, with pomp and ceremony adding to the entertainment. Those who show the most talent compete for athletic scholarships for college or university. At college or university, performers receive top-level coaching and support, along with increased pressure to win in a highly competitive environment. College sport is very commercialised, with funding from television and sponsorship deals. The best college athletes are drafted into professional sport.

Professional sport receives a huge amount of interest from the public, which makes it ripe for commercialism. Television and advertising fund professional sport, and sometimes govern sporting procedures and influence its rules. The American sporting culture demands high-scoring, action-packed, short bursts of activity, which are followed by commercial breaks to keep the television sponsors happy. Most Americans therefore have contact with sport through the medium of television. Television channels transmit hours of sport each week. The Super Bowl registers the highest audience of any television programme each year.

Key term

Pro-draft system: professional clubs select the best college players when they become available after graduation.

Commercialism and sport in American society

Commercialism in Americal sport is driven by the following:

- The USA is a capitalist society based on material values and a market economy.
- Commercial enterprise is admired and the USA has been seen as the land of opportunity for the individual to make good and achieve the 'rags to riches' ideal.
- Corporate sponsorship of top sport gives opportunity for advertising.
- The media have a high impact on promotion and advertising revenue.

The American Dream

The top US professional sports stars in basketball, American football and baseball are among the richest people in the world. The American Dream assumes that anyone can be a success in society irrespective of age, gender or ethnic background, and sport is a particularly useful vehicle for such success. Sport can shatter stereotypes and smash through the restrictive glass ceiling of opportunity. Role models on multi-million dollar playing contracts are created, giving others from all sections of society something to aspire to.

> **Key terms**
>
> **Capitalism**: an economic system that enables private enterprise to accumulate wealth and power.
>
> **Individualism**: taking opportunities and standing for oneself.
>
> **The American Dream**: anyone can achieve success, wealth and status.

Socioeconomic influences on sport in the USA

It is important to understand that US society is driven by capitalism, which directly influences all that happens in sport from high-school level, through sport at college and on to professional sport. Capitalism allows an individual to accumulate wealth.

The social history of the USA is reflected by individualism. The USA attracted many early settlers because the land was rich and resources were plentiful. However, before resources can be converted into wealth, they have to be won, often single-handedly. This attitude of every man for himself has steered the USA towards capitalism, with accompanying ideologies such as:

- everyone has the chance to succeed
- freedom is given to all individuals to pursue the wealth and happiness to be gained from capitalism
- happiness is secured through the generation of wealth and achieving the American Dream
- 'win at all costs'/Lombardianism as the mainstream competitive culture

American football

American football emerged from the European game of rugby in 1879. Walter Camp, a player and coach of Yale University, instituted the early rules of the game.

The key features of American football are as follows:

- It is a professional sport, played to the highest standard.
- Huge financial rewards are available for success.

- It has major exposure via the media.
- As a professional sport it gives every player an equal opportunity to go from rags to riches.
- Massive stadiums accommodate large numbers of spectators, with a family-orientated environment
- There is support entertainment alongside the sporting event.

Professional American football games tend to be of a violent nature. A number of factors can account for this:

- Protective body armour reduces physical inhibition (e.g. the helmet and mask dehumanise performers).
- Head-on contests are confrontational.
- The language is provocative (e.g. 'sack the opponent').
- The culture of the USA — for example: the individual desire for excitement and sensationalism; sports such as American football can be linked to sport as the 'last frontier' (e.g. toughness); the rules and ethos of American football encourage contact, which often leads to violence.
- Media influence — sensationalism and violence in American football sell sport to the public.
- The Lombardian ethic (win at all costs) prevails, with violence seen as necessary for success in many cases.

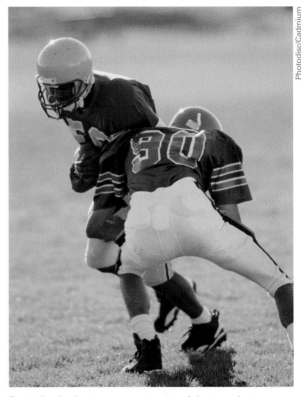

Photodisc/Cadmium

Protective body armour encourages violent conduct

Key term

Sack the opponent/sack the quarterback: to tackle and bring down a quarterback before he has passed the ball.

Top tip

Questions may be set requiring you to give reasons why high-level sports in the USA, such as American football, are more violent than in the UK.

Sport as a reflection of Australian culture

Australia became independent from the UK in 1901 but it retains links to the UK and evidence of its colonial roots still exist, for example in education and sports. Although it is a relatively young country, Australia has used its colonial history (see below) to develop and foster a high quality of life. Cities such as Sydney and Melbourne contain a wide range of theatres, galleries and opera houses, reflecting high-culture pursuits. However, sport dominates most Australian households.

Australia in the twenty-first century has a strong egalitarian (i.e. equal opportunities) ethos, with a powerful sense of nationalism. Its ideology focuses on the capitalist democratic society of the Western world.

When considering the sporting ethos of Australians, it is important to try to comprehend Australia's great size. This has impacted upon the culture and sporting pursuits of the nation.

- Travelling distances made the widespread development of sport in the nineteenth century difficult — both for playing and watching.
- Most of the population live on low-lying coastal planes with excellent accessibility to the sea. This is aided by favourable climatic conditions.
- Advanced technological communications in the twenty-first century have increased accessibility. For example, satellite links enable sport to be viewed all around the world.

Colonial influence and immigration

The original inhabitants of Australia were the Aborigines. In 1788, however, around 1000 men and women — mainly convicted criminals — landed by ship at Port Jackson under sentence of transportation from England. Australia became a penal colony of the British Empire.

After the establishment of the first colony, many free settlers left Britain for Australia. Their numbers increased as the benefits of this new continent were published in Britain. The British government promoted emigration. Its assisted passage scheme helped to cover travelling costs to the new colony. Immigration gained pace in the 1850s when gold was discovered in many areas of southwestern Australia.

The Australian colonies witnessed spectacular growth between 1870 and 1918, with the population growing rapidly as immigration increased and more people left Britain to start a new life in Australia. But after the First World War, Britain's hold on the Australian colonies began to dwindle and Australia has slowly pulled away from Britain, though it still has the Queen as its Head of State and remains a member of the reformed Commonwealth.

Top tip

To understand the development of sport in Australia you need to be aware of the significant influence the UK has had on its evolution. For example, its major games remain as straightforward adaptations of those from the UK.

The popularity of colonial games

Cricket was the first sport to be imported to Australia from the UK. The first game was played in Sydney around 1825. It has remained a mass spectator sport and has done much to unite and build the confidence of the nation. Cricket was imported without adaptation but was never seen as the preserve of any one class. Unlike the UK, there was no reference to 'gentlemen and players' and no privilege given to the school tie, that is, the school you attended.

Rugby was also imported during the period of colonial settlement. As in the UK, educational institutions were foremost in introducing rugby, and Sydney University played the first game in 1863. Parallels between the two countries can also be drawn in the fact that games on both sides of the world were strictly amateur and catered for the middle classes.

The nature of sport in Australia

Sport in Australia is a high-status national preoccupation. A number of factors influence the Australian national desire to achieve sporting success:

- Settlement and colonialism — the historical influence of Britain.
- Bush culture — the old frontier image of individuality and ruggedness is exhibited through sport.
- Political support — successive governments have recognised the enormous potential of sport to increase Australia's international status and have invested in it. Such investment is seen as reflecting a strong economy and affluence.
- Enlightenment — a healthy lifestyle is important and individuals are keen to take part in sport, particularly in outdoor activities in such a favourable climate. Sport is fashionable and is enjoyed by the majority of the population.
- Unity and nationalism — sport has united a small population in a large land. It has brought together different cultural groups to celebrate sporting success, for example at the Olympics.
- Egalitarian society — sport reflects equality of opportunity in society and supports the 'land of the fair go' image.
- Ambition — desire to be a world sports power and increase its influence as a nation via sporting success, for example in rugby league, rugby union, cricket and Olympic sports.

Australian rules football

Australian rules football (Aussie rules) has developed into the prominent new game of Australia. There is evidence to suggest it is a genuine Australian game, adapted from an Aborigine 'leaping' game with an animal skin in Queensland. It was codified as the sport of 'Melbourne rules' in 1858. It was originally designed as a game to help cricketers keep fit in winter.

Many factors have shaped its development into a highly popular sport in Australia include:

- It is known as 'the people's game' and is accessible to all; it blends all cultures and celebrates its ethnic appeal (endorsing the egalitarian nature of society).
- Spectators are from all classes and backgrounds, which suits the egalitarian nature of society.
- It reflects the manly image of the bush in the physical, aggressive way it is played.
- It has an image of fair play, which suits Australia and its recognition for the 'best and fairest' (the Brownlow medal is presented to the best and fairest player each year).
- The large open spaces available throughout Australia are reflected in Aussie rules being played on huge cricket ovals with 18-a-side.

- Aussie rules gives opportunities for commercialism through sponsorship and media coverage. It is a good product for television as it allows opportunities for commercial breaks during games. Sport accounts for 15% of television time in Australia and broadcasting games aids various sports, including Aussie rules, by gaining commercial sponsorship. Sky TV is an example of excellent media promotion of the sport and provides extensive coverage. Its recent impacts include:
  - games being played at strategic times throughout the week, to attract the largest television viewer ratings
  - the referee restarting play after goals are scored only when a light on the scoreboard indicates that the commercial break on television has ended

Top tip

The specification lists the influence of commercialism and the media as important factors that have shaped the development of Aussie rules.

Practice makes perfect

1 A large number of ethnic sports such as the Highland Games still occur in the UK today. Give four reasons for the survival of such activities. *(4 marks)*

2 Discuss the positive and negative outcomes of commercialisation of sport in the USA. *(4 marks)*

3 Explain why Australian rules football has developed into the prominent new game of Australia. *(6 marks)*

Chapter 14

Sociocultural studies relating to participation in physical activity

Contemporary sporting issues

What you need to know

By the end of this chapter you should be able to:

- demonstrate knowledge and understanding of the different sources of funding of physical activity — public, private and voluntary (including the National Lottery)
- demonstrate knowledge and understanding of UK Sport
- demonstrate knowledge and understanding of the UK Sports Institute and devolved National Institutes of Sport
- demonstrate knowledge and understanding of home country organisations (e.g. Sport England)
- demonstrate knowledge and understanding of current government and national governing body initiatives
- critically evaluate initiatives that affect the aspirations and participation of young people
- explain the sports development pyramid from mass participation to sports excellence
- explain opportunity, provision and esteem and how they affect participation and the achievement of sports excellence
- give a critical evaluation of sociocultural factors affecting participation and achievement of sporting excellence by young people, the elderly, people with disabilities, women and ethnic minority groups
- describe possible measures to increase participation and the achievement of sports excellence
- explain the reasons for the use of drugs in sport and describe the consequences of drug use on the health and wellbeing of young people and negative role models for young people
- describe possible solutions to the problem of drug use in sport
- explain the impact on performance in sport of modern technological products (with reference to particular products and activities)
- explain the roles of the media
- critically evaluate the impact of the media on sport
- explain the relationship between sport, sponsorship and the media (the 'golden triangle')
- show knowledge and understanding of violence in sport (players and spectators) — and possible causes and solutions
- demonstrate knowledge and understanding of the modern Olympic movement and key organisations within it
- explain the commercialisation of the Olympics: pre- and post-1984 (Los Angeles)
- describe the opportunities and implications for sport in the UK arising from London 2012
- explain how the Olympic Games is a vehicle for 'nation building' (e.g. China) — the shop window effect

Funding of physical activity in the UK

Raising participation levels for all and winning gold medals costs a lot of money. Traditionally, government funding for sport has been low, with politicians in Britain regarding sport as a low-status activity. Increasingly, however, politicians have seen the vote-winning potential of providing quality sporting facilities for all and achieving international success in sport.

Funding for sport in the UK can be gained from a variety of sources. These can be divided into three main sectors:

- The public sector funds sport via central and local government.
- The private sector involves companies and businesses sponsoring a team, event or individual in the hope of commercial benefit.
- The voluntary sector is where individuals and clubs fund their own training and participation, for example via club membership fees. The National Lottery is an important source of funding for local sports clubs/individuals participating in sport in the voluntary sector.

The increased funding of sport via the lottery has led to increased success in sports such as sailing and cycling. However, some top-level athletes have been critical of such funding, claiming that it decreases the drive for success if finance is guaranteed for a number of years. Under the new 'no compromise' approach of UK Sport, however, funding is reduced if sports do not meet the targets set. This new stricter approach to funding elite sport is explored in more detail on p. 138.

> **Top tip** It is important to be able to analyse critically how sport is funded in the UK.

Organisations promoting participation

Sport England

Sport England has a Royal Charter, which means that although it is free from political control, it is still accountable for its actions. It is a government-funded agency with responsibility for 'creating an active nation through sport'. Sport England views its primary role as sustaining and increasing participation in community sport.

> **Top tip** Sport England does not build sports facilities, but it does improve them by investing lottery funds.

The key objectives of Sport England are for people to:

- **start** — increase participation in sport by 1% annually, to improve the nation's health (particularly in various target groups such as women and ethnic minorities)
- **stay** — retain people in sport, and increase club membership and numbers receiving coaching
- **succeed** — become the 'best nation' in the world by 2020 in terms of participation

Sport England is therefore trying to sustain and increase participation in community sport by promoting, investing in and advising on high-quality sports pathways that release potential through community sports activities, sports clubs, coaches and officiating and sports facilities.

Sport England makes an important contribution to the success of raising participation in school sport. A target was set to ensure that by 2008 at least 85% of school-aged children spend a minimum of 2 hours each week on high-quality PE and school sport. Sport England has a particular role to play in supporting the 2-hour 'community element' of the 2010 target minimum of 4 hours of sport offered to children. The target is measured annually through the National School Sport Survey. Sport England's contribution focuses on the school–club links, Step into Sport and competition managers strands within the National School Sport Strategy. Data published in October 2006 showed that good progress is being made.

Sport England's target of increasing participation in sport for 2 million people by 2012 is divided between nine regional sports boards in England. Regional sports boards work with the county sports partnerships and community sports networks in their regions. Their role is to deliver government aims for sport in their regions and allocate resources given to them with maximum effectiveness.

The Youth Sport Trust and UK Sport

All these organisations are aiming to ensure smooth pathways to releasing the sporting potential (including volunteering, coaching, effective leadership and officiating) of as many people as possible.

- The Youth Sport Trust is primarily responsible for sustaining and increasing the quality and quantity of school sport (including curriculum PE).
- Sport England is primarily responsible for sustaining and increasing participation in formal and informal community sport.
- UK Sport is primarily responsible for the development and performance of world-class elite athletes.

Historically, the transition from school sport to elite-level sport has not always been as smooth as the organisations would have wanted. This is shown by the massive decline in sport participation that occurs at 16, that is, the 'post-school gap' (see p. 150), and the difficulties some elite athletes from more deprived backgrounds face in getting to the podium. In order to make the transition from school sport to community sport smoother, Sport England needs to run alongside the Youth Sport Trust ahead of the handover at 16. Sport England's role in this area is to ensure through its work with sports nationally, regionally and locally that the sporting environment is attractive and supportive of young people. This will help to ensure that they stay in sport once they leave compulsory schooling. Attempts to ensure this are through:

- club development — making sure clubs are strong enough to reach out to schools and young people
- community sports provision — including non-sports youth clubs such as the Scouts
- helping NGBs develop effective competition frameworks for children and young people
- the development of NGB volunteering strategies for young people

Sport England therefore has a crucial role to play in the Club Links, competition managers and Step into Sport strands of the National School Sport Strategy. It also has an important role to play in linking with UK Sport's World Class Performance Programme. Sport England is responsible for funding elite sport for non-Olympic sports such as squash and netball. It also funds the Commonwealth Games Council of England. Sport England sees such links to elite sport as 'a modest element' of its role.

Active Sports 'Get Active' programme

Active Sports is a scheme coordinated by Sport England based on the following policies:

- Active Schools forms the foundation.
- Active Communities looks at breaking down the barriers to participation and considers sports equity issues.
- Active Sports — Sport England has targeted nine sports, including girls' football and rugby league, through which it hopes to encourage more young people to take part in, improve through and benefit from, extra-curricular involvement. It links participation to excellence, for example via the Millennium Youth Games, and encourages those interested in taking part in a sport to join a club.

Activemark, Sportsmark and Sports Partnership Mark

In 2004, Sport England was involved in discussions with government departments on proposals to develop and reintroduce from 2006 Activemark, Sportsmark and the new Sports Partnership Mark. The key changes were as follows:

- Delivery of kitemark rewards by the national PESSCL strategy. This means that only schools within a school sport partnership are eligible.
- The kitemarks are awarded annually, automatically through the National School Sport Survey, which all partnership schools take part in.

Top tip

To find out more information about the new kitemarks, go to www.teachernet.gov.uk/teaching andlearning/subjects/pe/ ActivemarkSportsmark.

Tasks to tackle 14.1

Name three policies that Sport England has developed to encourage increased participation in sport.

Other home country sports councils

The **Sports Council for Wales** is responsible for developing and promoting sport and active lifestyles in Wales. It is the main adviser on sporting matters to the Welsh Assembly Government and is responsible for distributing funds from the National Lottery to sport in Wales. The Council fully subscribes to the Welsh Assembly Government's vision for a physically active and sporting nation, as outlined in its strategy document *Climbing Higher*. To support *Climbing Higher*, the Council has published *Framework for the Development of Sport and Physical Activity*. This commits the Sports Council for Wales to a shift from grants management to sports development through the marketing of physical activity, advocacy for sport and innovation in programme development.

The main themes of the Council's work are:

- active young people
- active communities
- developing performance and excellence

Sportscotland is the national agency for sport in Scotland. Its mission is to encourage everyone in Scotland to discover and develop his/her own sporting experience, helping to increase participation and improve performances in Scottish sport.

Sportscotland operates three national centres through a trust company, providing quality, affordable, residential and sporting facilities and services for the development of people in sport. Sportscotland is also the parent organisation of the Scottish Institute of Sport (see p. 138).

Sport Northern Ireland is committed to 'making sport happen' for as many people as possible. It works to:
- increase and sustain committed participation, especially among young people
- raise the standards of sporting excellence and promote the good reputation and efficient administration of sport
- support individuals working in sport, from administrators and coaches/leaders to officials, so that as many people as possible can get involved in physical activity

Schemes supporting those working in sport in Northern Ireland include:
- the Junior Club Development Pack (underpinning club development)
- Running Sport Courses (improving club management and administration)
- Sport for All Leader Award Scheme (training community-based sports leaders)

Sports Leaders UK

Sports Leaders UK provides the opportunity and motivation for people to make a meaningful contribution to their local community through nationally recognised Sports Leader Awards.

Following the award of various government grants to encourage participation in volunteering, Sports Leaders UK has developed its partnerships with organisations working with young people in the 14–19 age range. It is involved in the Step into Sport initiative, working with the Youth Sport Trust and Sport England to train a new generation of volunteer coaches, mainly in this 14–19 age range.

Sports Leaders UK is responsible for:
- the Junior Sports Leadership Award for 14–16-year-olds, taught mainly within the National Curriculum for PE at Key Stage 4. The award develops young people's skills in organising activities, planning, communicating and motivating.
- the Community Sports Leadership Award, designed for the 16+ age group and delivered in a range of institutions such as schools, colleges, youth clubs and sports centres
- the Higher Sports Leadership Award, which builds on the skills gained through the Community Sports Leadership Award to equip people to lead specific community groups such as the elderly, people with disabilities and children of primary school age
- the Basic Expedition Leadership Award, designed for people interested in the outdoors, which develops the ability to organise safe expeditions and overnight camps

The core values of these awards include:

- developing leadership — teaching people how to organise activities, and to lead, motivate and communicate with groups
- developing skills for life
- providing a stepping stone to employment, as they offer a recognised qualification
- encouraging volunteering in communities
- reducing youth crime
- supporting more active, healthier communities, by providing sports leaders to organise a range of physical activity sessions

The Youth Sport Trust

The Youth Sport Trust is the key organisation with responsibility for developing school sport. It works with a range of partners such as Sport England and Sports Leaders UK.

The Youth Sport Trust believes strongly in the power of sport to improve the lives of young people. It believes that all youngsters should receive an introduction to PE and sport that links to their developmental needs. They should be able to experience and enjoy PE and sport as a result of high-quality teaching, coaching, equipment and resources, leading to progress along a structured pathway of sporting opportunities (see p. 136) and the development of a sporting lifestyle as the foundation for lifelong participation.

The Youth Sport Trust is involved in a number of initiatives to help achieve these aims.

TOP programmes

These are a series of linked, progressive schemes for people aged from 18 months to 18 years. Over 20 000 schools are involved in TOP programmes such as:

Tasks to tackle 14.2

TOP Sport is an example of a primary school PE initiative designed to improve the quality of a pupil's experience. Describe the key features of TOP Sport.

- TOP Tots — helping young children aged from 18 months to 3 years experience physical activities and games
- TOP Start — encouraging 3–5-year-olds to learn through physical activity
- TOP Play — supporting 4–9-year-olds as they acquire and develop core skills
- TOP Sport — providing 7–11-year-olds with opportunities to develop skills in a range of sports
- TOP Skill — allowing 11–14-year-olds to extend their sports skills and knowledge
- TOP Link — encouraging links between schools and encouraging 14–16-year-olds to organise and manage sport and dance festivals in local primary schools and special schools — this is part of the Step into Sport programme and is also connected to the Junior Sports Leadership and Community Sports Leadership awards
- TOP Sportsability — creating opportunities for young disabled people to enjoy, participate in and perform in sport

PESSCL

The Youth Sport Trust plays a central role in supporting the government's PESSCL strategy and its key aim of increasing sports activity among 5–16-year-olds. As part of the strategy, the Youth Sport Trust works with a range of partners, including government agencies, to support the development of specialist sports colleges (for example, by assisting schools in every aspect of the application process and working with schools to realise their potential on achieving sports college status) and school sport partnerships.

Step into Sport pathway

The Youth Sport Trust also plays an important role in the Step into Sport programme.

- Step 1: young people engage in a programme of sports education at school.
- Step 2: young people move on to undertake the nationally recognised Level 1 Sports Leader Award.
- Step 3: young people gain practical experience in volunteering through planning and running a TOP Link sports festival for primary-school-aged children.
- Step 4: young people undertake accredited community sports leadership training and sport-specific leadership training.
- Step 5: young people, supported by a teacher mentor, engage in a programme of volunteering in their local community. County sport partnerships help to ensure that volunteering opportunities are available, appropriate and of high quality.

UK Ambassadors

Eight hundred young ambassadors are being appointed to spread the Olympic message and to act as role models for other young people.

Each school sport partnership nominates two young people. One is a 'gifted and talented' young athlete, the other a young sports leader or volunteer. Selection takes place in Year 11, although the majority of their role is undertaken in Year 12.

Talent Matters project

The 'Talent Ladder' website, as part of the Talent Matters project, gives gifted young sports people access to comprehensive information, advice and support. It is a key part of the Youth Sport Trust's Gifted and Talented programme, which is part of the government's overall PESSCL strategy.

> **Top tip**
> You do not need to know the structure of organisations, but it is important that you know how they work in partnership to raise participation levels.

For more information on the Talent Matters project, go to: www.talentmatters.org.

School Sport Champion

Kelly Holmes was appointed School Sport Champion to encourage and promote achievement in competitive school sport, which is a key aim of the Youth Sport Trust's work.

Lifelong learning

Lifelong learning is a government policy that aims to enable people to take part in physical activities that will enrich their lives, and the community, for a long time. Traditionally, school PE programmes have involved team games, but research suggests that people give up these activities as they get older. In the last decades of the twentieth century, schools began to branch out and offer other activities, sometimes using community facilities to promote the opportunities available to young people in their wider community. Activities such as golf, bowls, badminton and swimming are sporting activities that people can continue with for the rest of their lives.

Swimming is enjoyed by people of all ages

If the youth section drops out of society, the social consequences are costly. Sport is seen as one way of including young people in positive activities, channelling their energies, and making them less likely to resort to drugs and alcohol. Sport can help them to acquire new skills and integrate into wider society.

Tasks to tackle 14.3

Why can golf be considered a lifelong sport?

Schools have been challenging the idea of teaching only the traditional activities and, with the help of national governing bodies, they are trying to introduce new sports into their curriculum. Adaptations in equipment and the development of mini-games have meant that more activities are suitable for teaching in schools.

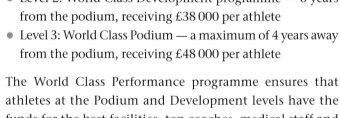

UK Sport

Top tip

For a free newsletter and up-to-date information on the work of UK Sport in relation to elite sport, visit www.uksport.gov.uk.

Key terms

Elite sport: sports performance at the excellence level of the sports development pyramid.

UK Sport: an organisation that focuses on the support and development of elite-level athletes in the UK.

World Class Performance programme: an initiative designed to support elite-level athletes with funding to enable full-time training.

Top tip

Although the figure per athlete looks generous, remember that it includes travel, coaching, physiotherapy costs etc.

Top tip

In questions relating to sporting excellence, you need to link the raising of standards to receiving top-quality coaching, facilities, equipment etc. Do not just write more facilities/better coaching as this will not earn marks.

UK Sport was established by Royal Charter in 1996. It works in partnership with a number of other organisations, such as national governing bodies of sport, to develop elite performance standards in the UK. Its mission is '...to work in partnership to lead sport in the UK to world class success'.

In 2006, UK Sport was given full responsibility for high-performance sport in the UK.

Investing in sport: World Class programmes

UK Sport began operating World Class programmes in 1997, with funding from the National Lottery. The aim of these programmes is to support leading Olympic and Paralympic athletes in their quest to win medals and world titles.

A 'no compromise' approach to funding elite sport has been adopted. This means that athletes/sports must reach the targets set, or funding has to be returned. For example, in 2006 the funding for hockey, athletics and basketball was cut as a result of failure to meet the agreed targets. The no compromise approach has led to an increased focus on resources for the most successful performers in the most successful sports.

The **World Class Performance programme** 2006 identified three stages of elite sport and designated a level of funding to be distributed at each level:

- Level 1: Talent programme — 8 years from the podium, receiving £48 000 per athlete
- Level 2: World Class Development programme — 6 years from the podium, receiving £38 000 per athlete
- Level 3: World Class Podium — a maximum of 4 years away from the podium, receiving £48 000 per athlete

The World Class Performance programme ensures that athletes at the Podium and Development levels have the funds for the best facilities, top coaches, medical staff and scientific services necessary to maximise performance. In addition, UK Sport makes a contribution towards the living costs of elite performers via Athlete Personal Awards. This funding allows top-class performers to concentrate on their sport full time and averages around £11 000.

Through the **World Class Events programme**, UK Sport distributes approximately £3.3 million of National Lottery funding each year to support the bidding and staging costs of major events on home soil — for example, the European Indoor Athletics Championships in March 2007 and London 2012 — as well as providing specialist support to organisers.

Promoting ethically fair, drug-free sport

UK Sport's initiative 'Sporting Conduct' is aimed at improving fair play in the competitive sporting arena. It is also responsible for the implementation and management of the UK's anti-doping policy. In 2006, nearly 8000 tests across 50 different sports were carried out, with results published quarterly on the UK Sport website. UK Sport started its '100% ME' campaign in May 2005. This is designed to provide a platform for athletes to celebrate their success as drug-free competitors and provide positive role models to future generations.

You can find out more about drug-free sport by going to:

www.100percentme.co.uk/home.php

UK Sport working in partnership

In July 2007, UK Sport and SportsAid, the sports charity, revealed a plan to offer support to emerging athletes across 35 sports in the build-up to the London Olympics and Paralympics in 2012. The new partnership is a result of changes to the Talented Athlete Scholarship Scheme (TASS), introduced to bring more certainty to the way in which the scholarships are awarded. Since TASS was introduced in 2004, over 3000 athletes have received financial support, helping them to maximise their sporting potential without compromising their academic careers. From April 2008, UK Sport will allocate £8million of TASS funding to athletes in summer Olympic sports over the 4-year cycle to London 2012. This money is part of the overall funding package for national governing bodies, designed to maximise medal opportunities at the London Games. SportsAid will administer a further £12 million in the same period to TASS and TASS 2012 athletes outside of those summer Olympic sports.

UK Sport and Performance Lifestyle

Performance Lifestyle is designed to help athletes create a unique environment necessary for success. Trained athlete advisers provide advice for competing athletes on how to maximise focus on their sport programme and yet still fulfil other important commitments such as work and family.

The approach is to work closely with coaches and support specialists as part of a team to minimise potential concerns, conflicts and distractions, all of which can impair performance and might even end a career prematurely. Lifestyle support, careers advice and educational guidance are all provided under Performance Lifestyle, often at UKSI centres, which are managed by UK Sport. Performance Lifestyle is available to all athletes on the World Class programme, as well as those nominated by their home country institutes.

The UK Sports Institute

In the spring of 1999, UK Sport, the four home country sports councils and the Department for Media, Culture and Sport initiated the formation of the UK Sports Institute (UKSI) network. This consists of ten regional centres in England with separate national centres in Scotland, Wales and Northern Ireland.

The UKSI network has been important in the establishment of world-class facilities for top performers to train and compete in. Programmes of excellence across the UK are coordinated at UKSI headquarters in London. The main role is to monitor and assess the quality of the service and facilities offered to athletes across the network. UKSI also coordinates research and development, drawing upon best practice from across the world and applying this to UK sports and elite athletes.

The primary role of each network centre is to help NGBs and their top performers to reach their targets in terms of world championships and medals. This requires the best coaches, facilities, equipment, sports scientists, medical professionals and various support personnel (e.g. lifestyle advisers). The network centres can also arrange facilities such as warm weather training, acclimatisation, altitude training and winter sports venues.

The **English Institute of Sport** (EIS) supports sports performers working at the very highest level, or having the potential to do so. At a regional level, the institutes of sport offer a range of services to give general sports science/sports medicine support — for example, acclimatisation, conditioning, sports massage and physiotherapy. Links are made with staff throughout the region to ensure a coordinated sports programme with the best coaches, equipment and facilities. To ensure educational and employment options are understood, links are also made to appropriate establishments.

> **Top tip**
>
> You can find out more about the work of each institute on the home country websites:
> www.sportengland.org.uk
> www.sportscotland.org.uk
> www.sports-council-wales.co.uk
> www.sportscouncil-ni.org.uk

The **Scottish Institute of Sport** was set up by sportscotland in 1998. It is funded by the sportscotland lottery fund and caters for over 200 athletes from a variety of sports. The University of Stirling became its main site in the autumn of 2000, offering a purpose-built facility acting as a hub centre for a network of six other centres, each of which is responsible for identifying and nurturing sports talent in its own region.

The Scottish Institute and the area institutes form part of the UK-wide network, thus ensuring that Scottish athletes have access to the very best support, wherever they are based in the UK. Athletes selected to receive institute support have tailor-made programmes to help them develop as world-class athletes, including technical support, sports medicine, sports science, performance analysis and lifestyle advice.

UKSI-Cymru is a network of services offered to athletes in Wales and is coordinated by the Sports Council for Wales. It also provides athletes with world-class facilities, as well as sports science, sports medicine and lifestyle support. As elsewhere in the UK, the institute operates a network of sites, with the Welsh Institute of Sport based in Cardiff acting as the hub.

The **Sports Institute Northern Ireland** (SINI) is a partnership between the Sports Council for Northern Ireland and the University of Ulster. SINI aims to provide specialist services and key facilities for over 100 able-bodied and disabled national and international sportsmen and women to improve their competitive capability. Services provided are similar to the other home country institutes.

Tasks to tackle 14.4

List the ways in which UK Sport influences sports excellence in the UK.

National governing bodies of sport

National governing bodies of sport, such as UK Athletics and British Swimming, have various responsibilities to fulfil. For example, they have to maintain rules and discipline in their sport, and promote their sport. To continue to receive UK Sport lottery funding and attract sponsorship and media deals, they must put in place initiatives that try to ensure success at international sporting events such as the Olympics. Some of the ways NGBs try to improve sports excellence include:

- talent identification schemes
- financial support
- selecting athletes for World Class Performance funding, SportsAid or TASS funding
- giving access to the best facilities and equipment
- training top-level coaches
- providing sports science support (e.g. medical support)
- organising and providing information about competitions at different levels
- providing lifestyle advice/mentors

Long-term athlete development

Long-term athlete development (LTAD) involves NGBs providing a structure to encourage lifelong involvement in sport. Some common principles of player/performer development have been identified and applied by NGBs. LTAD emphasises preparing youngsters at the earliest opportunity for healthy, lifelong participation in sport. The LTAD structure includes the following progressions:

- FUNdamentals — excitement/fun introduction to a sport
- learning to train — the stage for developing sporting skills
- training to train — acquiring and building on sport-specific skills and fitness requirements
- training to compete — developing more advanced skills and experiencing competitive environments
- training to win — maximising performance skills to try to achieve success
- retention — implementation of lifelong participation or involvement in sport as a performer, official, coach etc.

Talent ID in the UK

Examples of talent identification programmes in the UK include:

- UK School Games — a multisport event aimed at replicating the feel of the Olympic/Paralympic events

- the Junior Athlete Education programme — led by Loughborough University, this programme provides a school mentor and lifestyle workshops for talented young pupils and their parents
- 20-4-12 — a London 2012 grassroots search to find 20 potential Olympic champions. Project leaders will sift through young hopefuls nationwide before selecting 1000 children to attend 100 talent camps
- UK Centre for Coaching Excellence — a network of new coaching centres established to maximise our coaching talents in the run-up to London 2012
- TASS/TASS 2012, which provides financial support for talented elite-level athletes for such things as travel expenses and physiotherapists. For more information on TASS visit **www.tass.gov.uk.**

Excellence and participation in the UK

Equal opportunities to participate

There are a number of key terms you need to understand when studying equal opportunities in sport and recreation. Three of these — prejudice, discrimination and stereotyping — are important reasons for inequality, both in the past and at present.

The lack of participation of the five groups identified in the Unit G451 specification — women, ethnic minorities, people with disabilities, the elderly and young people — can be linked to a number of different factors, including prejudice, discrimination and stereotyping.

Increasing participation in sport is helping to achieve an important aim for local and central government — to decrease exclusion (and therefore increase inclusion) in society. Local and national governments continue to invest resources in sport and recreation schemes to try to create a sense of value/worth in society in an effort to combat social exclusion.

> **Top tip**
>
> Sports excellence questions may relate to specific organisations (e.g. UK Sport) and their functions, or may require you to link what you know about a number of different organisations (e.g. UK Sport, SportsAid, NGBs) in relation to winning more medals. Try to make *relevant* points that answer the question set.

> **Tasks to tackle 14.5**
>
> How do national governing bodies of sport support and develop performers at elite performance levels?

>
> **Key terms**
>
> **Discrimination**: unfair treatment of a person, racial group, minority; action based on prejudice.
>
> **Prejudice**: to form an unfavourable opinion before meeting an individual, often based on inadequate facts.
>
> **Social exclusion**: when certain sections of society are left out of the mainstream; this can happen when people suffer from a range of linked problems, for example unemployment, low income, poor housing.
>
> **Stereotyping**: a set of simplistic generalisations about a group that allows others to categorise them and treat them accordingly.

A pyramid structure can be used to illustrate a continuum of development from mass participation at the base of the pyramid through to excellence at the top.

The performance pyramid has four levels. At the bottom is the **foundation** level, which is the first introduction to physical activity for young children, often during primary school PE. Basic movement skills and a positive attitude to physical activity are developed from an early age. It is sometimes referred to as the 'grassroots' stage of development.

The second level is **participation**, with an emphasis on fun, socialising and formation of friendships in a recreational manner. At school this may be through extra-curricular activities.

More dedicated individuals may reach the **performance** stage. Such individuals reach county or regional levels of performance and receive specialist coaching in order to try to improve their standard.

A limited few reach **excellence** as elite performers. Such individuals strive to represent their country and are fully committed to their sport. In some cases they receive financial support to enable them to train full time, and achieve success in international sporting competitions.

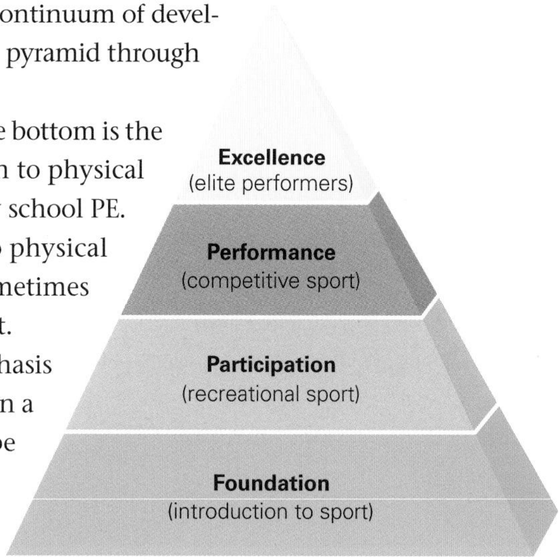

Excellence
(elite performers)

Performance
(competitive sport)

Participation
(recreational sport)

Foundation
(introduction to sport)

Figure 14.1 The performance pyramid

Key term

Inclusive sport: where all people have the right to equal opportunities according to their particular needs.

Top tip

Make sure you can identify and explain all levels of the pyramid in your own words, as this may be asked for in an exam.

Sport and mass participation

The focus of this section of Unit G451 is on how we can raise levels of participation at the bottom two levels of the performance pyramid, that is, how we can increase mass participation, and progression to the performance/excellence levels for those with the necessary talent.

The idea behind mass participation in sport is that everyone should have the chance to take part as often as they would like and at whatever level they choose. However, reality does not always match the principle of equal opportunities in 'Sport for All'. Target and special interest groups are sections of society identified by Sport England as needing special attention. The aim is to raise participation levels to try to ensure that these groups have equality of sporting opportunity.

Examples of target groups include ethnic minorities, women, young people (16–24), the elderly, lower social-class groups and people with disabilities. They are of special interest due to their under-representation in physical activity in relation to their numbers in society.

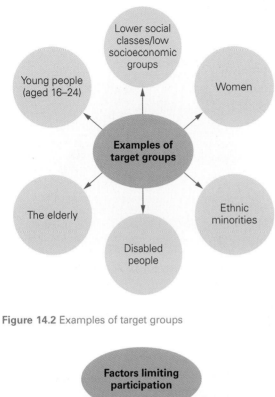

Figure 14.2 Examples of target groups

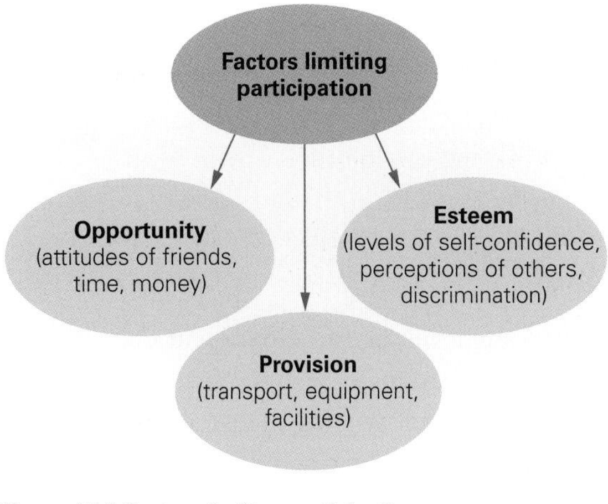

Figure 14.3 Factors limiting participation

Tasks to tackle 14.6

Consider your own experiences in sport and recreation and note any factors that have hindered your involvement in such physical activity.

Sport for All is a UK policy, initiated in the 1970s, aimed at achieving mass participation. In reality, however, not everyone is able to take up the sport of his/her choice. Various constraints limit regular participation. These can be grouped under three main headings:

- **opportunity** — factors that affect the chance to take part in sport or recreation, including time, money and the attitudes of friends and family
- **provision** — more tangible features that affect participation, including the availability of specialist facilities, equipment, coaching and appropriate activities
- **self-esteem** — the self-confidence to take part and the effects of perceptions held by others of an individual or group. Self-esteem is affected by an individual's status in a stratified society. It can lead to low expectations and under-achievement among lower social classes, people with disabilities and ethnic minorities. For example, social class may affect money available for equipment, coaching and transport.

Combinations of factors can lead to double deprivation and a greater likelihood of under-representation. For example, if you are a woman with disabilities, you are less likely to participate than if you are a man with disabilities or if you are a woman without disabilities.

Under-representation of women in sport

Not all women want to perform in all activities. The key issue is when discrimination or gender stereotyping *denies* women the freedom to choose. Women should have the same opportunity as men both to participate and to excel in their chosen sport.

A variety of different reasons can be given to explain the under-representation of women in sport. These include:

- stereotypical myths, for example the belief that physical activity could damage fertility, or that women are not aggressive
- less media coverage
- fewer role models and sponsorship opportunities
- lower prize money
- negative effects of school PE programmes, for example lack of choice, rules on kit
- lack of time due to work and family responsibilities
- lack of disposable income
- fewer female coaches and officials

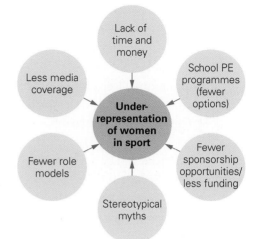

Figure 14.4 Under-representation of women in sport

Although women's representation in sport is still relatively low in relation to their numbers in society, improvements are being made. Reasons include the following:

- There is greater social acceptance of women having jobs and financial independence.
- Media coverage of women's sport has increased and positive role models have been promoted (e.g. Kelly Holmes).
- Stereotypical myths are refuted through education.
- More women are qualifying as coaches and to officiate in women's (and in some cases men's) sport.
- There are more clubs for women to join and more competitions to enter.
- Childcare is provided at some leisure centres.
- The Women's Sports Foundation (see **www.wsf.org.uk**) promotes the benefits of participation in exercise, raises the profiles of British sportswomen, and works with other organisations to develop campaigns and policies such as Sports Coach UK and Women into High-Performance Coaching.

The Women's Sports Foundation has produced a fact sheet that illustrates why raising levels of participation in sport among women is important. It points out that sport:

- improves body image and self-esteem
- reduces stress and depression, and increases energy levels
- develops skills necessary for success in the workplace, for example strategic thinking, goal setting, teamwork
- lowers the risk of obesity and initiation of cigarette smoking in adolescent girls
- increases the chance of academic success
- increases the overall quality of life

For case studies of initiatives in the UK that have worked to increase women's participation in physical activity, see www.whatworksforwomen.org.uk.

Women's participation in indoor activities such as badminton and aerobics is relatively high compared with outdoor activities such as rugby and hockey. Reasons for this include:

- a comfortable environment (dry and warm)
- seen as good for health and fitness/body toning
- improved provision in school PE programmes and clubs (preparation for leisure)
- activities can be performed recreationally, as lifetime activities
- they are non-contact activities
- they are more socially acceptable and fit female stereotypes

However, it should be noted that association football is gaining in popularity among women. A number of socio-cultural factors can help to explain this:

- increased equal opportunities in society in general
- increased media coverage of women's football, for example the women's World Cup in China, 2007
- more female role models
- more opportunities for girls to play football in school PE programmes
- more clubs to join
- rejection of stereotypes affecting female participation in contact activities such as football
- more leisure time and disposable income available

Race and religion in sport

Britain is a multicultural, multiracial, egalitarian society. Equal opportunities to participate and excel in sport should exist for all racial groups. Such equality is not a reality due to many factors, including racism.

Racism is illegal but it still exists in society (and therefore in sport as a reflection of society) on the basis of colour, language or culture. Racism stems from prejudice linked with the power of one racial group over another. This leads to discrimination, or unfair treatment. For example, teachers might assign students to certain sports or positions on the basis of ascribed ethnic characteristics rather than interests and abilities.

Top tip

Exam questions often require knowledge of causes of under-representation of women in sport and suggested solutions to these barriers. For example, if lack of time due to childcare responsibilities is a continuing barrier to participation, provision of crèches at leisure centres is one solution.

Top tip

Do some informal research on media coverage of women's sport by comparing a few newspapers to see how much coverage women get compared with men.

Tasks to tackle 14.7

How might women be discriminated against in sport?

Key term

Racism: a set of beliefs based on the assumption that races have distinct hereditary characteristics that give some races an intrinsic superiority over others. It may lead to physical or verbal abuse.

Other causes of under-representation of certain ethnic groups in sports and physical recreation include:

- conflict with religious observances
- a higher value placed on education (less support from family for sports participation)
- racist abuse
- fewer role models (particularly as coaches and managers)
- lower self-esteem and fear of rejection

Possible solutions to racial disadvantage and discrimination include:

- training more ethnic minority sports teachers and coaches, and educating them on the effects of stereotyping
- ensuring there is single-sex provision for Muslim women
- publicising and punishing more severely any racist abuse
- organising campaigns against racism in sport, for example the Kick It Out campaign
- making more provision in PE programmes for different ethnic preferences, for example by relaxing kit and showering rules to accommodate cultural norms

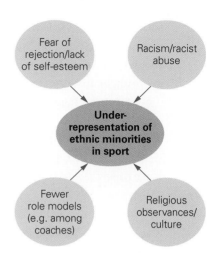

Figure 14.5 Barriers to participation for ethnic minority groups

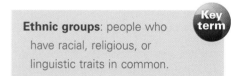

Ethnic groups: people who have racial, religious, or linguistic traits in common.

Under-representation of the disabled in sport

Generally, people with disabilities have a low level of participation in sport. Disability may be physical, sensory or mental in nature, with all of these potentially affecting participation in a negative way. Society continues to discriminate against, and impose barriers on, disabled people's participation in physical activity and possible progression up the performance pyramid.

Reasons why individuals with disabilities do not participate in physical activity include:

- negative self-image — this often adversely affects the confidence to take part, particularly when reinforced by negative comments and reactions from the public
- lower income levels — three-quarters of disabled people rely on state benefits as their main source of income
- lack of appropriate transport and access into and around facilities
- lack of specialist coaches
- lack of specialist equipment to meet the needs of disabled people
- fewer competitive opportunities
- low levels of media coverage

For some disabled individuals, inclusiveness is best realised by integration, while for others segregation may be better.

Integration has potentially a number of benefits for disabled individuals, such as increasing their self-esteem, breaking down negative stereotypes and helping them feel more valued in society. However, integration can also affect people with disabilities in negative ways, including safety concerns that have to be addressed and lower self-esteem if they are continually unsuccessful.

Segregation may lead to positive outcomes for the disabled, such as increased success. The negative aspects of segregation include reinforcement of the notion that the disabled are different from the rest of society, which may make them feel less valued and excluded from mainstream society.

The Paralympic Games have had a positive impact on the involvement of disabled people in sport. Media coverage has raised the profile of disabled sport and educated the general public about how disabled athletes compete in various sports, for example through adaptations.

> **Key terms**
>
> **Inclusiveness**: the idea that all people should have their needs, abilities and aspirations recognised, understood and met within a supportive environment.
>
> **Integration**: able-bodied and disabled people taking part in the same activity at the same time.
>
> **Segregation**: people with disabilities participating separately among themselves.

Table 14.1 Causes of, and solutions to, under-representation of disabled individuals in sport

Cause	Solution
Negative self-image, lack of confidence	Provide opportunities for success
Lower income levels	Increase investment in disabled sport to make it more affordable
Poor access to facilities; poor access in and around them	Provide transport to facilities; improve access in and around them
Low levels of media coverage, few role models	Increase media coverage of disabled sport, e.g. the Paralympics
Low levels of funding	Increase funding from the National Lottery
Few competitions and clubs	More competitions at all levels; more clubs for the disabled in a wider variety of sports
Myths and stereotypes	Educate people about the myths concerning disabled individuals and challenge inappropriate attitudes

Disability Sport England (www.dse.org.uk) works to increase participation among people with disabilities. It has a number of important functions, including:

- promoting the benefits of exercise to the disabled
- supporting organisations that provide sport and recreation facilities for the disabled
- increasing awareness and knowledge in society about the capabilities of people with disabilities
- encouraging disabled people to play an active role in the development of their sport

Benefits of participating in sport for disabled individuals include:

- raised levels of confidence and self-esteem
- improved levels of physical skill
- increased health and fitness
- inclusion and integration into society
- more role models to encourage participation
- reduce myths and stereotypes about the disabled

Effects of social class

In Britain, social class, wealth discrimination and the consequent inequality of opportunity are centuries old. In pre-industrial times (early 1700s), the upper and lower social classes pursued separate sports. For example, hunting was exclusively for the upper classes and mob football was for the lower classes. As a result of the Industrial Revolution, a new middle class was created that participated in sport 'for the love of the game' and played a key role in the formation of the national governing bodies and subsequent rule development. A three-tier society is still broadly in evidence in the UK today and can be linked to sporting participation as follows:

- upper class — polo, equestrianism and field sports
- middle class — hockey, tennis, golf and rugby union
- working class — football, darts, snooker and rugby league

There is also evidence that lower socioeconomic background leads to less participation in sport. This is due to factors such as cost, lower levels of health and fitness, low self-esteem and lack of opportunities to take up sport or to become role models in positions of responsibility. People from lower socioeconomic backgrounds are more likely to suffer from social exclusion as they have less power, income and self-confidence — they suffer from a range of linked problems such as higher unemployment, lower income and poor health.

Subsidised provision that encourages participation in local community schemes can help to overcome these barriers, for example Sport Action Zones set up by Sport England in some inner-city areas. These are particular areas with high levels of social and economic deprivation that have been targeted to try to raise participation in sport and recreation. Such schemes also serve important functions as diversions from crime and general social disorder.

Top tip

There are five clearly defined target groups you need to study — ethnic minority groups, women, people with disabilities, young people and the elderly. You need to consider causes of lower levels of participation in sport and recreation among these groups and possible solutions to such problems. Social class is included for interest and because it is sometimes seen as an additional barrier to participation and excellence in today's society.

Under-representation of the elderly in sport

The UK has a tradition of little or no involvement in physical activity of a recreational or sporting nature by older people (aged 60+). All age groups should enjoy the same opportunity and provision for recreation and sport, and try to overcome the barriers that prevent participation.

The following factors may explain the lower numbers of the over-60s taking part in sport:

- Poor health, for example heart problems, leads to cautious attitudes in relation to participation in physical activity.
- Low income levels mean that funds for recreational purposes may be limited.
- They may be unable to drive or may lack their own transport.
- Local leisure centres may offer activities that are unappealing to older people.
- Some people in this group may suffer from a lack of self-esteem and feel that physical activity is only for the young.

Solutions to these problems might include:

- specialist coaches catering for the needs of the elderly
- free or subsidised activities and transport
- taster programmes of new activities in response to the needs of the elderly
- increased media coverage of veteran events, creating positive role models

It is important to relate causes and solutions to the target group being discussed. For example, time is not as much of a problem for the elderly as it might be for working mothers.

The 'post-school gap'

In 1960, the Wolfenden Report identified a post-school gap of non-participation into which many school leavers fell as they progressed from school/childhood into work/adulthood, that is, the 16–24 age group.

This gap still exists today — as soon as physical activity becomes optional at the end of Key Stage 4, many teenagers 'drop out'. Part-time work, personal relationships and academic pursuits take over.

The fall in sports participation with age is worrying because individuals reduce their chances of maintaining health and agility and of being able to live independently into their old age. Research shows that people who are exposed to a wide range of sporting activities in their youth are more likely to continue to participate throughout their lives.

It is therefore important for school children to have a positive PE experience to ensure that they pursue 'active leisure' on leaving school. This can be achieved through varied and appealing PE programmes, school–club links, links to leisure centres and experiencing different roles, such as coach or official.

Post-school gap: the drop in sports participation when young adults leave full-time education at 16 and do not return to sport until their mid-20s.

Young people are often overlooked as a target group but the importance of the 16–24 age group should be recognised, since sedentary lifestyles can cause health problems later in life.

Current government policies in school PE/sport

Various initiatives have been set up to improve the quality of school children's PE experiences. These include:

- PE, School Sport and Club Links (PESSCL) strategy
- sports colleges
- school sport partnerships
- school sport coordinators
- Step into Sport
- Club Links

PE, School Sport and Club Links (PESSCL)

The Sport England website reports government investment of £978 million between 2003 and 2008 to deliver the PESSCL strategy:

www.sportengland.org/index/get_resources/schoolsport/pesscl.htm

PESSCL is a national strategy aimed at increasing the uptake of sporting opportunities by 5–16-year-olds so that 85% of them experience a minimum of 2 hours of high-quality PE and school sport each week. It is being delivered through nine interlinked strands:

- sports colleges
- school sport partnerships
- professional development
- Step into Sport
- Club Links
- Gifted and Talented
- sporting playgrounds
- swimming
- the QCA's PE and School Sport Investigation

Sports colleges

Sports colleges are part of the specialist schools programme, which is run by the Department for Children, Schools and Families (formerly the Department for Education and Skills, DfES). Sports colleges help to deliver the government's plans for PE and sport. They provide high-quality opportunities for young people in their neighbourhood.

> **Key term**
>
> **Sports colleges**: part of the government's specialist schools programme; sports colleges are secondary schools that have achieved specialist status for sport.

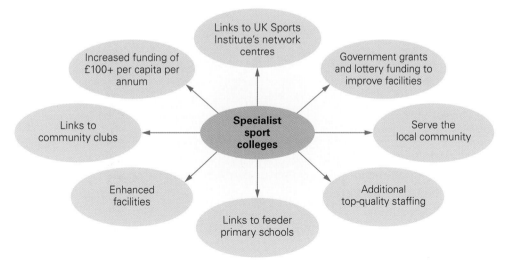

Figure 14.6 Features of specialist sports colleges

Sport is one of ten specialisms within the specialist schools programme. The programme helps schools to establish a distinctive identity through their chosen specialism. Sports colleges aim to raise standards of achievement in PE and sport for all their students. They are regional focal points for:

- promoting excellence in PE and sport in the community
- extending links between families of schools, sports bodies and communities, sharing resources and developing and sharing good practice
- helping young people to progress to careers in sport and PE

School sport partnerships

School sport partnerships are groups of schools that receive funding from the government to come together to enhance sporting opportunities. There are 450 partnerships across schools in England. Each partnership is individual but a 'partnership model' has been devised to develop new partnerships and expand existing ones (Figure 14.7).

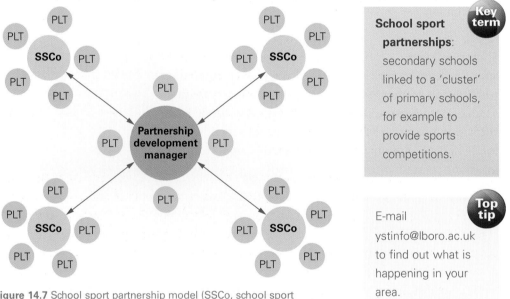

Key term

School sport partnerships: secondary schools linked to a 'cluster' of primary schools, for example to provide sports competitions.

Top tip

E-mail ystinfo@lboro.ac.uk to find out what is happening in your area.

Figure 14.7 School sport partnership model (SSCo, school sport coordinator; PLT, primary link teacher)

The aims of a school sport partnership team are to:

- enhance opportunities for young people to experience different sports
- access high-quality coaching
- engage in competition

Typically, partnerships:

- are clustered around a specialist sports college and managed by a full-time **partnership development manager**, whose role is to develop links with the LEA, other sports organisations and the wider community

- include around eight secondary school partners, each of which appoints a **school sport coordinator** (SSCo). SSCos are PE teachers who are released from the timetable for 2 days each week to work with their cluster of primary schools, developing after-school activities and links with the local community and sports clubs.
- include around 45 primary or special school partners (clustered in families of five around the sports college and secondary schools), each of which appoints a **primary link teacher** who is released from timetable for 12 days each year to help develop PE and school sport within the primary school

Each partnership receives a grant of nearly £300 000 per year, which pays for the different teacher posts and teacher release. The Big Lottery fund has given each partnership an additional grant — on average £75 000 over 3 years — to kick-start additional out-of-hours sports activities designed to widen participation.

The overall aim of the partnerships is to help schools to enable their pupils to spend at least 2 hours each week on high-quality PE and school sport. Six objectives have been set to help achieve this aim:

- strategic planning — develop and implement a PE/sport strategy
- primary liaison — develop links, particularly between Key Stages 2 and 3
- out-of-school hours — provide enhanced opportunities for all pupils
- school to community — increase participation in community sport
- coaching and leadership — provide opportunities in leadership, coaching and officiating for senior pupils, teachers and other adults
- raising standards of pupil achievement

The quality and amount of school sport is rising each year. In September 2004, the prime minister, Tony Blair, announced that **competition managers** would be added to the network of school sport partnerships. As a result of investment from the PESSCL strategy, the first 20 competition managers took up post in September 2005, to plan, manage and implement a programme of inter-school competition across their school sport partnership and others.

The Youth Sport Trust, Sport England and the National Council for School Sport have developed a framework to complement the principles of athlete development in the long term. It aims to provide consistency in competition structure for the following:

- Key Stage 3–4 (ages 12–16), inter-school leagues and cup competitions
- Key Stage 3 (ages 11–12), multi-sport competition, central venue leagues
- Key Stage 2 (ages 9–11), multi-sport competition, central venue leagues
- Key Stage 2 (ages 7–9), multi-skill festivals each term
- Key Stage 1 (ages 4–7), annual multi-skill festivals (off-site)

Each NGB is working closely with its National Schools Association to develop a new, integrated structure of competitions, from inter-school (local) to inter-district (county level) and above, using the new families of schools as geographic units for competition.

Step into Sport

Step into Sport and Club Links are the key strands of PESSCL that aim to provide the links from high-quality school sport to high-quality community sport, and to ensure that all young people have the best possible experience either as a participant or as a volunteer.

> **Key term**
>
> **Step into Sport**: a Youth Sport Trust scheme to increase the number of sports leaders in the 14–19 age range.

Step into Sport is part of the National School Sport Strategy, which was produced jointly by the Department for Culture, Media and Sport and the DfES. It is managed by Sport England and the Youth Sport Trust with Sports Leaders UK and provides a high-quality sports leadership training service. School sport partnerships work with county sport partnerships and national governing bodies of sport to target 14–19-year-olds by providing opportunities for young people to get involved in leadership and volunteering in sport.

The community volunteering aspect of Step into Sport enables 16–19-year-olds to take part in a range of activities staged by sports clubs and other organisations. Young people can play a variety of roles, including managing events and facilities, media duties and running a club, as well as assistant coach or referee roles. The aim is to support young volunteers in developing key life skills and in gaining new skills, knowledge, self-confidence and qualifications.

Club Links

A school–club link is an agreement between a school or a school sport partnership and a community-based sports club to work together to meet the needs of all young people who might want to get involved in their sport/club. It helps young people to realise their ambitions in sport and dance by providing pathways for them to follow. A

> **Top tip**
>
> For more information on multi-skill clubs see www.youthsporttrust.org/linkAttachments/scuk-multi-skils-faqs.pdf

school–club link can provide new and varied opportunities for people and put in place quality controls to ensure that standards remain high.

The main aim of the Club Links programme is to increase the number of children participating in sports clubs. A target was set to increase the percentage of 5–16-year-olds who were members of sports clubs from 14% in 2002 to 25% by 2008. The PESSCL survey for 2004–05 showed that an average of 22% of pupils in school sport partnerships participated in at least one sports club with links to the school, surpassing the 2006 target of 20%.

Twenty-two NGBs receive funding to work with and support their accredited clubs and help them to make sustainable and effective links with schools by working in partnership with county and school sport partnerships.

Progress has already been made with this scheme, including 800 multi-skill clubs being set up for primary school children in the 7–11 age range. Delivered through the network of school sport partnerships, these clubs provide additional opportunities for children to develop fundamental motor and movement skills, and act as a stepping stone into club sport.

Dance Links is a dance-specific project within Club Links. Its aim is to help improve links between school sport partnerships and dance providers to increase the number of young people participating in dance. Dance Links is also working to enhance the choice and quality of children's dance experience to increase the likelihood of maintaining their lifelong participation in this area.

Tasks to tackle 14.8

How can schools and community sports clubs work together to increase the levels of participation in sport and recreation?

NGBs and whole sport plans

In 2003, Sport England identified 30 priority sports, based on their ability to contribute to Sport England's vision of an active and successful sporting nation. Sport England is working with the NGBs of these sports to develop and implement their whole sport plans (WSPs).

Whole sport plans identify how a sport will contribute to Sport England's 'start', 'stay' and 'succeed' objectives from grass roots through to elite level. The plans identify what help and resources NGBs need to deliver their whole sport plans. They enable Sport England to direct funding and resources to NGBs and offer the opportunity to measure how well the NGBs are performing.

Seven key performance indicators (KPIs) have been agreed that reflect proposals and feedback from Sport England, UK Sport, NGBs and other relevant partners. These link to Sport England's 'start', 'stay' and 'succeed' objectives (p. 131):

- level of participation
- the number of active accredited clubs within the sport
- the number of active club members within the sport
- the number of qualified and currently active coaches and individual members delivering instruction in the sport
- the number of active volunteers supporting the sport
- performance by teams and/or individuals in significant international competition and world rankings
- the percentage of English athletes in GB teams in sports competing as GB

Increasing participation

NGBs are required to open their sport to all sections of society, including those at grass-roots participation levels. Ways of achieving increased participation and sports equity include:

- developing policies linking to specific target groups, for example disabled and ethnic minorities
- training more sport-specific coaches to encourage participation
- developing mini-games and modified versions of their sports to encourage participation at all levels of ability, for example high 5 netball and short tennis
- making facilities more accessible, affordable and attractive, targeting funds at grass-roots levels and inner-city schemes
- improving awareness of the sport through publicity, advertising and use of positive role models

Performance-enhancing products

There are various reasons why performers may be tempted to use drugs, including:

- the potential for improving physical performance and therefore increasing the chance of winning
- pressure from coaches and/or peers
- the belief that everybody else is doing it (negative role models)
- a 'win at all costs' attitude fostered by the prospect of high rewards (e.g. money and fame)
- a lack of deterrents or a perceived low risk of being caught

In the fight against the continued use of illegal drugs in various sports, possible solutions include:

- stricter, random testing
- harsher deterrents and punishments (e.g. lifelong bans)
- the use of positive role models to reinforce the anti-drugs message
- coordinated education programmes to highlight to athletes and coaches the health and moral issues surrounding drugs in sport

The use of performance-enhancing drugs is associated with modern-day sport, particularly at elite level.

Recent summer and winter Olympic Games have seen numerous drugs scandals, in which athletes have broken their oath by illegally enhancing their performance. The 2007 Tour de France was nicknamed the Tour de Farce following a number of drug scandals.

Some examples of performance-enhancing drugs and their effects are outlined below.

- Diuretics are used by athletes who want to lose weight (e.g. jockeys and boxers).
- Narcotic analgesics are used to reduce pain and mask injury (e.g. football and tennis players). Long-term health damage/ injuries may result if too much pain relief is applied.
- Beta-blockers have a relaxing effect and are used in high-precision sports where it is important to be calm (e.g. archery and snooker).
- Erythropoietin (EPO) is used to increase endurance (e.g. long-distance cyclists and runners).
- Anabolic steroids build muscle and bone mass and are therefore used to increase strength and power (e.g. weightlifters and sprinters).

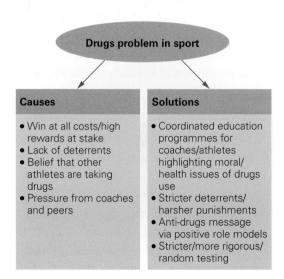

Figure 14.8 The drugs problem in sport

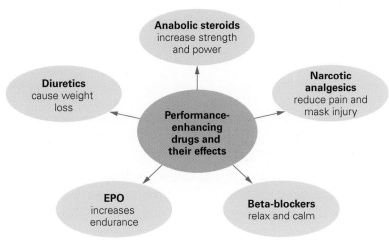

Figure 14.9 Performance-enhancing drugs

Top tip

Implementing the solutions listed is difficult in practice, because of the inaccuracy of tests, the massive costs of introducing widespread improved testing, the use of masking agents and the continued high rewards available for winning.

Modern technological products

In the increasingly competitive and financially rewarding world of sport, performers and their coaches constantly seek to gain an edge over their rivals. Technological developments can improve performance — a specially designed swimsuit might decrease the drag through the water and improve swimming times as a result, or a pair of football boots might have improvements designed to improve your touch and feel for the ball. For example, the Nike Total 90 Laser boot worn by Wayne Rooney has a number of technological benefits that help improve performance, such as:

Top tip

There is a covert, regular, systematic, multi-million pound drugs industry operating with the sole purpose of helping sports competitors to enhance their performance illegally in various ways. It costs millions of pounds to try to combat such illegal acts, but it is a cost worth paying to ensure fair competition between athletes.

- spinal bars to minimise the roll-in motion of the foot
- dual-density inner soles for stability and flexibility
- EVA insert to reduce stud pressure and provide responsive cushioning
- a 'power zone' to amplify ball power and shooting accuracy
- off-centre lacing for good ball control

Rowing is one sport that has embraced technology for performance improvement and experienced more success in world games as a result. The **biomechanical boat** uses instrumentation to measure and record forces exerted on the rowing boat. This allows the rower and coach to receive precise feedback on the rate and pattern of force produced. In conjunction with observation and video analysis, this can prove a useful tool for improving technique. The forces in different phases of the rowing stroke can be examined, and force profiles can be compared between different rowers in a crew to examine whether there are individual differences that can be corrected and improved. **Virtual reality goggles** allow the rower to see the image transmitted from the coach's video camera while rowing. This visual feedback is immediate and can be combined with the rower's feelings of performing the activity, so that he/she can both see and feel what it is like when making a particular change in technique.

Sport science has transformed the cricket bat in the last decade. The weight is typically between 2 lb 8 oz and 2 lb 12 oz, much lighter than previously. Ten years ago, bats were dried to 16% moisture, now they are dried to 12–14%, so that you get more wood at a lighter weight. Bats are now pressed harder to create an exaggerated bow effect to the blade. The edges are almost half as thick again as they were ten years ago, so many edges go to the boundary for four runs. The profile has also changed — along with the big edges comes a huge 'sweet spot' in the middle, with a chunk of prime willow behind it. The sweet spot can be moved along the blade, depending on where the player wants it. Batsmen often use three bats these days — a heavy one for the 20–20 game because they just want to smash the ball, a heavier one for 50 overs, and a lighter blade for games of 3–5 days' duration.

Roles of the media

The media (newspapers, magazines, television, radio, internet etc.) have four main roles in relation to sports coverage:

- informing
- educating
- entertaining
- advertising

> **Key term**
>
> **The media**: forms of mass communication, usually comprising the press, television, radio and the internet.

Live coverage gives factual information about what is happening and what has happened in sport, informing the public about fixtures and results in a variety of sports. The media can educate the public about sporting issues such as drugs in sport, and about sporting skills and coaching techniques. Large amounts of television and radio airtime and newspaper column coverage, as well as a huge number of websites, are devoted to entertaining people and helping them to enjoy their leisure time by watching, listening or reading about sport.

The Olympic Games and football World Cup can generate audiences of over 25 million people in Britain. The media are important in generating income for sport via advertising, for example through product endorsement or sponsorship.

The media can encourage participation in sport and healthy lifestyles in a number of ways, including:

- providing positive role models to inspire participation
- promoting events to participate in — for example the Great Northern Run and Sport Relief
- educating the general public about different sports and their health benefits
- promoting 'lifetime activities' such as golf and badminton by giving them exposure on television

Top tip

Make sure you can relate the four roles of the media to sporting examples. In any particular media feature, one role can dominate or a number of roles may be evident. For example, *Match of the Day* informs, entertains, advertises by giving publicity to sponsors around a ground, and sometimes educates (e.g. on rule changes).

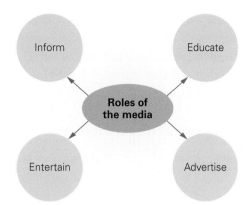

Figure 14.10 Roles of the media in sport

The media may discourage participation and healthy lifestyles owing to:
- passive spectatorism — the tendency to consume sport inactively rather than taking part
- promotion of unhealthy products that are not part of a healthy lifestyle — for example, alcohol (the Welsh rugby team is sponsored by Brains brewery)
- a high proportion of media coverage is given to sports that are unlikely to be part of an individual's lifelong involvement in physical activity, for example rugby and football

Sport and the media

Professional sport has become a media commodity, driven by market forces, but it also benefits from its relationship with the media. This relationship between sport and the media has both positive and negative outcomes.

On the positive side, sport is available to millions of people in the comfort of their own homes. Positive role models are created, who may inspire participation. Advanced technology can provide detailed analysis of sport and slow-motion replays. Rule changes can result from media pressure to make sport more exciting — examples include 20–20 cricket and the back-pass rule in football. Deviant practices can be more clearly identified and subsequently scrutinised, for example with video evidence available to officials.

On the negative side, audiences may suffer from sporting overload (for example, too much football), and sports stars may lose their privacy. Television can encourage passive viewing and discourage participation. Advanced technology may be intrusive, for example stump microphones might pick

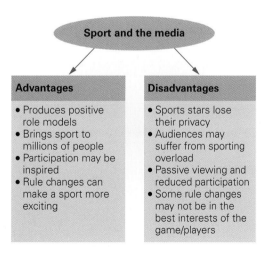

Figure 14.11 The impact of media on sport

up arguments among players. In addition, rule changes are not always in the best interests of a sport or the performers (e.g. in football referees insist that an injured player should leave the pitch for treatment).

Sport, sponsorship and the media

Elite sport has been commercialised in a number of ways. The most obvious is through the high financial rewards available for top performers in sports that receive media attention, for example tennis, golf and soccer. Sport is sold as a product to the media (Premiership football, Super League rugby etc.) on which Sky television maintains a monopoly in relation to live coverage. This may lead to an increase in the pressure to win, fostering a 'win at all costs' attitude and perhaps even cheating.

Companies can become involved in sport in a variety of ways. This might include sponsoring:

- a stadium, for example the Reebok stadium at Bolton
- a league or competition, for example the Barclaycard Premiership
- an individual, for example Nike sponsors Tiger Woods
- a team, for example Nike's sponsorship of Manchester United's kit and Adidas's sponsorship of Real Madrid's kit for the 2007–08 season

Top tip

The media have the power to make or break sports. Regular television coverage, in particular, with its associated sponsorship opportunities, is what many minority sports, such as netball, aspire to. One way in which television (i.e. Sky) has benefited a sport and created interest and excitement along with major financial benefits is via the invention of 20–20 cricket.

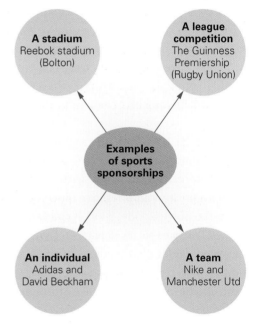

Figure 14.12 Examples of sports sponsorship

Such investment/sponsorship in sport is undertaken for a financial return in the future, but it can have risks if the performers underperform or behave badly.

Top tip

You need to be able to illustrate your knowledge of the commercialism of sport with different types of sports sponsorship and examples of these, e.g. kit, equipment, grounds, competitions, training costs. Sponsors and sponsorship do change and you need to keep up to date so that you are using current relevant examples.

The 'golden triangle'

The presence of the media has turned sport into a commodity that can be bought and sold. Television companies pay huge amounts of money to cover sports, and advertisers and sponsors back sport because of the exposure they will get in the media. Many sports have either been adapted to suit the needs of television or have changed their structure to attract television coverage.

There is a direct link between the funding of sport and the media. Media coverage brings sponsors and advertising to a sport, which are now essential for a sport to remain viable. Companies sponsor sports mainly as a means of cheap advertising, a way of getting into the public's living room. This relationship between sport, sponsorship and the media is referred to as sport's 'golden triangle' and it is becoming increasingly essential in the success of sporting events.

Key term

The **'golden triangle'**: the association between sports events, sponsorship and the media.

Top tip

Sports sponsorship needs to be considered in a critical manner. It has a number of benefits for sport (e.g. increased financing) but can also have negative implications (e.g. sponsors gaining too much control). Sport and sponsorship go hand in hand as they generally form a mutually beneficial relationship.

Violence in sport

Controlled aggression can be a fundamental and necessary part of many sports as performers strive to assert their authority. However, aggression sometimes spills over into uncontrolled situations, with fights or high tackles possibly resulting in injuries and penalties.

Performer violence can be defined as, 'any aggressive act by an individual outside the rules of sport'. The causes for such violence include:

- a 'win at all costs' attitude
- frustration with the officials, opponents, team-mates or the crowd
- local rivalry with the opposition
- receiving verbal or physical abuse
- high rewards of winning
- the physically robust nature of some sports, for example ice hockey

Solutions to the problem include:

- severe penalties, such as bans, fines or 'sin bins'
- the use of video technology by a panel to assess and adjudicate on unfair play
- education and an emphasis on the ethos of fair play
- a greater number of officials
- more authority for the officials

Table 14.2 Causes of, and solutions to, violence in sport

Causes	Solutions
Importance of winning/rewards encourage violence and cheating	Educate on the ethos of fair play; encourage sportsmanship
Frustration with officials making poor decisions	Use of video technology to adjudicate on decisions and spot aggressive acts
'Acceptance' in certain sports; poor role models to follow at all levels of a sport (e.g. ice hockey, soccer)	Harsher penalties for offenders (e.g. penalty tries and sin bins in rugby); promotion of positive role models

Crowd violence

Aggressive and rebellious behaviour at sporting events existed in pre-industrial times and throughout the Victorian period, that is, the nineteenth century. Hooliganism became a major social problem again in the 1960s with the collective aggressive behaviour of predominantly white, unskilled, teenage males at football matches.

Dysfunctional spectator behaviour involves violence with the intent to harm others. A key example is football hooliganism. A variety of different causes can be suggested to explain why football hooliganism occurs. These include:

- consumption of alcohol
- violence by performers on the field of play
- pre-match hype increased by media coverage
- poor refereeing
- behaviour of opposition fans (abusive chants)
- an unfavourable score or result
- diminished individual responsibility as part of a crowd
- religious or partisan differences (e.g. Celtic versus Rangers)

Top tip

Top-level commercialised sport involves highly pressurised situations. Comparison of such a 'win at all costs' attitude with the old amateur ethic of 'it's not the winning but the taking part that counts' is important. Many national governing bodies of sport try to encourage fair play, for example before Premiership football matches, the opponents shake hands.

Top tip

In the wake of football crowd tragedies, stadiums have been made safer (e.g. by the removal of fences) and more welcoming to appeal to all sections of society and to encourage families to attend matches.

Table 14.3 Causes of, and solutions to, dysfunctional spectator behaviour

Causes	Solutions
Alcohol	Control of alcohol sales
Violent performers	Encourage 'fair play' by performers
Organised gangs	Use of 'police intelligence'
Poor policing/lack of segregation	Improve policing/stewarding
Abusive/racist chants	Use of CCTV to identify troublemakers; harsher punishments

A number of solutions to the problem are in place, such as the use of CCTV, improved policing and security, tougher deterrents, stricter control of alcohol sales, family membership schemes and all-seating stadiums.

The Olympic Games

Baron Pierre de Coubertin, founder of the modern Olympic Games, found his inspiration in the Much Wenlock Games in Shropshire. This is a multi-sports festival, which began in 1850 and is still held annually to the present day. Great Britain has been intricately linked with the success and ideals of the modern Olympic Games since they started in 1896.

Great Britain is one of only five countries to have competed at every summer Olympic Games of the modern era, and one of only three countries (along with France and Switzerland) to have taken part in every winter Olympic Games to be held since 1924. London, has hosted the Olympic Games twice (in 1908 and 1948), and will again have the privilege of hosting it in 2012.

The British Olympic movement

The **British Olympic Association** (BOA) was formed in 1905. Today its members include elected officials representing the governing bodies of the summer and winter Olympic sports and professional staff. The professional staff, led by the Chief Executive, oversee the day-to-day running of the BOA. The BOA develops and protects the ideals of the Olympic movement throughout Great Britain in line with the Olympic Charter, and supports and leads the best-prepared Great Britain Olympic team (Team GB) to compete in each summer, winter and youth Olympic Games.

Working with the national governing bodies, the BOA selects Team GB from the best sportsmen and women. Every aspect of Team GB's preparation is planned in detail. This involves organising visits to the host city prior to the Olympic Games and creating an exclusive preparation camp with the best facilities for Team GB to use in the weeks before the Games. This helps Team GB athletes to prepare and acclimatise before they settle into the Olympic Village.

The BOA runs programmes to assist athletes throughout their training, not just in the lead-up to an Olympic Games. Athletes are helped to find jobs that fit around their training and competition, and discounts are provided at national and local sports centres.

Team GB athletes have access to the best medical advice and support whenever they need it at the **Olympic Medical Institute**. The team of experienced doctors, nutritionists, physiotherapists and other medical personnel ensures that athletes recover from injury quickly and are in top condition to compete at the Games.

Youth Olympic festivals give young Team GB athletes a taste of the Olympic experience and the opportunity to compete at a multi-sport event. In association with the Olympic governing bodies, the BOA selects and manages a team for the youth festivals.

The **British Olympic Foundation** (BOF) is the charitable arm of the BOA. It is committed to inspiring through sport and education. The BOF aims to raise the profile and understanding of the Olympic principles and ideals through a wide range of activities. The BOF also aims to encourage participation in sport and hosts many events to promote physical activity and the benefits of leading a healthy lifestyle.

For London 2012, the BOA aims to field the largest and most competitive Team GB ever. Its ambition is to finish fourth in the overall medal table.

Four organisations are responsible for delivering the 2012 Olympic Games. Known as key stakeholders, they are the BOA, the UK government, the Mayor of London, and the London Organising Committee of the Olympic Games (LOCOG). Each organisation has specific commitments to fulfil and its own dedicated role in the project.

The BOA's role is defined by three commitments:
- to secure success in the Olympic Games
- to promote, through sport, the Olympic ideals across the 2012 programme
- to deliver a viable London Olympic institute

The International Olympic Committee

The International Olympic Committee (IOC), based in Lausanne, Switzerland, is the supreme authority of the Olympic Movement. It has a variety of aims including:
- to ensure the regular celebration of the Olympic Games
- to fight against any form of discrimination affecting the Olympic Movement
- to support and encourage the promotion of sports ethics
- to lead the fight against doping in sport
- to oppose any political or commercial abuse of sport and athletes
- to see that the Olympic Games are held in conditions that demonstrate a responsible concern for environmental issues
- to support the International Olympic Academy

There are 21 special working groups, known as Commissions, appointed by the President of the IOC to facilitate the IOC's work in specific areas. The Commissions have an advisory function and include:

- Athletes
- Ethics
- Press
- Olympic Solidarity
- Culture and Olympic Education
- Programme
- Radio and Television

The IOC has created a number of symbols and practices to spread the values and ideals of the Olympic message. The following message appears on the scoreboard at every Olympic Games:

> The most important thing in the Olympic Games is not to win but to take part, just as the most important thing in life is not the triumph but the struggle. The essential thing is not to have conquered but to have fought well.

The Olympic symbol, designed by de Coubertin in 1913, is five interconnected rings, three on the top and two below, representing the five continents involved in the Olympic Games. Each ring is a different colour.

The motto of the Olympic Games is 'Citius, Altius, Fortius', which means 'swifter, higher, stronger'. It was created by Father Didon, a friend of de Coubertin.

At each opening ceremony, a representative of all the competitors must repeat the Olympic oath:

In the name of all competitors, I promise that we will take part in these Olympic Games, respecting and abiding by the rules which govern them, in the true spirit of sportsmanship, for the glory of sport and honour of our teams.

Commercialisation of the Olympic Games

The most successful era of corporate sponsorship began in 1984 at the Los Angeles Olympic Games. For the first time, the organising committee for the Games separated sponsors into three categories:

- official sponsor
- official supplier
- official licensee

The profit from the LA Games was over $US200 million. In contrast, Canadian taxpayers were paying for the 1976 Montreal Games for decades afterwards.

Sponsorship is now an important source of financial support to the Olympic movement. Sponsors also provide other support services, such as products, technical support and staff development. Futhermore, public awareness and support for the Olympic movement is increased through the promotional activities of the sponsors.

As the sponsors' roles have increased, the biggest challenge has been to ensure that the Games do not become uncontrollably commercial. To this end, the IOC is responsible for the overall management of the Olympic marketing programmes of the Games. It has decreased the number of major corporate sponsors of the Games and insists on no advertising within the stadiums or on the competitors.

In 1985, the IOC created The Olympic Partner Programme (TOP) to diversify the revenue base for the Games and the Olympic movement. TOP is made up of multi-national organisations. TOP sponsors, in return for their financial commitment, are guaranteed exclusive and worldwide marketing opportunities within an agreed category, for example soft drinks and Coca-Cola. This is a unique benefit to sponsors, which ensures that their competitors may not associate themselves with an Olympic team or the Olympic Games anywhere in the world. TOP sponsors also have the opportunity to use the Olympic symbols, as well as appropriate Olympic designations. For example, Kodak can use 'Proud sponsors of the Olympic Games' on their merchandise. The Games can also be used for hospitality opportunities and for the show-casing of products.

TOP revenue is shared: 50% goes to the organising committees of the Olympic Games and Winter Olympic Games, 40% to National Olympic Committees and 10% to the IOC itself. In addition to sponsorship, the sale of broadcasting rights and ticket revenues also fund the Games and National Olympic Committees.

London 2012

There is no doubt that hosting the Olympic Games has a massive impact on sport and society in general for the host country. London 2012 will have a number of potential benefits to the UK including:

- improvement in sports facilities in London and the rest of the UK
- urban regeneration and new housing — for example, a purpose-built Olympic Park will be built for 2012 to include 9000 new homes around the deprived area of Stratford in east London
- improved transport links and infrastructure
- economic benefits and increased tourism
- raised participation levels
- national pride
- healthier nation, social control
- integration, social inclusion

Young people in particular will also benefit from positive role models inspiring participation and from extra sporting opportunities such as UK School Games.

However, critics have been quick to point out that London 2012 also has some possible negative aspects, including:

- relocation of homes and businesses — for example, compulsory purchase orders will be required to clear land for the 2012 Olympic Park
- increased cost to taxpayers and diversion of funds from other areas of society — council tax rises of around £20 per household are expected
- a legacy of debt if it is not commercially successful
- increased security risk, threat of terrorism
- disruption of normal life due to large numbers of tourists
- legacy of unused and expensive facilities
- future bids for Games may be affected if hosting them is unsuccessful

The Olympic Games and nation building

The role of sport in nation building is multi-faceted: a victory in a major sporting event is of national importance. Sporting success attracts international attention and leads to exposure and respect for the country on the world stage. Appeasement of the population is an important feature of nation building and success at the Olympics keeps the nation happy and content and leads to national pride.

www.london2012.com

An artist's impression of the 2012 Olympic stadium in London

Communist cultures such as China have traditionally used sport for political motives. The 'shop window effect', a form of propaganda, is a key feature of sport in communist cultures, where success in world events such as the Olympics is highlighted while internal problems are often ignored.

Sporting success often equates with political success, so positive role models are used to promote the country's status.

Shop window effect: where sporting success equates with political success and a country is shown in its best possible light.

Key term

A key feature of sport in communist cultures is authoritarian control by the state rather than the pursuit of sport for self-fulfilment, that is, it is functional. Sport is controlled centrally (centralised, government controlled) to promote collectivism — everyone works together to achieve the same (communist) goals.

The Olympic Games are often the chosen stage on which communist countries have tried to prove their superiority in sport and hence show the world that their political system works best. High-profile Olympic sports are therefore chosen for investment by the state, which is often disproportionate in relation to such issues as health and education.

Economic benefits arising from hosting the 2008 Beijing Olympics may also be important for China's nation building, for example through increased tourism, a higher level of media attraction and advertising, and more investment in industry.

Figure 14.13 Features of nation building

Top tip

Communist countries like China use sport for both internal and external political motives. Success in world events like the Olympics is used to appease the population in the face of hardship and to promote the success of communism to the rest of the world.

Practice makes perfect

1 Explain what is meant by the term **mass participation**. *(2 marks)*

2 Which factors have led to the increase in opportunities for women to participate in football in the UK? *(4 marks)*

3 Identify a range of factors that can influence an individual's participation in sport and recreation. *(5 marks)*

4 Describe the structure of the UKSI and explain its functions. *(3 marks)*

5 Explain how a home country sports organisation such as Sport England influences mass participation in the UK. *(3 marks)*

6 How can the media help to develop sports participation and excellence in the UK? *(3 marks)*

7 Discuss the suggestion that elite sports performers should be allowed to use performance-enhancing drugs just like other training aids. *(6 marks)*

Unit G452

Acquiring, developing
and evaluating practical
skills in physical education

Chapter 15
Coursework

Performance, coaching and officiating

You will be assessed in *two activities* from *two different* activity profiles. You have three choices:

- you can perform two activities from two different activity profiles
- you can perform one chosen activity and coach or lead one chosen activity from two different physical activity profiles
- you can perform one chosen activity and officiate one chosen activity from two different physical activity profiles

The specification classifies physical activities into different activity profiles. These activity profiles are those identified in the National Curriculum with the addition of combat activities. The activity profiles are described as follows:

- **Athletic activities** The performance and refinement of a range of dynamic skills with the intention of improving personal and collective bests in relation to speed, height, distance and accuracy, for example athletics.
- **Combat activities** Performers select, develop, apply and adapt skills, strategies and tactics with the intention of outwitting their opponent in a range of different combats, for example boxing and tae kwon do.
- **Dance activities** Performers use their imagination and ideas to create, perform, appreciate and develop dances with an awareness of historical and cultural contexts. The artistic intention makes use of rhythm, space and relationships, expressing and communicating ideas, moods and feelings.
- **Game activities** Performers select, apply and adapt skills, strategies and tactics, on their own and in teams, with the intention of outwitting the opposition in a range of different game types. The game activity context is subdivided into:
  - **Invasion game activities** such as football, rugby, netball, hockey and basketball
  - **Net/wall game activities** such as tennis, badminton, volleyball and squash
  - **Striking/fielding game activities** such as cricket and rounders
  - **Target game activities** such as golf
- **Gymnastic activities** Performers devise aesthetically pleasing sequences using combinations of skills and agility, which they repeat and perform with increasing control, precision and fluency, for example gymnastics and trampolining.

- **Outdoor and adventurous activities** Performers develop, individually and in teams, the ability to analyse, plan and then respond effectively and safely to physical challenges and problems they encounter in familiar, changing and unfamiliar environments, for example canoeing.
- **Swimming activities and water safety** Performers develop the confidence and ability to stay afloat and to swim unaided for sustained periods of time, selecting, adapting and refining their skills so that they can swim safely and engage in a variety of different activities in and around water.
- **Safe and effective exercise activities** Performers exercise safely and effectively for the benefit of health and wellbeing, for example weight training.

Invasion games, such as basketball, form one category of games in which OCR students can be assessed

Performing an activity

In all activity profiles the emphasis is on acquiring and developing skills to the highest level, both in isolation and under more pressurised situations, for example when player, space or skill restrictions are applied. You need to be able to perform skills consistently, precisely and with control and fluency. It is important that you demonstrate clearly an understanding of the perceptual requirements of an activity that you are performing, that is, decision-making. You should have a clear knowledge of the rules, regulations and codes of practice of your chosen activity.

Chapter 15 Coursework

You will be assessed on a range of skills in a conditioned, competitive situation. You need to be able to:

- perform skills from simple to complex level
- develop and improve your skills
- select and apply the relevant skills and tactics if you have chosen a game or open environment
- select and apply the relevant choreography/compositional ideas in activities such as dance, gymnastics and trampolining
- understand and apply the relevant rules, regulations and codes of practice of the activities chosen
- understand the fitness and health benefits of the activity

Coaching or leading an activity

When coaching or leading an activity, you will be assessed on your ability to lead a safe, purposeful and enjoyable session. You need to show qualities such as motivation, responsibility, control and confidence.

It may be that you work with primary school children in TOP Sport or Dragon Sport sessions, or with youth groups or local clubs. Whatever the context, you need to:

- structure your sessions so that the participants are challenged
- be well organised in the planning and delivery of sessions
- communicate appropriately and clearly
- be aware of health and safety procedures
- utilise appropriate risk assessment procedures
- understand the fitness and health aspects of the activity
- evaluate each session and plan for the next one
- be aware of child protection issues and procedures
- ensure that all those present are included in the session as fully as possible

Throughout these sessions you need to keep a detailed log that should include the following:

- a 3-month record of your coaching/leading
- a scheme of work that should include a description of 10 hours of session plans — make sure that you evaluate each of these sessions and design an overall risk assessment
- a personal video record of at least 40 minutes' duration
- details of the health and safety issues relevant to the activity, for example checking equipment, looking at the safety of using the facility, performing warm-ups and cool-downs etc.
- details of child protection procedures
- evidence of any first-aid qualifications you have
- details of the health and fitness benefits of the activity — as a coach you should be a positive role model in terms of your own health and fitness levels, and physical demonstrations will give you the opportunity to improve your own levels of fitness — and what you gain while coaching/leading the activity, such as a sense of achievement and development of leadership skills

Officiating an activity

When officiating an activity you will be assessed on your ability to officiate in a safe, purposeful and enjoyable manner and will need to show qualities such as responsibility, control and confidence. You need to ensure you select an appropriate officiating style and show consistency and adaptability. You should:

- be able to officiate in challenging situations
- display a knowledge of the rules and regulations of the activity
- be able to communicate appropriately
- understand and appreciate health and safety procedures
- be able to implement a risk assessment
- be aware of child protection issues and procedures
- understand the fitness and health aspects of the activity
- be able to evaluate your officiating after each session and plan for improvements

Throughout these sessions you need to keep a detailed log that should include the following:

- a record of your officiating over a 3-month period
- a minimum of four evaluations of your officiating by qualified assessors
- evidence of risk assessments
- a personal video of 40 minutes of officiating
- details of health and safety issues relevant to the activity you are officiating
- details of child protection procedures
- details of the health and fitness benefits of the activity — for example, as a football referee you will improve your speed and cardiovascular endurance — and what benefit you receive while officiating the activity

Simon Marshall

A PE student prepares to officiate in a netball game, as part of her coursework

Evaluating and planning for the improvement of performance

Assessment for this coursework takes place via a verbal interview. To prepare for this interview, you will need to observe a live performance by another candidate in one of your own assessed activities. You will then need to consider the factors that make an effective and efficient performance in this activity (for example, perfect technical models of skills).

You will be required to critically evaluate the following:

- the **quality** of the acquired and developed **skills**. Here, you need to look at the strengths and weaknesses of skills such as passing (different types), shooting (different types), dribbling, intercepting, defending and marking, heading, tackling, footwork etc. In individual sports, these skills will be different. For swimming, look at the arm action, the leg action, head position, body position, breathing and overall efficiency of the stroke.
- the success of the **selection** and **application** of **skills**, **tactics** or **compositional ideas**. Look at any tactics relevant to your activity, for example in rugby league kicking the ball at the in-goal to force a drop out from the opposition so that you can regain possession, or in hockey working on short corners as an important way of scoring. Knowledge of tactics will come from participating in your activity and from coaching manuals, internet sites and your coach or teacher.
- the **fitness** and **health** aspects of the activity observed. Make sure the fitness components you evaluate are relevant to your sport. There are many to choose from:
  - physical/health components — stamina, maximum strength, explosive strength, muscular endurance, flexibility
  - skill/motor components — coordination, agility, speed, balance and reaction time

Preparation for the verbal interview

When making your evaluative responses you need to use appropriate technical language, and discuss the **strengths** and the **weaknesses** of the performance observed in terms of skills, tactical/compositional ideas and fitness.

Skills

Watch the skill closely and list the coaching points of the skill under the phases relevant to your activity. Then use these coaching points to state the strengths and weaknesses you can see in the performance (see Table 15.1). If you have two or three coaching points under each heading, you will then have about nine strengths and weaknesses to comment on. When looking at skills it is important to look at the phases. For example:

- games — preparation, execution, recovery and result, overall efficiency
- competitive swimming — arm action, leg action, body position, breathing, overall efficiency
- athletics: track — posture, leg action, arm action, head carriage, overall efficiency; jumps — approach, take-off, flight, landing, overall efficiency; throwing — initial stance, grip and preparation, travel and trunk position, throwing action, release, overall efficiency

The following table design might help you if you are evaluating a game. For this part of the interview you can write down what you see and refer to your notes.

Tactics and compositional ideas

Look at any tactics/compositional ideas relevant to your activity. Be aware of some before the interview so that you can comment on them. Knowledge of tactics and compositional ideas

Table 15.1 Evaluating performance

Phase	Coaching points	Strengths/weaknesses
Preparation	1	1
	2	2
	3	3
Execution	1	1
	2	2
	3	3
Result and recovery	1	1
	2	2
Overall efficiency	1	1
	2	2

will come from participating in your activity, from coaching manuals and from your coach or teacher.

Fitness

Make sure that the fitness components are relevant to your sport. These components are defined below, so choose which you think are the most appropriate.

Stamina

Stamina is also referred to as aerobic capacity, VO_2 max or cardiovascular endurance. It can be defined as the ability to take in and use oxygen. Stamina is important for participation in continuous submaximal activity, such as swimming, running or cycling. In team games such as hockey and football, it helps the performer to withstand fatigue and last the duration of the game.

Simon Marshall

A PE student undergoes a fitness test

Maximum strength

Maximum strength is the maximum force a muscle is capable of exerting in a single voluntary contraction. It is used in weightlifting, for example. Men can exert a greater maximum strength than women because they have a larger muscle mass, due to higher levels of testosterone. Fast glycolytic fibres are important for maximum strength as they can produce more force than slow-twitch fibres.

Explosive/elastic strength (power)

Power is the amount of work performed per unit of time (power = strength × speed). It is the ability to overcome resistance with a high speed of contraction. This can be seen in explosive events such as sprinting, throwing or hitting, where a high percentage of fast glycolytic fibres is needed for a good performance.

Strength endurance

Strength endurance is the ability of a muscle to perform repeated contractions and withstand fatigue. It is important for rowers and swimmers, where the same muscle action is repeated. In addition, when a team game goes to extra time, the players with better strength endurance are in a stronger position to maintain a high level of performance. This type of strength is characterised by a high proportion of type 1 (slow oxidative) and type 2a (fast oxidative glycolytic) fibres.

Flexibility

Good flexibility helps to improve performance and avoid injury. It can also help to generate faster and more forceful muscle contractions. There are two main types of flexibility:
- **static** flexibility is the range of movement around a joint, for example doing the splits
- **dynamic** flexibility is the resistance of a joint to movement, for example kicking a football without hamstring and hip-joint resistance

Coordination

Coordination is the ability of the motor and nervous systems to interact so that motor tasks can be performed accurately. Examples include the hand–eye coordination required to hit a tennis ball, and being able to coordinate the swing of a golf club to hit the ball correctly. Speed, balance, control, agility, precision, rhythm and fluency of execution are all important components of coordination.

Agility

Agility is the ability to move and position the body quickly and effectively while under control. The combination of speed, coordination, balance and flexibility is very important. For example, it is used in netball for catching and passing on the run, or in basketball for dribbling around opponents.

Speed

Speed refers to how fast a person can move over a specified distance, or how quickly a body part can be put into motion. Speed is important in most sports. For example, a winger in rugby needs to be able to sprint quickly and a pace bowler in cricket needs to be able to move his arm quickly. Fibre type plays a major role in terms of speed. A greater number of fast glycolytic fibres means that stimuli are received more quickly and energy is released anaerobically, making the performer faster than someone with a greater number of slow-twitch fibres. The proportion of fast glycolytic fibres is determined genetically.

Balance

Balance is the ability to keep the centre of gravity over the base of support. Balance can be static, such as in a handstand in gymnastics, which has to be kept still, or dynamic, where balance is retained while in motion, for example when side-stepping in rugby to get around an opponent.

Reaction time

Reaction time is the time taken from detection of a stimulus to initiation of a response, for example the time taken between the starting pistol going off and movement from the blocks, or reacting to a tennis serve.

Areas for improvement

Having looked at skills, tactical/compositional ideas and fitness, you will have an idea of which parts of the performance can be improved. You now need to devise an action plan detailing what the performer needs to do in order to improve. Your action plan should contain the following points:

- **goals** — what you are aiming to achieve
- **time scale** — how long your action plan will take. It may also be useful to suggest how long it might take to perfect each part of a skill and how long you might spend on each practice to try to improve the skill.
- **method of achieving goals.** Give a detailed description of the coaching points and drills you would use to help the performer improve his/her level of skill, starting with the easiest. Make sure that your practices are progressive, starting at a level that is appropriate to the performer you are observing and gradually becoming more difficult to reflect improvements.
- **method for evaluating achievement of goals.** It is a good idea to mention how you will check your

Simon Marshall

The handstand is not an easy skill to master

success in achieving your goals. A specific test will help, for example Cooper's 12-minute run if you have looked at stamina, or a stats sheet before and after your action plan if you are looking at a game skill. The sport you are looking at may have specific skills tests you can use to monitor improvement.

Opportunities to participate

There are several national agencies that promote sporting activity in the UK, for example Sport England, the national governing bodies of sport and the Youth Sport Trust. These agencies provide funding, resources, coaches and sports leaders, giving people the opportunity to take part in sport. Look at what is available in your area. The following list is a helpful guide:

- school PE and extra-curricular activities
- School Sports Coordinators
- local clubs
- leisure centres (activities, competitions, leagues)
- specialist coaching

Fitness aspects

Decide which of the components of fitness are relevant and then look at the performer and highlight his/her strengths and weaknesses. It might be a good idea to try some fitness tests to confirm your judgements.

Short- and long-term health benefits

You need to understand that physical activity is an essential component of a healthy lifestyle. It can impact upon your physical, mental and social wellbeing. Physical activity can give you confidence, determination to succeed, mental alertness and enable you to deal with emotions (mental benefits). Physically, it can benefit the muscular and skeletal systems, the heart, lungs and the vascular system. These are all discussed in detail in the anatomy section of this book. It is important that you relate such detail appropriately to your chosen activity.

Answers

Tasks to tackle

1.1 (page 5)

Joint	Joint type	Articulating bones
Ankle	Hinge	Tibia, fibula, talus
Knee	Hinge	Tibia, femur
Hip	Ball and socket	Head of femur and pelvis (acetabulum)
Spine	Gliding	Vertebral arches
Shoulder	Ball and socket	Humerus, scapula (glenoid fossa)
Elbow	Elbow	Humerus, radius, ulna
Wrist	Condyloid	Carpals, radius, ulna

1.2 (page 8)

	Wrist	Elbow	Radio-ulnar	Shoulder	Spine	Hip	Knee	Ankle
Flexion		✔		✔	✔	✔	✔	
Extension		✔		✔	✔	✔	✔	
Abduction				✔		✔		
Adduction				✔		✔		
Rotation				✔	✔	✔		
Horizontal flexion				✔				
Horizontal extension				✔				
Plantar-flexion								✔
Circum-duction				✔		✔		
Dorsiflexion	✔							✔
Palmar-flexion	✔							
Supination			✔					
Pronation			✔					
Lateral flexion					✔			

1.3 (page 18)

	Movement	Muscle	Type of contraction
1	Flexion	Triceps brachii	Eccentric
2	Extension	Triceps brachii	Concentric
3	—	Triceps brachii	Isometric

1.4 (page 18)

Joint	Joint type	Articulating bones	Movement	Agonist muscle	Antagonist muscle	Type of contraction
Right elbow	Hinge	Radius, ulna, humerus	Extension	Triceps brachii	Biceps brachii	Concentric
Right shoulder	Ball and socket	Head of the humerus and scapula (glenoid fossa)	Flexion	Anterior deltoid	Posterior deltoid	Concentric
Spine	Gliding	Vertebral arches	Flexion	Rectus abdominus	Erector spinae (sacrospinalis)	Concentric
Right hip	Ball and socket	Head of femur and pelvis (acetabulum)	Extension	Gluteus maximus	Iliopsoas	Concentric
Left knee	Hinge	Tibia, femur	Extension	Rectus femoris	Biceps femoris	Concentric
Left ankle	Hinge	Tibia, fibula, talus	Dorsiflexion	Tibialis anterior	Gastrocnemius	Concentric

1.6 (page 22)

Elite athlete	Predominant fibre type
Marathon runner	Slow oxidative
100 metres sprinter	Fast glycolytic
Centre in netball	Fast oxidative glycolytic/fast glycolytic
Speed cyclist	Fast glycolytic
Endurance swimmer	Slow oxidative

2.2 (page 27)

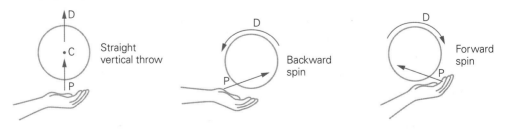

180

2.3 (page 28)

    (a) No. The centre of mass moves forward outside the body and causes you to fall forward.

    (b) No. Your centre of mass moves forward outside the base of support and causes you to nose dive.

3.1 (page 31) gastrocnemius → vena cava → right atrium → tricuspid valve → right ventricle → semilunar valve → pulmonary artery → lungs → pulmonary vein → left atrium → bicuspid valve → left ventricle → semilunar valve → aorta

4.1 (page 46)

	Before exercise	During exercise	Recovery
Blood pressure changes	Increases	Increases at first and when steady state is reached, decreases	Decreases

5.1 (page 50)

nose → pharynx → larynx → trachea → bronchi → bronchioles → lungs → alveoli

6.1 (page 60)

Ability	Skill
Innate	Learned
Enduring	Consistent
Foundation of skill	Goal-directed
Specific to the task	Aesthetic

6.2 (page 61) Any skill may be chosen with associated abilities and fundamental skills, as long as there is a link between them.

6.3 (page 64) The answers depend on the skill chosen. Refer to the criteria on pp. 61–64 to make sure that your answer is correct.

7.1 (page 65)

Task	Performer
Danger	Motivation
Open or closed skill	Ability
Organisation	Age
Complexity	Experience

7.2 (page 69) The answer depends on the skill chosen. Refer to the text to ensure that the answer is correct.

Answers

8.1 (page 76) The display is the sporting environment from which information is gathered. Selective attention is the process by which information is filtered into relevant and irrelevant items.

8.2 (page 77) The types of feedback required for a novice are positive, extrinsic and knowledge of results.

8.3 (page 78) The short-term memory is the working memory. It has a limited capacity, receives information from the sensory stores, and passes information to and receives information from the long-term memory.

The long-term memory stores motor programmes, has an infinite capacity and lasts for a lifetime. It receives information from the short-term memory and passes this information back to the short-term memory when required.

9.1 (page 85) A motor programme can be developed by practising key points both mentally and physically, and by using intrinsic and extrinsic feedback.

9.2 (page 85) Any skill with appropriate subroutines, e.g. tennis serve — grip, ball placement, the hit, trunk rotation, footwork

10.1 (page 89) The coach could offer praise, reinforcement and rewards, set attainable goals, use role models, vary practice, allow success in practice, attribute success internally and use positive feedback.

11.1 (page 94)

Phase of learning	Practice	Feedback	Guidance
Cognitive	Part practice, distributed practice, varied practice	Extrinsic, positive and knowledge of results	Mechanical and manual
Associative	Whole–part–whole, whole, progressive part	Intrinsic and extrinsic using information from the coach, knowledge of performance	Visual and verbal
Autonomous	Whole, fixed, massed	Intrinsic and extrinsic in terms of the coach improving the finer details	Verbal

11.2 (page 95) Whole approach — the skill should be studied in its entirety, not in parts; so the solution to winning the 1500 m race should not be based just on the last lap.

Problem solving — performance should solve questions that are posed by the situation, such as how you overcome a powerful serve in tennis.

Experience/insight — performers should use what they already know to arrive at the answer, for example how did you combat the serve of a powerful player in your last tennis match?

Understanding — the performer should know the reasons for the answer, for example I will reduce the power of the powerful server by making her move around the court to drain her energy before serving.

11.3 (page 104) Positive reinforcement is the use of a pleasant stimulus after a correct response to strengthen the S–R bond. Negative reinforcement is the withdrawal of either a pleasant stimulus after an incorrect response or the withdrawal of criticism after a correct response.

12.1 (page 106)

(a) Yes

(b) Yes

(c) No — you have to do this

(d) No — you have obligations as you are paid to do sport for a living

(e) No — you have to go once you have enrolled

12.2 (page 109)

- It can be played at any age or ability level.
- It is physically active with health benefits.
- It is a sociable game.
- It can be played recreationally.
- It is accessible to everyone via a range of public or private facilities.

12.3 (page 110) Any three from:

- availability of equipment/facilities
- availability of time
- availability of money
- availability of coaching
- level of self-confidence
- PE experience/status of PE in school
- geographical location
- friends/peer pressure

12.4 (page 112)

(a) Health and fitness, less strain on the NHS, social integration, friendships formed

(b) As (a) plus social control/less crime

12.5 (page 113) Any four from:

- develop physical fitness and skills; improve motor skills in a range of different activities such as games and gymnastics
- develop social skills; improve teamwork in games such as rugby and netball
- prepare for active leisure or a career via enjoyment, skills and qualifications gained during a PE programme (e.g. Community Sports Leadership Award)

- improve quality of life via outdoor and adventurous activities, where pupils gain an aesthetic appreciation of the natural environment
- develop cognitive skills — PE involves many activities, that require decision-making (e.g. tactics) and understanding of rules

12.6 (page 116)

(a) Yes, mountain biking in the natural environment could involve being taught safe techniques of descent (coming down mountains and steep natural hills safely).

(b) No, hockey is normally played on Astroturf, which is artificial.

(c) Yes, as orienteering in the natural environment — being taught how to read a map and take a compass bearing could be part of a pupil's OAA experience.

12.7 (page 116) Examples: mountain biking, sailing, skiing, orienteering, *if* it is competitive, strict rules are applied (which help determine a winner), there is a national governing body to oversee the activity as a sport, judges or officials are present and extrinsic rewards are available (possibly professional opportunities available).

12.8 (page 117) None, as this answer is irrelevant to the question set. The answer links to functions and benefits to society, not to the characteristics. The key to success in exams is to answer the question set.

13.1 (page 120) It would potentially earn you 7 marks. Some of these words are similar and would therefore only earn you 1 mark because they would appear under the same point on a mark scheme, for example rural/isolated, festival/ritual.

13.2 (page 122) You need to make some relevant key point and give a brief elaboration of them:
- large amounts of time available/boarding influence
- money — regular income from fees
- facilities — specialist facilities provided, such as swimming baths
- staff expertise — specialist coaches/teachers were employed
- positive role models — participation was encouraged by sixth formers and games masters
- regularity of play, for example games afternoons
- competitive play, for example inter-house/inter-school fixtures
- compulsion — daily games were compulsory in many public schools

14.1 (page 133) Any three from:
- Active Schools/Active Communities/Active Sports
- Sports Colleges/SSCos
- Activemark/Sportsmark/Sports Partnership Mark
- PESSCL
- National Junior Sport Programme/TOPs
- Sport Action Zones

14.2 (page 135)

- Run by Youth Sport Trust/for 7–11-year-olds/part of Sport England's Active Schools Project
- In partnership with LEAs/SSCos/NGBs
- Supports National Curriculum PE
- Provides sport-specific/age-related equipment in a range of activities
- Provides illustrated resource cards for teaching skills
- Provides training for teachers by qualified trainers

14.3 (page 137)

- It can be played at any age.
- It is a physical activity with health benefits.
- It has a handicap system of play, so all abilities/ages/genders can play/compete together.
- It is a sociable game.
- It can be played recreationally for social benefits.

14.4 (page 141)

- Oversees the UKSI
- Runs the 100% ME programme/doping control
- Distribution of lottery funds to the elite/World Class Performance programme
- Runs the World Class Events programme
- Talent ID programmes

14.5 (page 142)

- Talent ID schemes
- Select performers for World Class programme/Sports Aid/TASS funding
- Support them financially
- Give access to top-level facilities/equipment
- Train specialist coaches/provide specialist training camps
- Provide sports science support
- Organise/provide information about competitions
- Provide lifestyle advice/mentors

Note: it is important that in your answers to questions about elite-level performance you refer to top-level/specialist provision and avoid simply writing 'more facilities', 'more coaches' etc.

14.6 (page 144) Factors negatively affecting your participation will obviously be personal to you, but may include:

- lack of free time due to academic/work commitments
- lack of money
- norms/stereotypes of society against you participating in certain activities (e.g. rugby if you are female, dance if you are male)
- lack of clubs to pursue the activities of your choice
- poor PE experiences, putting you off participation

14.7 (page 146)
- Verbal/sexual harassment
- Fewer clubs/restrictive membership clauses/fewer competitions
- Lower funding/costs too high
- Less media coverage/fewer role models

14.8 (page 155)
- Increase school–club links/share coaches/facilities
- Observe government policy (e.g. PESSCL/sports colleges/SSCos)
- Offer discounts/subsidised use of facilities
- Taster days
- Offer different ways of participating
- Increase awareness of health and fitness issues

Practice makes perfect

Chapter 1 (page 23)

1 **(a)** Agonist is gastrocnemius/soleus (1 mark); type of contraction is concentric (1 mark)

(b) Eccentric contraction (1 mark); muscle is lengthening under tension/acting as a brake/performing negative work (1 mark)

2

Joint	Joint type	Articulating bones	Movement produced	Agonist
Ankle	**Hinge**	Talus, tibia and fibula	Plantarflexion	**Gastrocnemius/ soleus**
Knee	Hinge	**Femur and tibia**	Extension	**Rectus femoris/ vastus lateralis/ vastus intermedius/ vastus medialis**
Hip	Ball and socket	**Acetabulum and pelvis**	**Extension**	Gluteus maximus

(max. 6 marks)

3 Any four for 4 marks:
- biceps femoris/semi-membranosus/semitendinosus
- is the agonist

- rectus femoris/vastus lateralis/vastus medialis/vastus intermedius
- is the antagonist
- work in opposition/when one contracts the other lengthens/returns to resting length

4 Fibre type — fast glycolytic/type IIb (1 mark)
Structures (sub-max. 2):
- large size
- low myoglobin concentration
- large glycogen store
- few capillaries
- high elasticity (or equivalent)
- few mitochondria

Functions (sub-max. 2):
- quick contraction speed
- produce a vast amount of force
- tire quickly/fatigue quickly
- high anaerobic capacity/low aerobic capacity   (max. 5 marks)

5 Mark only the first two answers.
Any two for 2 marks:
- muscle temperature increases, which enables oxygen to dissociate more easily from haemoglobin
- increase in the speed of nerve impulse conduction
- greater elasticity of the muscle fibres occurs through the increase in muscle temperature
- reduction in muscle viscosity improves coordination between antagonistic pairs
- increase in enzyme activity in the warmer muscle fibres increases speed and strength of muscle contraction

6 Identification of any repetitive activity (1 mark)
Implications — any two for 2 marks:
- inflammation of bursae
- wearing down of articular/hyaline cartilage
- muscle strain/tissue damage
- growth-plate injuries in children, common sites — elbows/knees/shoulders/heels

Chapter 2 (page 29)

1 **(a)** The direction of the force must go through the centre of mass of the object to produce linear motion (1 mark), with example (1 mark).

(b) The position of application of the force must be outside the centre of mass of the object to produce angular motion (1 mark), with example (1 mark).

2 • Size — the larger the force the further and/or faster an object will go.
  • Direction — if a force is applied through the middle/centre of mass of an object, it will travel in a straight line.
  • Position of application — applying a force outside the middle/centre of mass of an object will allow it to spin.

  3 marks for the above explanations or similar, but examples must be given or marks cannot be awarded.

3 Any three for 3 marks:
  • centre of mass must be over base of support
  • on balance in the set position
  • centre of mass needs to be as close to the edge of the area of support as possible
  • when hands are removed the athlete will overbalance/centre of gravity moves outside the base of support

4 1 mark for each of the following, with a sporting example:
  • Law of inertia — unless a force is applied, an object will remain stationary or continue moving in the same direction.
  • Law of acceleration — the greater the force applied, the further and faster the object will travel.
  • Law of reaction — whenever an object exerts a force on a second object there will be an equal and opposite force from the second object on the first.

5 1 mark for a named gymnastic balance.
  1 mark each for any three of the following:
  • centre of mass needs to be over the base of support
  • line of gravity should be through the middle of the base of support
  • the number of contact points, for example a handstand has two, a headstand has three
  • the lower the centre of mass, the more stable the balance

Chapter 3 (page 39)

1 Any three for 3 marks:
  • diastole phase
  • heart is relaxed
  • blood enters the atria during ventricular diastole
  • bicuspid and tricuspid valves are shut

  Any three for 3 marks:
  • systole phase
  • heart is contracted
  • atrial systole — blood is forced through the bicuspid and tricuspid valves into the ventricles

- ventricular systole — the pressure of blood in the ventricles increases, opening the semilunar valves
- blood is ejected into the pulmonary artery and aorta

2

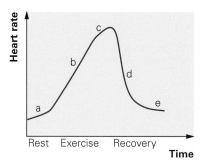

1 mark for labelling each of the following (max. 4):

a = the anticipatory rise due to the hormonal action of adrenaline

b = a sharp rise in heart rate at the beginning of exercise due mainly to anaerobic work

c = the heart rate continues to rise due to maximal workloads stressing the anaerobic system

d = a rapid decline in heart rate as soon as the exercise stops

e = a slower recovery as the body systems return to resting levels (but the heart rate is still above resting level)

3 Stroke volume is the amount of blood pumped by the heart ventricles/left ventricle (not the heart) per beat (1 mark).

Heart rate is the number of beats per minute (1 mark).

Cardiac output is heart rate × stroke volume, or the amount of blood pumped out by the heart ventricles/left ventricle (not the heart) per minute (1 mark).

They all increase (to supply the muscles with extra blood and therefore the extra oxygen they need) (1 mark).

4 1 mark for each of the following:
- chemoreceptors detect an increase in carbon dioxide
- medulla/cardiac control centre responds to this
- impulse is sent down the cardiac accelerator/sympathetic nerve to SA node
- heart rate increases

5 1 mark for the name of a disease.
Any two of the following for 2 marks:
- regular aerobic exercise
- reduces cholesterol and lipid levels/LDL
- increases HDL

- resistance training can lower heart rate and blood pressure
- exercise that can train and strengthen the chest muscles

Chapter 4 (page 48)

1 Any two for 2 marks:
- (97%) combines with haemoglobin
- to form oxyhaemoglobin
- (3%) dissolves in plasma

2 Any two for 2 marks:
- vasodilation occurs, so more blood flows to the working muscles
- an increase in temperature results in an increase in the transportation of enzymes necessary for energy systems and muscle contraction
- a decrease in blood viscosity improves blood flow to the working muscles
- oxygen dissociates from haemoglobin more quickly
- decrease in OBLA

3 Any four for 4 marks:
- vasomotor centre/medulla
- vasoconstriction of arterioles surrounding non-essential organs
- closing of precapillary sphincters supplying non-essential organs
- vasodilation of arterioles surrounding skeletal muscles
- opening of precapillary sphincters surrounding skeletal muscle

4

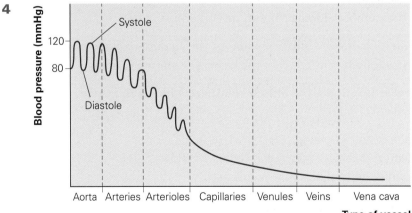

The graph should show:
- blood vessel names (1 mark)
- high pressure in arteries/arterioles (1 mark)
- rapid drop in pressure in capillaries (1 mark)
- low pressure in venules/veins (1 mark)

(max. 3 marks)

5   Any three for 3 marks:
- reduces the amount of oxygen available in the body
- carbon monoxide has a greater affinity for haemoglobin than oxygen (200 to 300 times greater)
- level of carbon monoxide absorbed in the blood increases
- level of oxygen decreases
- less oxygen is released from the blood into the muscles
- increases resistance of airways (often through the swelling of mucous membranes)

6   Any two for 2 marks:
- an active cool-down keeps the respiratory and skeletal muscle pumps working
- prevents blood pooling in the veins
- maintains venous return
- removal of lactic acid and carbon dioxide

Chapter 5 (page 57)

1   Any three for 3 marks:
- inspiration — increase the volume of the thoracic cavity/decrease the pressure
- diaphragm and external intercostals contract
- expiration — decrease the volume of the thoracic cavity/increase the pressure
- passive — diaphragm and the external intercostals relax

2 marks for:
During exercise more muscles are used in:
- inspiration — sternocleidomastoid/scalenes/pectoralis major
- expiration — internal intercostals/rectus abdominus

2   Any four for 4 marks:
- chemoreceptors/muscle receptors/baroreceptors/stretch receptors
- respiratory centre/medulla
- phrenic nerve/intercostal nerve
- inspiration: diaphragm/external intercostals contract
- expiration: internal intercostals/abdominals
- rate/depth/rhythm of breathing increases

3   Pectoralis minor (1 mark), sternocleidomastoid (1 mark)

4   Any four for 4 marks:
- gases flow from areas of high pressure to areas of low pressure
- (partial) pressure/concentration of oxygen is high in the lungs/alveoli and low in the blood
- therefore oxygen diffuses down the diffusion gradient into the blood

- (3%) dissolves in the plasma
- (97%) combines with haemoglobin
- one molecule of haemoglobin combines with four molecules of oxygen

5 4 marks in total, 3 marks max. from each section

Effects:
- haemoglobin saturation depends on partial pressure of oxygen in alveolar air/the lungs
- at altitude the pressure/concentration of oxygen is reduced
- therefore there is a reduction in the diffusion gradient
- haemoglobin is not fully saturated
- which results in lower oxygen-carrying capacity

Influences:
- therefore less oxygen is delivered to the working muscles
- so earlier onset of fatigue
- results in decrease in performance (of aerobic activities)

Chapter 6 (page 64)

1 There is no general ability in sport because abilities are specific ✔ to the task and occur in small groups ✔. For example, coordination and power are the abilities underpinning the tennis serve.

2 A continuum shows the range ✔ along which skills match certain criteria and the extent ✔ to which a specific skill matches those criteria. For example, in tennis, a return of serve is classified as an open skill because it is affected by the environment. A football pass is also open but because it involves more decision-making it is more open than the return of serve in tennis. A continuum also shows how skills can change with the situation ✔. For example, a basketball pass is open in a game but closed in practice.

3 1 mark for each of the following:
- several discrete skills are combined
- in order
- to give a more continuous task

Chapter 7 (page 72)

1 Organisation of a skill refers to the degree to which that skill can be broken down ✔. If the skill can be broken down — such as the clearly defined arm action and leg action in a swimming stroke — it can be taught in parts ✔. If the skill is hard to break down — such as the quick action of a golf swing — whole practice must be used ✔.

2 Whole practice is when the skill is taught in its entirety ✔ with the subroutines intact. It promotes fluency ✔ and understanding and may help to develop motor programmes ✔. The skill is learned with efficiency and the link between the stimulus and the response can be developed ✔.

Whole practice has the advantage that the essential links between subroutines are maintained — these links could be ignored during part practice. Part practice helps to eliminate danger ✔ — there could be a safety problem if the whole skill is attempted without prior knowledge. Some gymnastic skills are broken down into manageable sections before being attempted whole. Part practice can provide extra motivation ✔ if there is success on each small part. Whole practice may be best for experienced performers ✔ while part practice is more appropriate for novices ✔.

3 Mental rehearsal is the process of going through the skill in the mind ✔. It helps to store images in the memory, builds motor programmes ✔ and improves reaction time ✔. Mental rehearsal allows practice to take place even when the performer is injured ✔. There is evidence to suggest that a combination of mental and physical practice improves performance ✔.

Chapter 8 (page 82)

1 Any four for 4 marks:
- Use mental rehearsal to go over the performance in the mind.
- Use different types of practice to ensure the drills are stored in the memory.
- Point out similarities with information already stored, for example between a known tennis serve and an overarm volleyball serve.
- Use praise and reinforcement.
- Break the information into chunks, and make it relevant and meaningful to the performer.

2 Reaction time is the time from the onset of the stimulus to the onset of the response. (1 mark)

Movement time is the time from the start of the task to its completion. (1 mark)

Response time is the time from the onset of the stimulus to the completion of the task. (1 mark)

In a 100 m sprint, reaction time is the time from hearing the gun to leaving the blocks, movement time is the time from leaving the blocks to hitting the finish line, and response time is the time from hearing the gun to hitting the finish line. Response time is reaction time plus movement time.

Reaction time can help sports performers to gain an advantage over their opponents. They will be able to produce skilled movement at speed ✔ and they will have more time ✔ to select their options before making their play.

3 Any four for 4 marks:
- age
- gender
- experience
- performance-enhancing drugs
- fitness
- number of stimuli
- anticipation

Chapter 9 (page 86)

1 Open-loop control is when skills are controlled with almost automatic movements ✔. The skills are well learned and a motor programme ✔ may control the movements when the environment is closed so that the skill can be repeated habitually. In closed-loop control the skills may be less well learned. Closed-loop control can operate at two levels — level 2 when intrinsic feedback ✔ is used to adjust movements and level 3 ✔ when the feedback used is more conscious and movements may appear uncoordinated.

Open-loop control operates without the use of feedback ✔ during the execution of the task, although feedback can be used after the skill has been completed ✔, such as when a tennis player uses feedback from a first serve to adjust the second serve.

Open-loop control is used for fast skills ✔ where there is no time for feedback. Closed-loop control is used for continuous tasks so that the feedback is used to correct errors during the task. During closed-loop control, current movements may be compared with a memory trace as a measure of progress ✔.

2 1 mark for each of the following:
- can concentrate on the finer details of the task
- faster reaction times
- efficiency

Chapter 10 (page 92)

1 Gross skills require less muscular control than fine skills and so can be performed under high levels of arousal ✔. Fine skills need more control and a lower level of arousal. Complex skills are best performed at low levels of arousal ✔, because a number of decisions must be made. Simple skills can be performed at high levels of arousal, because few decisions are required. Beginners perform better at low levels of arousal because they may already be nervous ✔. More experienced performers are used to playing under pressure and will perform well at high levels of arousal ✔.

2 Intrinsic means from within the performer. (1 mark)
Extrinsic means from an outside source, e.g. a coach. (1 mark)

3 Any three for 3 marks:
- initial motivation and drive

- success satisfies this drive
- motivation is lost
- new challenge needed

Chapter 11 (page 104)

1 Positive transfer occurs when the learning and performance of one skill is aided ✔ by the learning and performance of another. When two skills have a similar shape, for example a tennis serve and an overarm volleyball serve, positive transfer might occur when knowledge of one is used to help the other ✔.

Negative transfer is when one skill hinders ✔ the learning and performance of another ✔. The skills may have some similarity. For example, a tennis serve and a badminton serve are both used in court games, but the actions are different and therefore confusion between the two causes negative transfer ✔.

Bilateral transfer can help performance because a skill from the stronger side of the body can be transferred to the weaker side ✔. For example, a predominantly right-footed footballer could learn to kick with the left foot.

Proactive transfer can help performance because skills that are already known are used to help skills that are currently being learnt. Retroactive transfer hinders performance because skills that are being learnt interfere with skills that are already known. Zero transfer implies no impact on the learning and performance ✔ of skills.

2 Any four for 4 marks:
- positive reinforcement, praise, rewards
- negative reinforcement
- punishment
- law of effect
- law of exercise
- law of readiness
- allow early success
- use mental rehearsal

3 1 mark for each of the following:
- initial conditions — information from the environment
- sensory consequences — information from the senses
- response specifications — what to do
- response outcome — the result

Chapter 12 (page 118)

1 Any four for 4 marks:
- competitive/serious
- structured/strict rules/time limit/space boundaries
- rules externally enforced/officials present
- extrinsic rewards available

- involves commitment/endeavour/dedication
- tactical/strategic
- high levels of physical skill/prowess
- sportsmanship

2   Physical activity in the natural environment (1 mark) in a person's free time (1 mark) with individuals having a choice (1 mark) of how to spend that time.

3   As physical recreation (1 mark): choice of whether to participate or not, winning or losing is of little importance, motives for taking part include improving health and fitness and socialising

As PE (1 mark): in lesson time at school/NC PE; teaching of skills to improve performance

As sport (1 mark): competitive game played to strict national governing body rules, high skill levels evident

4   Sportsmanship (max. 2 marks): playing by the unwritten rules/fair play; example — kicking the ball out of play if an opponent is injured/shaking hands at the end of a contest

Gamesmanship (max. 2 marks): the art of winning by 'cunning means' but without actually breaking the rules; example — time wasting/sledging

5   Any three for 3 marks:
- appreciation of the natural environment
- conservation awareness
- development of survival skills/assessment of risk
- develop cognitive skills/decision-making
- develop leadership skills/teamwork/trust
- preparation for active leisure/a career

Chapter 13 (page 129)

1   As a specific number of reasons are asked for, limit your answer to this number with a range of different points. For example, do not put social and community as two separate points — these will only earn 1 mark. Any four from:
- tradition
- religion/ritual/festival
- social/community event
- tourism
- geographical isolation
- particular to a local area
- annual/occasional

2   It is important to attempt to answer both parts of the question to earn full marks.

Positive outcomes of commercialism (max. 2 marks):
- Chances of success are improved due to high levels of funding.
- It fits in with the US culture's 'win ethic'.
- Events that might otherwise not happen occur due to commercial sponsorship.

Negative outcomes of commercialism (max. 2 marks):
- Performers become mobile adverts.
- Sponsors can dictate/control sport, e.g. venues, timings.
- Fair play values may be lost.
- Minority sports miss out; only the most profitable sports and successful performers benefit commercially.

3   With 6 marks available you should devote some time to carefully considering your answer. Devise a simple plan with a variety of points in it, along with a brief explanation of each. Use this structure to develop a well-organised, detailed response. Any six from:
- reflection of an egalitarian society/known as the 'people's game'/ accessible to all/blending all cultures
- spectators from all backgrounds
- 'frontier' is reflected in game, linking to manly image of the bush
- links to fair play image and recognition for the best and fairest
- played in a large open space, which reflects geography of Australia
- commercialised and attracts sponsorship deals
- promoted in the media, creating positive role models

Chapter 14 (page 168)

1   Mass participation means a lot of people taking part in sporting activities ✔, the grass-roots/foundation stage of the sports development pyramid ✔. This requires equal opportunity/elimination of discrimination ✔, which suggests social policy/ government agency involvement ✔.

(max. 2 marks)

2   Any four from:
- equal opportunities/war effort/changed perceptions of women's capabilities/Sex Discrimination Act
- more media coverage/role models
- encouragement via school PE programmes/extra curricular opportunities
- FA more approving/more clubs offering competitive opportunities
- reduced stereotypes/more socially acceptable
- more leisure time/disposable income available to women

3 Any five from:
- social status/working classes least likely to participate
- family/peer influence
- religion/culture/race issues
- amount of leisure time available
- gender
- age
- disability
- discrimination
- media coverage/role models
- access to facilities/clubs/coaches/amount of disposable income
- PE experience

4 There are two parts to the question, so you need to make clear your answers to both parts of it.

The structure of the UKSI can be described as consisting of a number of national institutes of sport throughout the UK (1 mark).

Its functions include (any two for 2 marks):
- increasing international sporting success (i.e. more medals/world titles)
- provision of high-class facilities
- provision of top-level coaches
- provision of sports science/medical support
- provision of lifestyle advice
- links to sports colleges/NGBs to develop excellence

5 You need to give a minimum of three different schemes/initiatives that one of the home country sports councils is involved in. For example, if you choose Sport England, the schemes and initiatives include:
- Active Communities 'Get Active' — increase physical activity opportunities in disadvantaged groups
- Sport Action Zones — target socioeconomically deprived areas
- funding of local facilities
- Start, Stay, Succeed
- other Get Active programmes (Active Schools/Places/People/Sports)

6 Any three for 3 marks:
- promote a sport and increase awareness of it
- provide positive role models
- increase income to a sport/increase sponsorship opportunities

- help eliminate stereotypes and increase the likelihood of minority groups participating
- provide videos/DVDs/websites to help improve performance and knowledge of how to play a sport
- influence on rules/timings/structure of a sport

7 'Discuss' questions have two sides, so you should try to give a balanced answer giving both sides of the argument. 6 marks for six separate points (sub-max. of 4 marks per section):

Agreement with legalising drugs:
- battle against drugs expensive/time-consuming
- detection of drugs often ineffective
- difficulty in defining difference between a drug and a nutritional supplement
- leads to higher performance levels/spectators/sponsors more likely to be attracted
- gives a level playing field for all

Disagreement with allowing drugs:
- dangerous side effects/health implications
- negative role models to the young
- pressure from coaches to take drugs against their will
- unethical/cheating — sport should be about using your natural talents

Index

OCR AS Physical Education

Index

Index

OCR AS Physical Education